The New Testament
in Its Literary Environment

Library of Early Christianity

Wayne A. Meeks, General Editor

The New Testament in Its Literary Environment

David E. Aune

The Westminster Press
Philadelphia

Scripture quotations from the Revised Standard Version of the Bible are copyrighted 1946, 1952, © 1971, 1973 by the Division of Christian Education of the National Council of the Churches of Christ in the U.S.A. and are used by permission.

Book design by Gene Harris

First paperback edition 1989

Published by The Westminster Press®
Philadelphia, Pennsylvania

PRINTED IN THE UNITED STATES OF AMERICA

9 8 7 6 5 4 3 2

Library of Congress Cataloging-in-Publication Data

Aune, David Edward.
   The New Testament in its literary environment.

   (Library of early Christianity ; vol. 8)
   Bibliography: p.
   Includes indexes.
   1. Bible. N.T.—Criticism, interpretation, etc.
1. Title.   II. Series: Library of early Christianity ; 8.
BS2361.2.A96   1987   225.6'.6   86-18949
ISBN 0-664-21912-8
ISBN 0-664-25018-1 (pbk.)

To my mother,
  Anna Skar Aune,
and in memory of my father,
  Edward Marius Aune

Contents

Foreword

This series of books is an exercise in taking down fences. For a number of years the study of ancient Christianity, and especially of the New Testament, has suffered from isolation, but happily that situation is changing. For a variety of reasons, we have begun to see a convergence of interests and, in some instances, real collaboration by scholars across several academic boundaries: between Roman historians and historians of Christianity, between New Testament scholars and church historians, between historians of Judaism and of Christianity, between historical and literary scholars.

The Library of Early Christianity harvests the fruit of such collaboration, in several areas in which fresh approaches have changed the prevailing view of what the early Christians were like. Much of what is presented here has not been brought together in this fashion before. In order to make this information as accessible as possible, we have not burdened the books with the sort of argument and documentation that is necessary in scholarly monographs, in which such new work is ordinarily presented. On the other hand, the authors do not condescend to their readers. Students in colleges and seminaries and at more advanced levels will find in these books an opportunity to participate in a conversation at the growing edge of current scholarship.

There was a time when nearly every New Testament scholar had been trained in the Greek and Latin classics. Comparing the genres and styles of the early Christian writings with other ancient literature was for them natural and obvious, though such comparison did not always produce better understanding. The differences between the New Testament books and the literary works of the Golden Age were so great that often the result of comparing the two was that the Christian documents were put in a class by themselves. By the turn of the century, however, the discovery of hoards of papyri in

Egypt and decades of labor in editing the less well-known authors of the Hellenistic and Roman periods had brought increased awareness of the great variety of literary forms and styles and of popular language in the time when Christianity began. Pioneers like Eduard Norden explored the place of characteristic types and individual documents of early Christian literature within that variety, and Hans Wendland, Martin Dibelius, and others brought together the results of such studies in fine handbooks on the literary context of early Christian writings.

Much has happened in the study of early Christian literature as well as the classics since those handbooks were written. Today, unfortunately, the New Testament student who has a classical education adequate for accurately locating the texts in their literary context is a rare exception. David Aune is such an exception, and his analysis of forms, genres, and styles available to early Christian writers, and of their own modifications of them and special solutions to their special literary problems, goes far beyond anything previously available.

WAYNE A. MEEKS
General Editor

Abbreviations

AJP	*American Journal of Philology*
AMW	David Hellholm, ed., *Apocalypticism in the Mediterranean World and the Near East* (Tübingen: J. C. B. Mohr [Paul Siebeck], 1983)
ANRW	*Aufstieg und Niedergang der römischen Welt,* ed. by H. Temporini and W. Haase (Berlin and New York: Walter de Gruyter, 1972–)
ATR	*Anglican Theological Review*
Beginnings	F. J. Foakes-Jackson and Kirsopp Lake, eds., *The Beginnings of Christianity,* Part I: *The Acts of the Apostles.* 5 vols. (London: Macmillan Co., 1920–33)
BJRL	*Bulletin of the John Rylands Library*
CBQ	*Catholic Biblical Quarterly*
CPJ	*Corpus Papyrorum Judaicarum*
CRINT	*Compendia Rerum Iudaicarum ad Novum Testamentum,* ed. by S. Safrai and M. Stern et al. (Fortress Press, 1976–)
HTR	*Harvard Theological Review*
JAAR	*Journal of the American Academy of Religion*
JBL	*Journal of Biblical Literature*
JHS	*Journal of Hellenic Studies*
JJS	*Journal of Jewish Studies*
JR	*Journal of Religion*

JRS	*Journal of Roman Studies*
LCL	Loeb Classical Library
NTS	*New Testament Studies*
NovT	*Novum Testamentum*
RAC	*Reallexikon für Antike und Christentum*, Stuttgart, 1950–72
RE	A. Pauly, G. Wissowa, and W. Kroll, *Real-Encyclopädie der klassischen Altertumswissenschaft*, 1893–
TAPA	*Transactions of the American Philological Association*
TB	*Tyndale Bulletin*
VC	*Vigiliae Christianae*
ZNW	*Zeitschrift für die neutestamentliche Wissenschaft*

Introduction

Christianity began as a Jewish religious reform movement launched by Jesus of Nazareth, a rural Palestinian teacher and holy man who was executed as a revolutionary by the Roman occupation authorities about A.D. 29. His followers believed that God had delivered him from death and exalted him to heaven and regarded him as the Messiah whom Judaism expected to appear in the last days. Christianity spread rapidly. Within two decades Christian congregations were scattered throughout nearly every major urban area of the Roman world, and converts from paganism had begun to outnumber Jewish Christians.

Many dramatic changes took place during this relatively short period: Christianity changed (1) from a movement confined to Palestine to one found throughout the entire Mediterranean world; (2) from an eastern to a western cultural setting; (3) from a primarily rural to an almost exclusively urban setting; (4) from a largely Aramaic-speaking to a predominantly Greek-speaking constituency; and (5) from an exclusively Jewish sect to one that admitted an increasing number of converted pagans. Most significant of all, however, is a theological factor: the early recognition of Jesus as the Jewish Messiah was transformed in a remarkably short time into the conviction that Jesus Christ was the preexistent Son of God sent to redeem and transform those of any national origin who believed that God had acted through him to achieve the salvation of the world.

The earliest surviving Christian documents permitting glimpses of what early Christianity was like (the authentic letters of Paul, written between ca. A.D. 49 and 64) indicate that all of the major changes mentioned above were already taking place. An inclusive term for the direction these changes were taking is "Hellenization." Actually, the Judaism from which Christianity emerged was already

Hellenized. Early Judaism not only was diverse religiously but had undergone an increasing though uneven process of Hellenization since the late fourth century B.C. The Christianity reflected in Paul's letters is consciously rooted theologically in this Judaism and yet is struggling to discard the cultural markers of Jewish ethnic identity (e.g., circumcision, Sabbath observance, dietary restrictions, the wearing of religious paraphernalia). Paul's letters were written in a popular form of literary Greek using Hellenistic arguments, styles, and forms. In fact, every book of the New Testament reflects to varying degrees an accommodation between Jewish religious and ethical values and traditions and Hellenistic forms of linguistic, literary, rhetorical, and conceptual expression. The Christianity of the New Testament is a creative combination of Jewish and Hellenistic traditions transformed into a *tertium quid* ("a third something"): that is, a reality related to two known things but transcending them both.

The extent of the influence that Hellenistic literary culture had on first-century Christianity is just now beginning to be recognized. The purpose of this book is to compare the literary genres and forms found in the New Testament with those of the literary cultures of the ancient Mediterranean world, particularly Hellenism. A generation ago this task would have been judged difficult if not impossible. Nineteenth-century New Testament scholars confidently contrasted *Hochliteratur* ("cultivated literature"), produced by and for the educated upper classes of the Greco-Roman world, to *Kleinliteratur* ("popular literature"), which originated with the lower classes and to which the compositions of the New Testament were assigned. Most of the surviving Greek and Latin literature was produced and preserved by the educated upper classes. Since ancient literature written for popular consumption has largely perished, this dichotomy had the effect of putting the literature of the New Testament in a class by itself.

Recent studies have made it increasingly apparent that the antithetical categories of *Hochliteratur* and *Kleinliteratur* have value only as ideal types at opposite ends of a complex spectrum of linguistic and literary styles and levels. The pyramidal character of ancient society had an impact on literary culture as well as on other aspects of social and cultural life. The literary conventions and styles of the upper classes percolated down to lower levels, and they occur in attenuated and simplified forms in popular literature. For elevated literary forms and styles were not locked away in the libraries and salons of the rich and educated, they were on public display. During the first and second centuries A.D., public performances by rhetoricians were in great demand, and they (like contemporary movie stars or rock musicians) received wealth and prestige along with fame. Listening to the public recitation of literary works was also a popular form of entertainment. All levels of the population of the Roman world were exposed to the variety of structures and styles found in the rhetoric, literature, and art that were on public display throughout the Empire. While many of the sophisticated styles of the literature and rhetoric of the upper classes are missing from the popular literature (for example, linguistic Atticism—an attempt to write in the style of fifth and fourth century B.C. Greek literature— is absent from the New Testament writings), there are some basically similar literary and rhetorical patterns and genres found in all strata of ancient society.

Literary genres and forms are not simply neutral containers used as convenient ways to package various types of written communication. They are social conventions that provide contextual meaning for the smaller units of language and text they enclose. The original significance that a literary text had for both author and reader is tied to the genre of that text, so that the meaning of the part is dependent upon the meaning of the whole. Four major literary types are represented in the New Testament: gospels, acts, letters, and apocalypse. They obviously correspond to ancient biographical, historical, epistolary, and apocalyptic literature. These literary types will be analyzed at some length in the following chapters. While each form has its own complexity, all have one important feature in common. Each is a "complex" or "inclusive" literary genre used to frame a variety of shorter literary forms. A *literary genre* may be defined as a group of texts that exhibit a coherent and recurring configuration of literary features involving form (including structure and style), content, and function. *Literary forms*, on the other hand, while exhibiting similar recurring literary features, are primarily constituent elements of the genres that frame them.

Even though the New Testament is published between two covers like any other book, it is not quite as homogeneous as it first appears. Actually, it is not a "book" in the usual sense but a collection of twenty-seven compositions in various literary genres by roughly a dozen authors written over a hundred-year period (ca. A.D. 50 to 150) in an ancient language (Greek) and within an alien culture (the ancient Mediterranean world). Unless we understand the ways in which these historical factors conditioned the production of the literature of the New Testament, it will remain a closed book. The twenty-seven individual compositions that make up the New Testament were not all regarded as canonical by the major branches of the Christian church until the late fourth century A.D. Many relatively early writings were highly regarded but eventually excluded from the New Testament canon. Since the content of the canon was determined by ecclesiastical decisions based mainly on theological considerations, any study of the literary character of the New Testament writings cannot reasonably exclude a discussion of early noncanonical Christian literature. The early Christian literature most relevant for our purposes includes the Apostolic Fathers (a heterogeneous collection of fifteen compositions by nine Christian authors written from ca. A.D. 90 to 140) and the many apocryphal gospels, acts, and apocalypses written from ca. A.D. 125 to 400.

For Further Study

On Literature and Literary Genres: For a general discussion of literary theory see René Wellek and Austin Warren, *Theory of Literature,* 3rd ed. (Harcourt Brace Jovanovich, 1977). See also W. W. Robson, *The Definition of Literature and Other Essays* (Cambridge: University Press, 1982), and J. M. Ellis, *The Theory of Literary Criticism: A Logical Analysis* (University of California Press, 1974). A useful dictionary of literary terms and concepts is available in C. Hugh Holman, *A Handbook to Literature,* 3rd ed. (Odyssey Press, 1972). A popular introduction to genre criticism is Heather Dubrow, *Genre* (London: Methuen, 1982). An important treatment of genre theory is found in E. D. Hirsch, *Validity in Interpretation* (Yale University Press, 1967). See also his *The Aims of Interpretation* (University of Chicago Press, 1976). A useful survey of genre criticism in relationship to biblical studies is M. Gerhart, "Generic Studies: Their Renewed Importance in Religious and Literary Interpretation," *JAAR* 45 (1977), 309–325.

On the New Testament and Early Christian Literature: The best introduction to the history and literature of early Christianity within its historical and cultural setting is Helmut Koester, *Introduction to the New Testament,* 2 vols. (Fortress Press, 1982). Also important are W. G. Kümmel, *Introduction to the New Testament,* rev. ed., tr. by H. C. Kee (Abingdon Press, 1975), and Philip Vielhauer, *Geschichte der urchristlichen Literatur* (Berlin: Walter de Gruyter, 1975), which also treats early noncanonical literature. The standard English translation and introduction to the New Testament apocryphal literature is Edgar Hennecke, *New Testament Apocrypha,* ed. by Wilhelm Schneemelcher, tr. by R. McL. Wilson et al., 2 vols. (Westminster Press, 1963–66).

On New Testament Genres and Forms: For an encyclopedic treatment of Hellenistic literary forms with an extensive bibliography, see Klaus Berger, "Hellenistische Gattungen im Neuen Testament," *ANRW* II.25.2

(1984), 1031–1432, 1831–1885 (index). Equally important is Berger's *Form-geschichte des Neuen Testaments* (Heidelberg: Quelle & Meyer, 1984).

On the Old and New Testament Canon: The most comprehensive recent discussion of the Old Testament canon of Judaism and early Christianity is Roger Beckwith, *The Old Testament Canon of the New Testament Church* (Wm. B. Eerdmans Publishing Co., 1985), with extensive bibliography and a detailed discussion of important texts. The best recent discussion of the New Testament canon is Harry Y. Gamble, *The New Testament Canon: Its Making and Meaning* (Fortress Press, 1985). See also the more detailed discussion of Robert M. Grant, *The Formation of the New Testament* (Harper & Row, 1965). Old but indispensable is B. F. Westcott, *A General Survey of the History of the Canon of the New Testament,* 6th ed. (Baker Book House, 1980 [originally published 1889]).

On Hellenistic Literature and Culture: Two useful surveys with many articles on various aspects of literature by specialists are David Daiches and Anthony Thorlby, eds., *The Classical World* (London: Aldus Books, 1972), and M. I. Finley, ed., *The Legacy of Greece: A New Appraisal* (Oxford: Clarendon Press, 1982). An older work that is still important is Paul Wendland, *Die hellenistisch-römische Kultur in ihren Beziehungen zum Judentum und Christentum,* 4th ed. (Tübingen: J. C. B. Mohr [Paul Siebeck], 1972). The best discussion in English of Greek literature is Albin Lesky, *A History of Greek Literature,* tr. by J. Willis and C. de Heer (Thomas Y. Crowell Co., 1966). The standard handbook on Latin literature reflecting recent research is now E. J. Kenney and W. V. Clausen, *Latin Literature,* vol. 2 of *The Cambridge History of Classical Literature* (Cambridge: University Press, 1982). Also important is B. P. Reardon, *Courants littéraires Grecs des IIe et IIIe siècles après J.-C.* (Paris: Belles Lettres, 1971). See also B. A. Van Groningen, "General Literary Tendencies in the Second Century A.D.," *Mnemosyne* 18 (1965), 41–56, and E. L. Bowie, "Greeks and Their Past in the Second Sophistic," in *Studies in Ancient Society,* ed. by M. I. Finley (London: Routledge & Kegan Paul, 1974), pp. 166–209.

On Greco-Roman Education and Rhetoric: One of the more competent surveys of Greco-Roman education is Stanley F. Bonner, *Education in Ancient Rome* (University of California Press, 1977). Also important are M. L. Clarke, *Higher Education in the Ancient World* (London: Routledge & Kegan Paul, 1971), and H. I. Marrou, *A History of Education in Antiquity* (Mentor Books, 1964). George Kennedy has written several important works on ancient rhetoric including *The Art of Persuasion in Greece* (Princeton University Press, 1963), *The Art of Rhetoric in the Roman World: 300 B.C.–A.D. 300* (Princeton University Press, 1972), *Classical Rhetoric and Its Christian and Secular Tradition from Ancient to Modern Times* (University of North Carolina Press, 1980), and *Greek Rhetoric Under Christian Emperors* (Princeton University Press, 1983). Also important is D. A. Russell, *Greek Declamation* (Cambridge: University Press, 1983).

On Israelite-Jewish Literature: Two comprehensive introductions to the Old Testament are Georg Fohrer, *Introduction to the Old Testament,* tr. by D. Green (Abingdon Press, 1968), and Otto Eissfeldt, *The Old Testament: An Introduction,* tr. by P. R. Ackroyd (Harper & Row, 1965). A comprehensive survey of developments in Old Testament scholarship between 1950 and 1979 is found in G. W. Anderson, *Tradition and Interpretation: Essays by Members of the Society for Old Testament Study* (Oxford: Clarendon Press, 1979). The most important recent discussion of postbiblical Jewish literature is now the comprehensive handbook edited by Michael E. Stone, *Jewish Writings of the Second Temple Period: Apocrypha, Pseudepigrapha, Qumran Sectarian Writings, Philo, Josephus,* vol. 2, sec. 2 of *CRINT* (1984). Another competent introduction to this literature is George W. E. Nickelsburg, *Jewish Literature Between the Bible and the Mishnah* (Fortress Press, 1982). An excellent discussion focusing on Diaspora literature is John J. Collins, *Between Athens and Jerusalem: Jewish Identity in the Hellenistic Diaspora* (Crossroad Publishing Co., 1983). The standard translation of Old Testament pseudepigrapha, with extensive introductions and bibliographies, is J. H. Charlesworth, *The Old Testament Pseudepigrapha,* 2 vols. (Doubleday & Co., 1983–85). A more limited selection of texts is found in H. F. D. Sparks, ed., *The Apocryphal Old Testament* (Oxford: Clarendon Press, 1984). Charlesworth has also compiled an extensive bibliography on the subject: *The Pseudepigrapha and Modern Research: With a Supplement* (Scholars Press, 1981). Also important is Charlesworth's *The Old Testament Pseudepigrapha and the New Testament* (Cambridge: University Press, 1985).

On Judaism and Hellenism: The most important discussion is that of Martin Hengel, *Judaism and Hellenism,* 2 vols. (Fortress Press, 1974). Hengel has stated his views more succinctly in *Jews, Greeks and Barbarians: Aspects of the Hellenization of Judaism in the Pre-Christian Period* (Fortress Press, 1980). See also Victor Tcherikover, *Hellenistic Civilization and the Jews* (Atheneum Publishers, 1970). Still important is S. Lieberman, *Hellenism in Jewish Palestine* (Jewish Theological Seminary, 1950). For an opposing view see D. Flusser, "Paganism in Palestine," *The Jewish People in the First Century: Historical Geography, Political History, Social, Cultural, and Religious Life and Institutions,* vol. 2, sec. 1 of *CRINT* (1976), pp. 1065–1100.

1

The Genre of the Gospels: Nonliterary and Literary "Parallels"

The word "gospel," originally an Anglo-Saxon term meaning "good news," literally translates the New Testament Greek noun *euangelion*, still surviving in "evangelist" and related English words. *Euangelion* was an important religious term for Paul; he uses the noun 52 times and the verb 19 times. In its Christian meaning, the term first occurs in his letters, though he certainly derived it from previous Christian usage. In fact, the concept "gospel" lies at the center of his theology. Paul often uses the expression "gospel of Christ," a theological abbreviation for "the good news (of the saving significance of the death and resurrection) of Christ" (e.g., Rom. 15:19; 1 Cor. 9:12; Gal. 1:7; Phil. 1:27; 1 Thess. 3:2). He favors the absolute or unqualified use of the term "gospel," which he uses 22 times (e.g., Rom. 1:16; 1 Cor. 4:5; Gal. 2:5, 14; 1 Thess. 2:4), an even more abbreviated technical term that he and his congregations understood to mean "the saving message about Jesus."

Like Paul, the author of Mark uses the technical term "gospel" (Mark 1:15; 8:35; 10:29; 13:10; 14:9). Here, however, the word implies the career of Jesus in addition to his death and resurrection, as Mark 1:1 suggests: "The beginning of the gospel of Jesus Christ" —that is, the message of good news about Jesus Christ proclaimed by the church (13:10; 14:9). Ancient literary parallels indicate that Mark 1:1 is not a book title ("beginning" means the point at which the narrative starts). However, the phrase "the gospel about Jesus Christ" is Mark's description of his subject matter. By transforming what had been an oral proclamation about Jesus into a literary work, he is primarily responsible for the eventual use of the term "gospel" as a generic designation.

Matthew and Luke were not impressed. Both favored more conventional literary terms. Matthew labeled his introductory genealogy a "book" (*biblos*, Matt. 1:1) and designated the kerygma (a Greek term meaning "proclamation [of the gospel]") as "the gospel of the kingdom" (4:23; 9:35; 24:14), but he fails to give his entire work any specific designation. Luke described his as a "narrative" (*diēgēsis*, Luke 1:1) and referred to the oral gospel as "the word" (*logos*, Luke 1:2), a term suitable for both oral and written speech.

"Gospel" as a Literary Form

Justin Martyr (d. A.D. 165) was the first to refer to "gospels" in the plural, meaning literary texts rather than oral proclamation (*1 Apology* 66, written ca. A.D. 155). After the middle of the second century the singular noun *euangelion* often refers to a written gospel (Justin, *Dialogue with Trypho* 10.2; 100.1; Irenaeus, *Against Heresies* 3.1.1; Clement of Alexandria, *Stromateis* 1.21). Christian authors through the fifth century pinned the "gospel" label to nearly fifty compositions. Origen (died ca. A.D. 254) found it necessary to sort through the variety of meanings which the term "gospel" had in his day (*Commentary on John* 1.1–9). To ancient Christians "gospels" were Jesus literature; that is, compositions which contained accounts of the words and/or actions of Jesus. Using content as a criterion, gospels were distinguished from acts of apostles, apocalypses, acts of martyrs, letters, and sermons or homilies. From the perspective of the modern understanding of genre, however, early Christianity produced few if any works fully comparable to the canonical gospels.

The four Gospels were written anonymously between A.D. 70 and 100, and assembled into a collection about A.D. 125. The authors did not provide them with titles; others added them later. The earliest Gospel titles consisted of just two words, the Greek preposition *kata*, "according to," followed by the name of the Evangelist in the accusative. Similarity in form suggests that they were formulated and affixed to all the gospels at the same time, i.e., when they formed a collection (ca. A.D. 125). The reasons for associating a particular Evangelist with each Gospel can no longer be known, but presumably such ascriptions were based on earlier tradition. Since ancient book titles usually consisted of a short title and the author's name in the genitive (at the end of the papyrus roll), the oldest titles of the Gospels appear unusual. Yet since the Greek preposition *kata* with the accusative can function as a genitive of possession, the titles reflect colloquial usage. The simple two-word titles were soon expanded to, for example, "the Gospel according to Mark," which should be understood as "the Gospel *by* Mark." The original sense of these expanded titles seems to be "the (one) gospel (in the version) of [e.g., Mark]." Later copyists expanded the titles even more.

Modern Scholarship and the Gospels

Almost every aspect of the study of the Gospels has been reassessed during the last twenty years. Not surprisingly, there is disagreement on almost every major issue. Nevertheless, some results of earlier research have proven remarkably durable. These can be supplemented by subsequent developments and summarized under the headings of literary criticism, historical criticism, form criticism, and redaction criticism.

Literary Criticism

Literary criticism deals with the interpretation and evaluation of a literary work through the careful examination and analysis of the work itself on the basis of both internal factors (e.g., genre, structure, content, style, sources) and external factors (e.g., historical setting, social setting, biographical data, psychological information). In the past, New Testament scholars have been preoccupied with the problem of the *sources* of the Gospels at the expense of other literary concerns. The first three Gospels (Matthew, Mark, and Luke) exhibit literary interdependence and for that reason are designated the *Synoptic* Gospels because they can be "seen together" when placed in parallel columns because of extensive verbal agreements. Mark (ca. A.D. 70) was the earliest Gospel. Matthew (ca. A.D. 85) and Luke (ca. A.D. 90), independently of each other, incorporated nearly the whole of Mark into their compositions (only thirty-one verses of Mark are not found in either Matthew or Luke). While keeping the outline of Mark intact, they added material at the beginning (birth narratives, genealogies) and end (resurrection appearances, the ascension story in Luke). Matthew inserted collections of sayings of Jesus in the form of five artificial sermons (Matthew 5–7, 10, 13, 18, 23–24), while Luke placed much of the same material at various junctures in an equally contrived travel narrative (Luke 9–18). In antiquity, when copyrights did not exist and plagiarism was not considered a vice, Matthew and Luke simply followed accepted literary procedures. Both share many parallel passages not found in Mark (up to 250 verses), collectively designated "Q" (from the German term *Quelle,* meaning "source"). This collection of Jesus' sayings, usually dated to ca. A.D. 50 and set in Palestine, probably existed in written form. The dependence of Matthew and Luke on Mark and "Q" is called the Two Source Theory.

The situation with John is somewhat different. Before the 1950s many scholars thought John both knew and was dependent on the Synoptic Gospels. Now the prevailing opinion is that John is independent of the Synoptics but that both are dependent on parallel traditions. If this is so it means that both Mark and John developed the gospel form independently. Scholars have proposed that John used two major sources, a Signs source (a collection of seven miracle stories) and a Discourse source.

Historical Criticism

Historical criticism emphasizes the examination and evaluation of sources useful for reconstructing the past. Applied to particular texts like the Gospels, this method focuses on such issues as when, where, why, by whom, and to whom they were written, factors preliminary to the evaluation of the historicity of events portrayed.

After the Enlightenment the assumption that divine inspiration guaranteed the historical and theological truth of Scripture was increasingly abandoned by liberal Protestants. During the nineteenth century, confidence in the historical method encouraged scholars to attempt a separation of fact from fancy in the Gospels with the object of producing a historically reliable biography of Jesus. The Gospel of John, with its marked theological emphases and striking differences from the Synoptics, was widely regarded as having little historical value. Scholars became increasingly skeptical about the traditional identities of the Gospel authors and about the supposed "eyewitness" character of their reports. In 1906 Albert Schweitzer wrote a celebrated book exposing the subjective character of this "quest for the historical Jesus." Rather than successfully separating the real Jesus from the legendary embellishments of early Christian piety and credulity, scholars unintentionally fabricated a "historical" Jesus reflecting (and thus justifying) their own theological and philosophical views; they fashioned a Jesus in their own image and likeness. The quest for the historical Jesus had reached an impasse, and many were skeptical about the possibility of writing a biography of Jesus at all. A contemporary of Schweitzer, Wilhelm Wrede, demonstrated that even Mark (the Gospel thought earliest and most historical) was a highly theological (hence historically tendentious) interpretation of Jesus.

After the First World War a reaction to the idealism of liberal theology emerged as dialectical theology. Associated with such European Protestant theologians as Karl Barth, Emil Brunner, and Friedrich Gogarten, dialectical theology become influential for New Testament studies when combined with existentialism by Rudolf Bultmann. Despite the Bible's errors, imperfections, and mythic modes of thought, it was argued, the Bible and the gospel it conveys can mediate an encounter with the transcendent Word of God. With the kerygmatic Christ thus insulated from the possibility or necessity of historical qualification or disconfirmation, there was little reason to worry about the so-called historical Jesus.

Form Criticism

Since a reliable portrait of Jesus was no longer historically feasible or theologically necessary, New Testament scholars focused on the Gospel traditions with their mythical embellishments as reflections of early Christian faith responses to Jesus. From this the discipline of *form criticism* emerged. It was a method for identifying and analyzing preliterary oral forms (i.e., units of folklore) that had been incorporated into literature (like the Gospels), in which community traditions played a more significant role than creative authorship. Various types of oral forms were identified and classified (such as sayings of Jesus, pronouncement stories, miracle stories, parables, and stories about Jesus). The Evangelists functioned as editors who incorporated these oral traditions into their Gospels relatively unaltered. As the author-editor of the first Gospel, Mark had created a temporal and geographical framework into which he inserted Jesus traditions where he thought appropriate. Since the various traditions originally circulated independently, Mark was not writing a "biography" (it was argued), since no coherent outline or structure of the career of Jesus had previously existed. Form critics were more interested in how and why early Christians had modified or even created Gospel traditions than in the historical Jesus himself. The Gospels, in a word, reveal more about post-Easter Christianity than about the historical Jesus.

By the mid-1950s a new quest for the historical Jesus was under way, based on the conviction that some historical ties between Jesus of Nazareth and the Christ proclaimed by the church must be demonstrated if Christianity was not to dissolve in myth. While the possibility of writing a biography of Jesus continued to be thought impossible, given the inadequacy of the Gospels as historical sources, attempts were made to peel away legendary embellish-

ments from each traditional unit in an attempt to reconstruct the
message and activities of Jesus. The result has been a spate of books
attempting to reconstruct the teachings of the historical Jesus.

Redaction Criticism

By the mid-1950s the Evangelists began to be appreciated as
creative authors and not just mindless collectors and organizers of
earlier Jesus traditions. The emerging discipline of *redaction* (or
composition) *criticism* focused on distinguishing received tradition
from the redactional (i.e., editorial) contributions of the Evangelists. This was easier with Matthew and Luke, which could be compared with Mark and a reconstructed "Q," than with Mark. Redactional features, it was thought, would reveal the theological and
literary intentions of each author-editor. It soon became apparent
that merely to distinguish tradition from redaction was inadequate
for understanding the Gospels as literary compositions, since it
could not be assumed that unmodified traditions were superfluous
to the design of each composition. The value of more conventional
forms of literary criticism became apparent during the mid-1970s.

Genre Criticism and the Gospels

Modern readers probably agree with the *Columbia Encyclopedia*
that the Gospels are "biographies of Jesus." They might be sur-
prised to learn that, until very recently, New Testament scholars
were nearly unanimous in the opinion that, whatever else they might
be, the Gospels were certainly not biographies. The foregoing survey of historical and form-critical views of the Gospels clarifies some
of the reasons behind this curious view. However, ancient biography is a complex genre consisting of many subtypes. It is reasonable
that the Gospels be compared to them. This chapter argues that the
canonical Gospels constitute a distinctive type of ancient biography
combining (to oversimplify slightly) Hellenistic form and function
with Jewish content. Several methodological problems are involved
in making the comparisons that result in these conclusions, and the
following paragraphs deal with some of them.

First, comparing Greco-Roman biographical literature with the
Gospels does not imply that literary forms (any more than other
cultural commodities) were taken over unmodified. Second Maccabees is an example of a Jewish historical writing (second or first
century B.C.) that is Hellenistic in form but Jewish in content. Analogous adaptations of Hellenistic and Jewish literary forms with dis-

tinctive Christian content are found in the New Testament Gospels and letters.

Second, Greco-Roman literary composition often departed from the prescriptions of ancient literary and rhetorical theory (though Israelite-Jewish tradition is almost wholly devoid of such theoretical reflections). Earlier in this century classical scholars widely assumed that an author's individuality and creativity were evident only in departures from the generic norms prescribed by ancient theory. Today it is more readily appreciated that theory did not exert such a stranglehold on creativity. Ancient theory, valuable as it is, must not be allowed to impede the understanding of actual texts.

Third, there are many perils in any comparative enterprise: what do we compare with what and how do we go about making the comparison? In discussions of Gospel genre there are two tendencies. One tendency insists that literary analogues to the Gospels must be very close. The result: no text can pass the test. This position reached its nadir with the claim that Mark is the only "true" Gospel (the view of Norman Perrin). The other tendency ignores or skews important distinctions between the Gospels and potential generic parallels and jumps to the conclusion that the Gospels are, for example, aretalogies (lists of accomplishments), or encomiums (formal praise), or Greek tragedies, or biographies of philosophers, and so on. A careful course must be steered between these twin perils.

The Gospels as a "Nonliterary" Genre

Those who regard the Gospels as unparalleled in Jewish or Greco-Roman biographical or historical literature usually propose that they constitute a unique literary genre which organically developed out of the inherently narrative potentialities of the kerygma ("proclamation"), or oral gospel. After discussing that hypothesis, we shall consider the less popular but potentially significant view that the Gospels were structured in lections for weekly reading.

The Gospels as Expanded Kerygma

From the turn of the century until very recently, Mark was regarded as a unique composition with no real connections with existing Israelite-Jewish or Greco-Roman literary forms. The singularity of the Gospel form is accounted for by supposing it to be an expanded literary expression of the oral kerygma of early Christians. Though no early Christian sermons have been preserved, this kerygma has been reconstructed on the basis of evidence in Paul's letters and Acts. In Paul the kerygma is a recital of the significance of the death and resurrection of Jesus within the framework of the fulfillment of Old Testament predictions, his exaltation to God's right hand and imminent return in glory (Rom. 1:1–4; 1 Cor. 15: 3–8; 1 Thess. 1:10; 2:8). Many speeches in the early chapters of Acts exhibit a kerygmatic pattern (e.g., 2:14–39; 3:12–26; 4:8–12; 5: 29–32; 10:34–43; 13:16–41). This kerygma could begin with optional references to John the Baptist (Acts 10:37b; 13:24–25) and the earthly ministry of Jesus (2:22; 10:36–39a; 13:31), but it always emphasized the death and resurrection of Jesus, included proofs from the Old Testament, and referred to Jesus' exaltation to the right hand of God and imminent return to save and to judge, concluding with a call for repentance and faith. Through evangelistic preaching and catechetical instruction, according to this view, the basic kerygma was expanded, illustrated, and commented upon by the addition of stories and sayings of Jesus. The movement from oral kerygma to written gospel was both gradual and inevitable. When Mark produced the first written "gospel," he was simply bringing the potentialities of the oral kerygma to fruition.

While there are continuities between the oral kerygmas (existing only as written texts!) and the written Gospels, there are also important discontinuities. The qualitative and quantitative differences between kerygma and gospel are no less significant than the contrast between ideas in a writer's notebook and a finished novel. Genre consists of the interrelated elements of form, content, and function, and a contrast can be drawn between oral kerygma and written gospel in each of these areas.

With regard to the *form* of the kerygmas in Acts, they are all *speeches* adapted by Luke to the various contexts and speakers (always using the first person to address audiences in the second-person plural). In Greek rhetorical categories, the earlier speeches have a strong legal element, but in the end they become persuasive with appeals for repentance (2:38–40; 3:19–26; 4:12). The speeches in Acts 10 and 13 are aimed at belief and not action.

The *content* of the reconstructed kerygma is problematic also because the ministry of Jesus is included in a kerygmatic setting only in Acts 10:36–39 (though briefly mentioned in Acts 2:22 and 13:31). Further, such elements as Jesus' exaltation to the right hand of God, his imminent return as savior and judge, and the appeal for repentance and faith are kerygmatic motifs *absent from the Gospels*. Acts 10:34–43 is a crucial text for the hypothesis of the Gospels' kerygmatic origin, for it has many similarities to the outline of Mark. It has even closer correspondences to Luke, however, suggesting that even if the speech contains pre-Lukan tradition it has been "adjusted" to its present context. Further, the narrative sections of the kerygmatic speeches lack a plot. Proportionally, the passion story in Mark (14–16) occupies about 20 percent of the narrative, with the ministry of Jesus taking up 80 percent (thus Mark has been called a passion story with an extended introduction). In Acts 10 the brief mention of John and Jesus occupies 20 percent and the rest 80 percent (a passion story with a brief introduction). Finally, with regard to *function,* Mark is not an evangelistic sermon meant to evoke repentance and faith, for its primary function is (as we shall argue below) the *historical legitimation* of the saving significance of Jesus.

The Liturgical Genre Hypothesis

The Gospels have an admittedly close connection with early Christian liturgy and worship. Not only did some segments of preliterary Gospel tradition have a setting in Christian worship before their incorporation into written Gospels (e.g., the Lord's Prayer and the eucharistic words of Jesus), but the Gospels themselves came to be read at services of worship (Justin, *1 Apology* 67; written ca. A.D. 155), though just how early cannot be determined. Proponents of various forms of the liturgical genre hypothesis, however, suggest that the Gospels were intentionally structured to complement or replace Jewish Sabbath or festival Scripture readings from the Torah (called *sedarim,* "divisions") and the prophets (called *haphtaroth,* "completions") arranged in annual or triennial lectionary cycles. The oldest system for serial reading of the Torah *(lectio continua),* practiced at least by A.D. 70 (cf. M. *Meg.* 3.6), was the triennial cycle that originated in Palestine. This system, which began either on 1 Nisan (Adolf Büchler) or 1 Tishri (Jacob Mann), consisted of 154 *sedarim;* if there were fixed *haphtaroth* they are difficult to determine. The triennial cycle was replaced by the annual cycle (developed in Babylon and still used in Judaism), consisting of 54 pericopes *(parashiyoth);* beginning and ending on Simhat Torah, 23 Tishri, the last day of the Feast of Sukkoth (17–22 Tishri).

This proposal offers a very specific setting for the origin of the Gospels by proposing they constitute a *liturgical* rather than a *literary* genre. This hypothesis makes two far-reaching assumptions: (1) Judaism developed fixed cycles of readings from the Torah and the prophets by the first century A.D. (2) Early Christianity took over this lectionary practice by complementing or replacing it with Gospels

composed in weekly lections with themes corresponding to the Old
Testament readings they supplanted.

Philip Carrington, struck by the possibility that the Markan pericopes isolated by form criticism might be accounted for in a different manner, proposed that they were designed as lections by the
compiler of Mark. He suggested thematic correlations between
Mark and the festivals of the Jewish liturgical year, such as the
Feeding of the Five Thousand and Passover (explicitly connected in
John 6:4) and the Feeding of the Four Thousand and Pentecost.
Mark 1–13 was based on the Jewish liturgical calendar, which began
on 1 Tishri (the seventh month, corresponding to September/Octo-
ber), replacing the lections of the Jewish scriptures with a presentation of the life of Jesus correlated with a church year yet retaining
thematic connections with the Jewish agricultural festivals.

Michael Goulder argues that Matthew wrote his Gospel for sequential reading during the church year by patterning his lections
on the Jewish festal cycle, not the sabbath cycle. Goulder proposes
that the sixty-nine paragraphs marked in Codex Alexandrinus (an
important fifth-century manuscript containing the whole New Testament) for the text of Matthew reflects the Evangelist's original
design. Luke presents a slightly different problem, and Goulder has
proposed that his Gospel was structured in readings emphasizing
the fulfillment of Old Testament lections following an annual Torah
cycle of readings, rather than the festal cycle.

Eileen Guilding has proposed liturgical structure for the Gospel
of John. Unlike Carrington and Goulder, she does not propose that
Johannine pericopes were designed for reading in Christian services, but rather that John is a Christian commentary on the Old
Testament lections of the triennial cycle. The Gospel of John frequently mentions, even emphasizes, Jewish festivals (2:13; 5:1; 6:4;
7:2; 10:22; 11:55–56; 12:1; 13:1). Further, commentators usually
correlate the Johannine Jesus' proclamation about living water (7:
37–38) with the water-pouring ceremony at the Feast of Sukkoth (M.
Sukk. 4.9), and his claim to be the light of the world (8:12) with the
ritual illumination of the Court of Women during Sukkoth (M. *Sukk.*
5.2–4).

The difficulty with these theories is that they assume more knowledge about Jewish lectionary practice in the first century A.D. than
the evidence permits. This is particularly true when lectionary theories are projected back centuries earlier than Jewish scholars are
willing to go. Liturgical genre theories tend to ignore or minimize
several critical issues. First, evidence for the influence of synagogue
worship on early Christian worship is often exaggerated (Christians

observed neither Jewish festivals nor Sabbaths, according to Justin, *Dialogue with Trypho* 10), and there is no first-century evidence that the Old Testament was read in services. Second, evidence for the reading of Christian writings in the early church is fragmentary or late (1 Thess. 5:27; Col. 4:16; Rev. 1:3; 22:8; cf. 1 Tim. 4:13; Justin, *1 Apology* 67). The use of *serial* readings is not attested before the fourth century. Third, the sacrosanct status necessary for regular inclusion of a book in cultic worship (like the Torah) makes it improbable that the Evangelists intended to compose a book to *immediately* replace the Torah. Fourth, while the liturgical genre theory explains (however inadequately) the episodic structure of the Gospels, it accounts neither for the use of Jesus' life as the lectionary framework nor for the dramatic and thematic elements that unify each Gospel.

Ancient Biographical Literature

The term "biography" (Greek: *biographia*) as a generic term was not coined until the late fifth century A.D. (Damascius, *Life of Isidore* 8). Greek writers used *bios* and the Romans *vita* (both meaning "lifetime," "mode of life," or even "career") as nontechnical designations of biographical literature. A biography relates the significance of a famous person's career (i.e., his character and achievements), optionally framed by a narrative of origins and youth, on the one hand, and death and lasting significance on the other. Specialists in ancient Mediterranean literature have emphasized the historical value, written sources, and murky origins of biography, often slighting literary considerations, including the issue of genre. Greco-Roman and Israelite-Jewish biographical conventions must be discussed separately, but that is easier done in theory than in practice. Judaism was but one of the native cultures of the Mediterranean world that borrowed far more than it contributed to Hellenism. The Jewish historian Josephus wrote the extensive work *Antiquities of the Jews* for a Greek audience, depicting figures like Saul and Solomon with Hellenistic biographical conventions. Philo's *Life of Moses* is really an encomiastic biography, topically arranged under the headings of king, lawgiver, high priest, and prophet.

Apart from the complications of cultural assimilation, there are four features of ancient biographical literature that differ strikingly from modern biography. (1) Obituaries were important in the development of ancient biography. In Greece and Rome dirges, eulogies, and epitaphs provided sketches of individual lives. In Egypt biographical inscriptions were incised on tombs of high officials from the third millennium B.C. to the Roman period. In epitaphs from both east and west the deceased speaks to posterity in the first person. In Israel, however, "biography" is anticipated in prophetic vision reports and collections of prophetic legends, but only at a later stage in the deathbed testament. (2) Ancient types of biographical literature, like many other narrative genres, tend to be complex or host genres serving as literary frames for a variety of shorter forms (anecdotes, maxims, speeches, and documents). In Greco-Roman tradition, biography usually took the form of autonomous texts, while in the Jewish tradition biographical literature tended to be used as episodic insertions into more complex narrative texts. (3) Ancient biographies focus on the public life of the individual and emphasize the stages of professional life.

(4) In ancient biography individuals are stylized as *types,* not depicted in terms of their historical particularity or individuality. The appearance of biographical writing in the ancient world is often thought to reflect a developing individualism. Regardless of the merits of this view, it must be emphasized that "individualism" was differently perceived then than now. To understand ancient biography one must be aware of ancient personality conceptions. Today it is assumed that human behavior can only be adequately understood in psychological terms. In the development of the individual personality, genetic and environmental factors interact from infancy through adulthood, with childhood as the most crucial period. In the ancient world, as in some modern third-world cultures, individuals were defined by the groups to which they belonged. Psychological factors were insignificant as explanations of human behavior. Human personality was thought as fixed and unchanging as the kinship and social groups that were primary sources of identity. Good people who became bad had not "changed," they just stopped masquerading (Livy 3.36.1–2). The Romans, for example, thought each nationality had its own indelible character (Quintilian 5.10.24); they stereotyped the Greeks as lazy, fickle, liars, foolish and inept (Cicero uses most of these racial stereotypes in *On Behalf of Flaccus* 10, 14, 42, 62–63). Modern biography is centrally concerned with personality development and the chronological framework within which it occurs. Ancients, with their static conception of the personality, rarely express interest in any such development. Further, chronology for the ancients functioned primarily to organize the external facts of a person's life, not as an explanation of behavior. Ancients approved of the "individual" who represented group norms and values; modern westerners value those who stand out from the crowd.

Greco-Roman Biographical Literature

Biography is a specific genre of Greco-Roman historical literature with broad generic features. Biography may be defined as *a discrete prose narrative devoted exclusively to the portrayal of the whole life of a particular individual perceived as historical.* It never attained a fixed form but continued to develop from ancient to modern times. Biographical and historical texts are difficult to describe generically, primarily because they are complex genres. While Greek biography has roots in the fifth century B.C. (e.g., biographical sections in Herodotus; collections of sayings of wise men and philosophers), the first surviving biographies are fourth-century products: Isocrates' *Evagoras* and Xenophon's *Agesilaus, Memorabilia,* and *Education of Cyrus* (the first two are prose encomia modeled after poetic eulogies; the last two mix fact and fiction). No biographies from the third and second centuries have been preserved except papyrus fragments of Satyrus' *Life of Euripides,* written (surprisingly) in dialogue form (P. Oxy. 1176). Some biographies of the Roman writer Cornelius Nepos have survived (first century B.C.). From the first through the fourth century A.D. biographies have survived by Plutarch, Suetonius, Lucian, Diogenes Laertius, Philostratus, Porphyry, and Iamblichus, as well as the twenty-five fictional imperial biographies of the *Historia Augusta* (ca. A.D. 395). Anonymous biographies reflecting popular tastes include the biography of Secundus the Silent Philosopher and the *Life of Aesop.* In addition there are numerous anonymous (even pseudonymous) lives of poets, mostly brief, largely fictional, sketches based on inferences from the literary works themselves and frequently intended as an introduction to the subject's works (e.g., *Life of Pindar,* P. Oxy. 2438; Pseudo-Hesiod, *Life of Homer*).

Biography and History

Herodotus has been called, not entirely accurately, the father of biography (in addition to his more secure reputation as the father of history), since character depiction was important for his conception of history. Thucydides (who normally excludes all biographical detail from his narrative) included a few "biographical" digressions (e.g., 1.126.3–12 on Kylon; 1.128–134 on Pausanias; 1.138 on Themistocles), and Xenophon included a few "biographical" epilogues in his *Anabasis* (e.g., 1.9 on Cyrus). Yet these biographical sketches are clearly subordinate to the suprapersonal historical concerns of these authors. Occasionally Greek and Roman writers theoretically distinguish biography from history in terms of content (Polybius

10.21.5–8; Plutarch, *Alexander* 1.1–3; *Nicias* 1.5; Cornelius Nepos, *Pelopidas* 1.1). In the Hellenistic and Roman periods, character was an important ingredient of historiography; in biography a person's achievements illustrate his character, while in history achievements are part of a broader historical framework. For Polybius, encomium (i.e., an oration or writing in praise of a person) was appropriately eulogistic in praising the character and achievements of individuals (i.e., idealizing them), whereas history was more pragmatic and objective. Plutarch and Nepos did not want to write *complete* accounts of the deeds of their subjects (that would be history), but wished to selectively emphasize sayings that reveal character (which is biography). Plutarch suggests that trivia (the insignificant deed, the chance remark) reveal character, though such material would be inappropriate for historiography. When Xenophon uses an anecdote about Theramenes in a historical account he is uneasy about its generic propriety (*Hellenica* 2.3.56). He did, after all, treat the life of Agesilaus twice, in the encomiastic biography *Agesilaus,* and historically in *Hellenica* 3–6.

Distinctions between history and biography, however, were more theoretical than practical. During the late Hellenistic period history and biography moved closer together with the increasing emphasis on character in historiography. Biography and history became more and more difficult to distinguish; encomium could and did pervade both. Dionysius of Halicarnassus (rhetorician, historian, and antiquarian) thought it appropriate to include discussions on the life *(bios)* of public figures complete with virtues and vices in addition to their public achievements (5.48.2–4 on Publicola; 8.60–62 on Coriolanus). Diodorus thought that historians should include the actions of states or kings which "are complete in themselves from beginning to end" (16.1). This could even involve the inclusion of birth legends (cf. his treatment of the fourth century B.C. Syracusan tyrant Agathocles, 19.2.1–7). On the biographical side, Plutarch depended on historians for much of his biographical information and could use a "digression" (*ekbolē* or *parekbasis,* technical historiographical terms, cf. Thucydides 1.97.1; Polybius 1.15.13; Plutarch, *Moralia* 855D), which he knew was appropriate only for history (*Dion* 21). The patriotic Roman historiography which denigrated other nations rankled Josephus (*Jewish War* 1.7) and was pejoratively labeled "encomium" by Lucian (*How to Write History* 7). Virtually all Greco-Roman history was written under the strong influence of rhetoric. The dominant form of oratory was the declamation in which epideictic rhetoric with its encomiastic tendencies predominated. These examples (which could be multiplied) reveal that neither history nor biography was constricted by static literary canons.

Biography and Rhetoric

Character representation *(prosōpopoiia* or *ēthopoiia)* was conventional for elementary rhetorical exercises *(progymnasmata)* and advanced exercises *(meletē,* or declamation, i.e., a complete speech). Ghostwritten juridical speeches, to be convincing, had to reflect the character of the speaker (whether an old man, young man, rich man, poor man, etc.). Aristotle provides examples of how to make verbal character sketches and correlate them with particular emotions like anger, pity, indignation, desire, etc. *(Rhetoric* 2.12–14). (In these sections, incidentally, Aristotle uses paratactic style, i.e., the use of "and" to connect clauses, a characteristic of three of the four Gospels.) In school exercises the student would have to speak as a famous historical or mythical character in critical situations, e.g., Andromache to Hector. Aristotle's pupil and successor, Theophrastus, wrote *Characters,* a series of paratactic thumbnail sketches, or notes *(hypomnēmata),* of thirty personified character defects (e.g., Stupidity, Talkativeness, Flattery). Since biographers, as antiquarians and historians, were primarily trained in rhetoric, that is the source of their skills in character depiction, skills more concerned with plausibility than with truth.

Types of Biography

According to Friedrich Leo, Plutarchian biography originated with the early Peripatetics (followers of Aristotle) and took the form of a largely chronologically ordered narrative with literary ambitions, appropriate for depicting statesmen, generals, and philosophers. The other variety of biography originated with the Alexandrian grammarians under Aristotelian influence. Particularly suitable for treating writers and artists, this type had no artistic pretensions, and contained a systematically arranged account of an individual and his accomplishments (Suetonius, Diogenes Laertius). This twofold distinction can also be found in ancient authorities. It is implicit in Xenophon's encomium *Agesilaus,* of which the first part (1–2) is a chronological account of his deeds, while the second (3–11) is a systematic account of his virtues. This pattern is also found in the epitaphs of ancient Egyptian dignitaries, the first part of which (in the first person) describes the life of the deceased as fulfilling idealistic rules of conduct, while the second part outlines the person's career. Quintilian explicitly distinguishes between two basic approaches to encomium or panegyric (an oratorical counterpart to biography), the chronological and the topical (3.7.10–18). The chronological account began with matters such as birth, parents, ancestors, and prenatal prophecies, while praise of the individual himself was based on character, physical characteristics, and external circumstances. In this framework words and deeds can be the basis of praise. The topical approach, on the other hand, focused on various virtues such as courage, justice, and self-control, as illustrated by deeds. Plutarchian biography developed out of Hellenistic historiography (with its emphasis on the chronological treatment of political and military matters), while the other type was an application of the topical approach of antiquarians, or "encyclopedists" (including everything from customs and ceremonies to names of persons and places). The titles of many of Suetonius' lost works suggest that he himself was an antiquarian (e.g., *Ludicra historia,* on Roman games and festivals, and *De variis rebus, "On Various Things,"* a catch-all title if ever there was one). These are not two distinct biographical genres, however, but two complementary variables within Greco-Roman biography.

Generic Features

The variety and complexity of Greco-Roman biographical literature requires another approach. Rather than propose another crude typology, we shall consider each generic aspect of Greco-Roman biography (i.e., content, form, and function) in terms of its primary and secondary constituents. Greco-Roman biography is a single genre exhibiting great variety. Biographers were faced with many mandatory elements each of which allowed a choice along a spectrum of possibilities, dependent on the subject matter or content (i.e., the specific *type* of individual being described), the form (i.e., the nature of available evidence), and the function (i.e., the purpose of the author).

Content

The most distinguishing feature of biography and that which allows it to be classified into various subtypes is the subject himself, i.e., the *content* of Greco-Roman biography. While the content can be described abstractly as an account of the stylized career and significance of a variety of public types of personalities (optionally framed by details concerning origins and youth and then by death and lasting significance), the importance of the *type* is suggested by the fact that series of biographies were written about particular types, e.g., statesmen (Plutarch), philosophers (Diogenes Laertius), emperors, literary figures, orators (Suetonius). The particular type of subject chosen determined to a large extent the topoi used to bring the individual portrayed into conformity with the type. The stylized presentation of the biographical subject has two related aspects: a typecast social role and the stereotypical virtues and/or vices associated with that role. Two types of "heroes" figured prominently in Greco-Roman biographies, public men (good citizens) who lived within and often controlled the structures of society, and philosophers who lived outside those structures. The latter became increasingly important as models in later antiquity. Since subjects of biography were conceptualized in terms of ideal types (e.g., monarchs, statesmen, generals, philosophers, poets, orators), the cluster of stereotypical features associated with each ideal type constituted a theme or *topos.* This suggests another link between biography and history: conventional features that constitute the *topos* of the ideal king or general, for example, are used in both history and biography. In the *Hellenica,* for example, Xenophon measures generals by *topoi* associated with the ideal military commander: wins and maintains loyalty of troops; feeds, cares for, and pays them; shares their lot; is affable and approachable, an example physically and morally, a persuasive speaker, an expert tactician. Xenophon uses these *topoi* in sketching the military careers of Hermocrates, Agesilaus, Teleutias, Iphicrates, and Jason. Ultimately drawn from Thucydides' summary characterization of Themistocles (1.138.1–3), the same *topoi* describe Alexander in Arrian's *Anabasis* 7.27, a work in which encomiastic history and biography merge.

The philosopher as a holy man was an important ideal type that became a popular biographical subject in late antiquity. The Greeks had always assumed the proximity of wisdom and deity. Pythagoras and Plato quite naturally became prototypical divine men in the late Hellenistic and Roman periods. Six biographies of Plato survive, of which the best known is found in Diogenes Laertius 3.1–47. Aristotle was considerably less illustrious in antiquity than Plato. Of his twelve surviving lives (two in Syriac; four in Arabic; five in Greek; one in Latin), that of Diogenes Laertius (5.1–37) is the most famous. By the second century A.D. philosophy had become a religious enterprise. Biographies that treat holy sages (all written during the third and fourth centuries A.D.) include (1) Philostratus' *Life of Apollonius;* (2) Porphyry's *Life of Pythagoras* and (3) *Life of Plotinus;* (4)

Iamblichus' *Life of Pythagoras;* and (5) the "Life of Origen" in Eusebius, *Ecclesiastical History* 6. Patricia Cox, who has investigated this type of biography in detail, proposes two basic biographical paradigms: holy men who were regarded as gods or sons of gods (nos. 1, 2, and 4), and those who were merely godlike (nos. 3 and 5). Both types were paragons of wisdom and pursued ascetic life-styles. Sages of the first type were given miraculous birth stories (confirming their divine origin), were depicted as miracle workers (confirming divine status), and because of their uniqueness were misunderstood by friends and foes alike. None of these features characterize the second type.

Content, like form and function, was subject to the traditional rules or conventions of the biographical genre. These rules involved a series of hierarchical *choices,* each selection presenting another level of options, but here again choices must be made along a range of possibilities: (1) from *fact* to *fiction,* (2) from *serious* to *comic,* (3) from *praise* to *blame,* (4) from *didactic* to *entertaining,* and (5) from *approval* to *disapproval.*

Form

Most ancient biographies were written with literary pretensions and reflect an appropriately high stylistic level, e.g., the use of appropriate vocabulary and syntax and the complex sentences of the periodic style. The formal structure of Greco-Roman biography consists of a fundamentally chronological framework provided by a person's life (true of Suetonian as well as Plutarchan lives), amplified by anecdotes, maxims, speeches, and documents. "Anecdote" (the Greek term *anekdotos* means "unpublished") is a general term including what Greeks called *chreiai* ("anecdotes"), *gnōmai* ("maxims"), and *apomnēmoneumata* ("reminiscences"), and novelle (i.e., short stories generically related to chreiai). Since the ancients regarded a person's actions and words as revelations of character (cf. Xenophon, *Memorabilia* 1.1.20), collections of chreiai (i.e., words and deeds of the wise), had a fundamentally biographical function from the fifth century B.C. on. Biographies could draw upon such collections for material. Sayings of Plato, however, did not circulate in separate collections but were transmitted individually in literary sources. *Gnōmologia* (collections of maxims) were later (fifth century A.D.) excerpted from Plato's lives. Some biographies were entirely fictional, fabricated out of inferences based on chreiai (such as the Life of Heraclitus in Diogenes Laertius 9.1–17). Others were collections of chreiai framed by biographical conventions (Lucian's *Demonax*). In Plato's case the 148 surviving anecdotes (144 in the six surviving Platonic lives) are fictional extrapolations from Plato's writings formulated to glorify or vilify Plato. Chreiai were transferable. An interchange between Diogenes and Aristippus is told of Metrocles and Theodorus (Diogenes Laertius 2.68, 102); a story about Thales by Hermippus is also told of Socrates (Diogenes Laertius 1.33). An anecdote told of the Samians by Herodotus (3. 46) is subsequently applied to the Chians by Sextus Empiricus (*Against the Professors* 2.25).

In the area of *form,* a biographer had at least four choices (the last two are involuntary because they depend on social level), each with a spectrum of possibilities: (1) from *continuous narrative* to *episodic narrative,* (2) from *chronological narration* to *topical exposition,* (3) from *elevated* to *popular diction,* and (4) from *periodic style* (with elaborate sentences) to *paratactic style* (with simple sentences). Continuous style was characteristic of historiography (despite the use of digressions), while episodic style typifies other types of narrative (ethnography, antiquities, novels). Chronological organization characterized political and military history, while topical organization was favored in the kinds of texts just mentioned. Style and diction were choices dependent on the author's social level.

Function

Greco-Roman biography has both obvious and latent functions. Among the manifest or conscious functions, the demonstrative (epideictic) is perhaps most common, though biographies can mix deliberative and forensic elements with it. Epideictic rhetoric, usually limited to praise or blame, is actually a broader category fundamentally concerned with persuading an audience to adopt or maintain a particular point of view in the *present.* Deliberative rhetoric is used to persuade an audience to take some *future* action, while forensic rhetoric uses the strategies of defense or accusation to persuade an audience to make a decision about *past* events or circumstances. The unconscious functions of Greco-Roman biography involve the historical legitimation (or discrediting) of a social belief/value system personified in the subject of the biography.

In the ancient world biography was a powerful propaganda tool. Given the ancient view of the significance of certain prominent individuals (such as founders and progenitors), biography was ideally suited for direct or indirect criticism or support of an established order. Cato the Younger (95–46 B.C.) was one such figure. He became an ideological symbol of the virtues of Republican Rome, and became the focus of a propaganda war, with laudatory pamphlets about him by Cicero, Brutus, Fadius Gallus, and Munatius Rufus, and hostile ones by Julius Caesar, Aulus Hirtius, and Augustus (all lost). The positive portrait in Vergil's *Aeneid* and Horace's *Odes* became a pattern for later authors.

In the Greek world, Socrates was a uniquely significant propaganda image, not for a political system (as was Cato the Younger), but for the philosophical systems of competing Socratic schools of thought. The Socrates of Xenophon is presented in several writings, the *Apology of Socrates,* the *Symposium,* the *Memorabilia* (a defense of Socrates in legal style), and the *Oeconomicus,* while the Platonic Socrates is the subject of the *Apology* (fictional autobiography), the *Symposium,* and more than a dozen dialogues in which Socrates figures prominently. There is in addition the Socrates of Aristophanes and Aristotle, making a total of four early myth-images of Socrates. Each "Socrates" is a composite figure consisting of the distinctive views of each author which are legitimated by projection upon the historical Socrates.

Greco-Roman biographies often have a teaching or didactic function, presenting the subject as a paradigm of virtue. Many Greek biographies are therefore *encomiastic,* i.e., the subject is praised in terms of his conformity to ideal patterns of virtue. Author and audience were more interested in the subject as a moral example and personification of professionally appropriate virtues than in his historical particularity. There was an enduring tension in Greek historical and biographical writing between the historical and the paradigmatic depiction of individuals. Greco-Roman biographers assumed that actions revealed character (Plutarch, *Alexander* 1.1–3; *Pompey* 8.6), exemplifying virtue *(aretē),* vice *(kakia)* or a combination of both. Plutarch selected statesmen and military leaders as subjects for his parallel lives because of their exemplary virtues, though two subjects, Demetrius and Antony, were negative examples. Suetonius inaugurated imperial biography, a subtype of Greco-Roman biography anticipated by Tacitus. His subjects presented inevitable restrictions. He portrayed the emperors in terms of their virtues and vices, correlating character with physiognomy (you are as you appear). Needless to say, many emperors were negative models.

Israelite-Jewish "Biographical" Literature

Few studies of Old Testament and postbiblical Jewish literature find the term "biography" a useful literary category. It is true that "biography" in the sense of an *independent* literary form narrating the achievements and significance of a person from birth to death is very rare. But that is not the end of it. Since early Christianity began as a religious renewal movement within Judaism and only gradually established a separate identity, many have proposed that antecedents of the Gospel form lie in Israelite-Jewish literature.

Character in Israelite-Jewish Narrative

Unified narrative, a narrative type seldom found in Israelite-Jewish literature (form-critically designated the "novella"), is exemplified by such short, self-contained dramatic structures as Ruth, Esther, and Jonah within the canon (cf. Dan. 1–6), and Judith, Tobit, and the expanded versions of Esther and Daniel in the Septuagint. Like many episodes in Genesis–2 Kings, these compositions focus on the adventures of a central protagonist. Yet unlike them they circulated independently and exhibit dramatic structure.

Episodic narration, reflecting the paratactic style of biblical prose, dominates the Torah (Genesis through Deuteronomy) and the Former Prophets (Joshua through 2 Kings). The form-critical category that closely corresponds to the episodic narrative type is the "saga," which is itself episodic and can incorporate such other literary forms as the tale, the novella, the legend, the history, the report, the fable, etiology, and myth. While the narrative sequence that extends from Genesis to 2 Kings (the Enneateuch) is not unified in terms of plot or action, individual episodes within that framework frequently are. Further, these episodes are often (though frequently loosely) dominated by a "biographical" interest. The patriarchal narratives are dominated successively by Abraham (Gen. 12–25), Jacob (Gen. 25–36), and Joseph (Gen. 37–50), while the remainder of the Pentateuch (Exodus through Deuteronomy) is dominated by the figure of Moses and framed by accounts of his birth and death. Joshua is the focal character of the book bearing his name, while various charismatic leaders figure prominently in the book of Judges. This biographical focus continues on through the books of Samuel and Kings, where the Elijah-Elisha cycle (anticipating later tendencies to emphasize the lives of prophets) contains numerous parallels to the canonical Gospels in both form and content (see below). This episodic style of historical writing found continuity within the Hebrew canon in the work of the Chronicler (1 and 2 Chronicles, Ezra, Nehemiah), as well as in the postcanonical 1 Maccabees. The same episodic technique is exhibited in the so-called midrashic rewriting of Israelite history in Jubilees, and in the *Jewish Antiquities* of Josephus.

The biographical interest in the prophetic figures in Genesis–2 Kings also characterizes portions of the Latter Prophets (Isaiah through Malachi), in which collections of oracles are often framed or punctuated by episodes from the lives of the prophets to whom the oracles or oracle collections were attributed. This oscillation between story and oracle permeates the Latter Prophets.

The characters depicted in the historical narratives of the Bible (particularly Joshua through 2 Kings) are primarily leaders of the people in the capacity of charismatic leaders, prophets, and kings. The Israelite conception of national leaders views them as bearers of divine mandates succeeding one another down through history by providential arrangement. The history of the nation is inseparable from the history of its leaders. Unlike Roman historians, however, who flattered contemporary emperors with encomiastic histories, Israelite historians depicted their leaders with more objectivity, doubtless because they were figures of the past. This is not really biography as compared with its Greco-Roman analogues, however.

Those who favor an Old Testament model for the literary pattern(s) of the Gospels usually focus on either the Moses stories of the Pentateuch or the Elijah-Elisha cycle. Before considering these possibilities, we shall first describe a more generic approach to the problem.

"Ideal Biography" in the Old Testament

Klaus Baltzer has recently identified an Old Testament literary form (using comparative material from Mari and Egypt) which he labels "ideal biography." The office and function of the subject are of central concern in this form, and little or no interest is shown in his personality. Examples of ideal biography are the short titular biography of David (2 Sam. 23:1–7, very close to the biographical epitaphs of Egyptian viziers), the longer narrative biography of Gideon (Judg. 6–8), and the Moses biography (Ex. 2 through Deut. 34), with many constituent topoi.

Baltzer specifically proposes that the Gospels share the genre of "ideal biography." Mark begins with an installation report (the baptism of Jesus, Mark 1:9–11), which contains a reference to time and place (1:9), an installation formula ("You are my beloved son," v. 11), and a calling ("with you I am well pleased," v. 11). Words and deeds of Jesus constitute the broader biography. Exorcisms may be a counterpart to the *topos* of the "securing of peace," and the cleansing of the Temple fits the *topos* of restoring cult purity.

Moses Stories as Literary Paradigms

Moses, in the Jewish estimate, towers over all other figures in Israelite-Jewish history. The figure of Moses influenced early Christian presentations and estimations of Jesus in two major ways, as a paradigm for presenting Jesus as a new Moses (the pattern found in the Gospel of Matthew), and as a means of conceptualizing Jesus as the eschatological Mosaic prophet, a pattern reflected in the Fourth Gospel. Yet the major issue is not whether Jesus was depicted using Mosaic imagery, nor whether the late Second Temple expectation of an eschatological prophet like Moses was used to conceptualize the significance of Jesus, but whether the *literary framework* of the story of Moses in the Pentateuch was influential in shaping the generic features of the Gospels as literature.

The central problem of relating the Gospels to antecedent literary types, according to Meredith Kline, is the presence of two different types of material juxtaposed in the Gospels, teaching discourse and historical narrative. Kline is of course correct that Exodus exhibits a combination of both narrative and sayings traditions in a manner not wholly dissimilar to the Gospels. Yet to regard the inauguration of a covenant as the center of gravity in the Gospels as Kline does is to press them into a mold they do not fit.

On the other hand, if we consider (as Kline does not) the entire complex of Moses legends and traditions from Exodus to Deuteronomy, some significant similarities to the Gospels emerge which are not as easily disposed of. First, the entire life of Moses from birth to death frames the books of Exodus through Deuteronomy. Further, the infant Moses is saved from the destruction intended by Pharaoh in a miraculous manner, and later as an adult must flee to Midian to escape death (Ex. 1–4). In Matthew, Jesus is saved from the murderous designs of Herod when his parents flee to Egypt after a divine warning (Matt. 2). Again, the death of Moses is a mysterious affair which was later transformed in an assumption tradition. The narrative framework of Exodus through Deuteronomy is essentially a travel narrative beginning in Egypt and concluding at the eastern side of the Jordan.

Yet in spite of the parallels just enumerated, the focus of the final version of the Pentateuch woven together by editors is *the presentation and explication of the Torah*, to which the career of Moses is essentially tangential. Like Jesus, Moses performs miracles (e.g., the ten plagues of Ex. 7–12), yet the basic generic features of Exodus through Deuteronomy are essentially dissimilar to those of the Gospels, though in both the process of legendary idealization and embellishment has occurred. While the parallels between the life of Moses and the life of Jesus (particularly in Matthew) are striking at first sight, parallels with other hero cycles with which they have no generic relationship considerably diminish their significance.

The Elijah-Elisha Cycle and the Gospels

The Elijah cycle in the books of Kings consists of six episodic narratives (1 Kings 17–19, 21; 2 Kings 1:1–17), to which six anecdotes have been added, while the Elisha cycle is contained in 2 Kings 2; 3:4–27; 4:1–8, 15; 9:1–10; 13:14–21). To designate these originally independent cycles as the Elijah-Elisha cycle suggests that in early Judaism these figures were merged in popular tradition. As in the case of Moses, Elijah (= Elisha) functioned as a paradigmatic figure in early Christian conceptualizations of Jesus. Popular traditions about eschatological Elijah *redivivus* were thought fulfilled in Jesus of Nazareth. The return of the prophet Elijah was a popular form of the expectation of a coming eschatological prophet, a notion encouraged by the concluding paragraph of the Latter Prophets (Mal. 4:5f.). The ancient Jewish expectation of a returning Elijah was based on the tradition that he was taken up alive into heaven in a whirlwind (2 Kings 2:9–12; Ecclus. 48:9, 12a; 1 Enoch 89.52; 1 Macc. 2:58). By the time of Jesus, Elijah had come to be regarded as the forerunner of the Messiah (Mark 9:11; 1 Enoch 90.31; Justin, *Dialogue with Trypho* 8.3f.; 49.1; 110.1).

Some elements in the Gospel tradition suggest that Jesus was regarded by some of his contemporaries as the eschatological Elijah (Mark 6:14f.; 8:28; John 1:19–21). J. Louis Martyn has argued at length that one of the sources of the Fourth Gospel conceptualized Jesus as the eschatological Elijah. Nevertheless, the early identification of John the Baptist as the eschatological Elijah who served as the forerunner of the Messiah Jesus made the older conceptualization of Jesus as Elijah inherently problematic so that the identification was suppressed.

Raymond Brown has proposed that an Elisha typology exerted a formative influence on the Gospel narratives. He makes the following points: (1) Elisha is depicted as traveling around the Northern Kingdom (Shunem, Gilgal, Jericho, Dothan), a parallel to Jesus' peripatetic ministry. (2) While Elijah and Elisha both provide parallels for the kind of miracles attributed to Jesus, twice as many miracles are attributed to Elisha as to Elijah. (3) Specific parallels between Jesus' miracles and those of Elisha include the following: (a) The miraculous cure of leprosy by Jesus (Mark 1:40–45 and pars.;

Matt. 11:4–5; Luke 7:21–22; cf. 17:11–19) is paralleled by Elisha's
cure of Naaman the Syrian (2 Kings 5). (b) Jesus' multiplication of
loaves (Mark 6:30–44; 8:1–10 and pars.; John 6:1–15) resembles
Elisha's multiplication of twenty loaves for one hundred men (2
Kings 4:42–44), including such motifs as the use of barley loaves,
the presence of a boy in the scene, and the objection that so little
could not feed so many. (c) The raising of the young man of Nain
(Luke 7:11–17) resembles Elijah's revival of the son of the widow
of Zarephath (1 Kings 17:17–24) and Elisha's raising of the son of
the Shunammite (2 Kings 4:18–37). Further, Brown notes that there
are many elements in the miracles of Jesus that have no parallel in
the Elisha stories (exorcisms, healings of the blind and the paralyzed), just as some features in the Elisha stories have no parallel
in the Gospels (the floating axhead, the purification of Jericho's
water, Elisha's induced ecstasy, etc.). In conclusion, Brown discusses recent research which suggests that an aretalogy (a collection
of miracle stories showing that various figures were in fact "divine
men") was prefixed to the passion narrative by Mark to counter an
incorrect view of Jesus as a wonder-worker. Brown proposes that
the early Christian conception of Jesus as an eschatological prophet
who worked wonders has a more appropriate model in the Elisha
cycle of miracles than in Greco-Roman aretalogies. The story of
Jeremiah is also relevant, he suggests, for it includes poetic oracles
connected to a prose biography of a prophet whose career began
with a divine call and concluded with his suffering and virtual martyrdom.

Postbiblical Biographical Traditions

The "biographical" interest in great prophetic figures of Israel's
past found renewed expression in the postbiblical period with the
composition of the *Lives of the Prophets* in Palestine during the first
century A.D. These *Lives* are thumbnail sketches of twenty-three
Israelite prophets, giving basic facts about their births and deaths
and including some anecdotes usually based on nonbiblical traditions. The superscription or title of the work provides a basic outline of each life: "The names of the prophets, where they came
from, where they died, and how and where they were buried."
There is some emphasis on the value and use of oral tradition by
the author (*Lives of the Prophets: Jeremiah* 5; *Daniel* 19), and many
anecdotes (chreiai) are included in some of the longer compositions. In some cases the sketches function as a summary of the
prophet's achievements (*Lives of the Prophets: Zechariah Son of Iddo*

1–6; *Ahijah* 1–5). The Greek lives of the poets are the closest literary parallel in form and function, while the content of both types of lives is culturally distinct.

Philo of Alexandria (ca. 20 B.C. to A.D. 50) was a prolific Hellenistic Jewish scholar who interpreted the Jewish Torah from the standpoint of an eclectic Hellenistic philosophy. Among his many writings are lives of Abraham, Joseph, and Moses (his lives of Isaac and Jacob are lost). Each patriarch is the allegorical embodiment of aspects of wisdom (*On Joseph* 1; *On Abraham* 56). Abraham is wisdom through study, Isaac is wisdom through nature, and Jacob is wisdom through practice. These lives combine chronological narratives based on the biblical text with the systematic discussion of exemplary moral qualities such as hospitality, kindness, courage, self-control (*On Abraham* 1–47; *On Joseph* 1–156). Despite the fact that the subjects are heroes of Judaism, the biographical treatment is thoroughly Hellenistic.

Louis H. Feldman has recently demonstrated that Josephus, in his retelling of the biblical narratives from Genesis to 2 Kings (blended with the work of the Chronicler), introduced Hellenistic biographical concerns into the narrative. His portrait of Saul, for example, emphasizes the traditional Greek moral qualities of wisdom, courage, temperance, and justice.

During the formation of the Mishnah and the Babylonian and Jerusalem Talmuds (second through sixth centuries A.D.), rabbinic Judaism produced no biographical literature. Rabbinic writings (none of which is attributed to particular authors) contain many sayings attributed to particular authorities and stories about specific rabbis. Yet there are no *collections* of sayings attributed to particular individuals or *sustained narratives* incorporating clusters of stories about individual sages. By Tannaitic times (second century A.D.), the emphasis on halakah (legal questions) had all but eliminated the biographical concerns of earlier periods. Most rabbinic traditions are attributed to specific authorities, and yet even these have usually been conformed to stereotypical literary forms, thus erasing individuality. Attributions that do exist in the material are therefore not historically reliable (the same sayings can be attributed to different authorities), a situation not dissimilar from Greek anecdotes. The connection of traditions with specific names from the past functions to underline the antiquity and authority of the traditions themselves.

Summary

Two major "nonliterary" models have been proposed for the Gospels: the Gospels as the kerygma in expanded form and the Gospels as written sequences of lections intended to replace the cycle of Old Testament Sabbath and festal readings of Judaism. The expanded kerygma hypothesis fails because in form, content, and function there are major differences between the written Gospels and the reconstructed versions of the oral kerygma. The liturgical genre theory is similarly deficient in that it too cannot explain the literary qualities of the Gospels.

There is no Old Testament literary form or tradition which can appropriately be labeled "biography." While many of the ingredients are present in the "ideal biography" described by Klaus Baltzer, they are never fully developed into a biographical genre. By the Hellenistic period the Jewish biographical literature produced by such writers as Philo and Josephus reflects a strong dependence on Hellenistic literary culture. By the late Tannaitic period (ca. A.D. 150–200), rabbinic Judaism had lost all interest in biography.

On the other hand, the features of Greco-Roman biography surveyed above offer many close if not exact parallels to the major literary qualities and features of the Gospels. In chapter 2 we will analyze the Gospels in terms of their distinctive literary qualities in the areas of form (including structure and style), content, and function. The results of this analysis will then be compared with the major features of Greco-Roman and Israelite-Jewish biographical forms and traditions discussed above to see if a literary pedigree of the Gospels can be proposed.

For Further Study

On Greco-Roman Biography: The classic study is Friedrich Leo, *Die griechisch-römische Biographie nach ihrer litterarischen Form* (Leipzig: Teubner, 1901). Also important are Ivo Bruns, *Die Persönlichkeit in der Geschichtsschreibung der Alten: Untersuchungen zur Technik der antiken Historiographie* (Berlin: Wilhelm Hertz, 1898), and Duane Reed Stuart, *Epochs of Greek and Roman Biography* (University of California Press, 1928). **Greek Biography:** The best discussion in English is Arnaldo Momigliano, *The Development of Greek Biography* (Harvard University Press, 1971). Important for the later period is Patricia Cox, *Biography in Late Antiquity: A Quest for the Holy Man* (University of California Press, 1983). Other important works include Albrecht Dihle, *Studien zur griechischen Biographie* (Göttingen: Vandenhoeck & Ruprecht, 1956); Janet Fairweather, "Fiction in the Biographies of Ancient

Writers," *Ancient Society* 5 (1974), 231–275; Mary R. Lefkowitz, *The Lives of the Greek Poets* (Johns Hopkins University Press, 1981) (the appendices contain translations of the lives of Homer, Pindar, Aeschylus, Sophocles, Euripides, and Aristophanes); Wolf Steidle, *Sueton und die antike Biographie*, Zetemata, 1 (Munich: C. H. Beck, 1951); Fritz Wehrli, "Gnome, Anekdote und Biographie," *Museum Helveticum* 30 (1973), 194–208. *The Image of the Holy Man:* An extensive survey of the problem and the literature is found in G. Fowden, "The Pagan Holy Man in Late Antiquity," *JHS* 102 (1982), 33–59. Another important treatment is Peter Brown, "The Rise and Function of the Holy Man in Late Antiquity," *JRS* 61 (1971), 80–101, reprinted in *Society and the Holy in Late Antiquity* (University of California Press, 1982), pp. 103–152. *Apollonius of Tyana:* For an excellent review of the literature see E. L. Bowie, "Apollonius of Tyana: Tradition and Reality," *ANRW* II.16.2 (1978). Particularly important is G. Petzke, *Die Traditionen über Apollonius von Tyana* (Leiden: E. J. Brill, 1970). *Aristotle:* Ingemar Düring, *Aristotle in the Ancient Biographical Tradition* (Göteborg: Almqvist & Wiksell, 1957). *Plato:* Alice Swift Riginos, *Platonica: The Anecdotes Concerning the Life and Writings of Plato* (Leiden: E. J. Brill, 1976). *Plutarch:* Barbara Bucher-Isler, *Norm und Individualität in den Biographien Plutarchs* (Bern and Stuttgart: Verlag Paul Haupt, 1972); Alan Wardman, *Plutarch's Lives* (University of California Press, 1974); and the classic study by Ulrich von Wilamowitz-Moellendorff, "Plutarch als Biograph," in idem, *Reden und Vorträge*, 4th ed., vol. 2 (Berlin: Weidmannsche Buchhandlung, 1926). *Suetonius and Latin Biography:* T. A. Dorey, ed., *Latin Biography* (London: Routledge & Kegan Paul, 1967). One of the best recent discussions of Suetonius is Andrew Wallace-Hadrill, *Suetonius: The Scholar and His Caesars* (Yale University Press, 1983).

On the Genre of the Gospels: *Expanded Kerygma Hypothesis:* Two competent surveys of the problem, both of which conclude that the Gospels are unique, i.e., kerygmatic in origin, are R. A. Guelich, "The Gospel Genre," in *Das Evangelium und die Evangelien,* ed. by P. Stuhlmacher (Tübingen: J. C. B. Mohr [Paul Siebeck], 1983), pp. 183–219, and Robert H. Gundry, "Recent Investigations Into the Literary Genre 'Gospel,' " in *New Dimensions in New Testament Study,* ed. by R. N. Longenecker and M. C. Tenney (Zondervan Publishing House, 1974), pp. 97–114. *Liturgical Genre Hypothesis:* Three important variants of the liturgical genre hypothesis include P. Carrington, *The Primitive Christian Calendar: A Study in the Making of the Marcan Gospel* (Cambridge: University Press, 1952); two books by M. Goulder, *Midrash and Lection in Matthew* (London: S.P.C.K., 1974) and *The Evangelists' Calendar: A Lectionary Explanation of the Development of Scripture* (London: S.P.C.K., 1978); and Aileen Guilding, *The Fourth Gospel and Jewish Worship* (Oxford: University Press, 1960). This theory is heavily criticized by Leon Morris in two studies, *The New Testament and the Jewish Lectionaries* (London: Tyndale Press, 1964) and "The Gospels and the Jewish Lectionaries," in *Gospel Perspectives,* vol. 3: *Studies in Midrash and Historiography,* ed. by R. T. France and D. Wenham (Sheffield: JSOT Press, 1983), pp. 129–156. See also W. D. Davies, "Reflections on Archbishop Carrington's *The Primitive Christian Calendar,*" in idem, *Christian Origins and Judaism* (Westminster Press, 1962), pp. 67–95. *Old Testament Patterns:* Raymond Brown, "Jesus and Elijah," *Perspective* 12 (1971), 85–104; Meredith Kline, "The Old Testament Origins of the Gospel Genre," *Westminster Theological Journal* 38 (1975), 1–27.

On the Gospels as Greco-Roman Biography: A negative assessment is provided by Albrecht Dihle, "Die Evangelism und die biographische Tradition der Antike," *Zeitschrift für Theologie and Kirche* 80 (1983), 33–49. Arthur Droge, "Call Stories in Greek Biography and the Gospels," in *Society of Biblical Literature: 1983 Seminar Papers,* ed. by Kent H. Richards (Scholars Press, 1983), pp. 245–254. Two important articles in support of the understanding of the Gospels as Greco-Roman biography: Hubert Cancik, "Die Gattung Evangelium: Das Evangelium des Markus im Rahmen der antiken Historiographie," and "Bios und Logos: Formengeschichtliche Untersuchungen zu Lukians 'Demonax,' " in *Markus-Philologie,* ed. by H. Cancik (Tübingen: J. C. B. Mohr [Paul Siebeck], 1984). The dubious view that the Gospel of Matthew is an encomium is argued by Philip L. Shuler, *A Genre for the Gospels: The Biographical Character of Matthew* (Fortress Press, 1982). Charles H. Talbert, *What Is a Gospel? The Genre of the Canonical Gospels* (Fortress Press, 1977), uses faulty arguments to prove that the Gospels conform to ancient lives of philosophers; cf. David E. Aune, "The Problem of the Genre of the Gospels: A Critique of C. H. Talbert's *What Is a Gospel?*" in *Gospel Perspectives: Studies of History and Tradition in the Four Gospels,* ed. by R. T. France and D. Wenham, vol. 2 (Sheffield: JSOT Press, 1981).

On Israelite-Jewish Biography: One of the few studies of Israelite biography is Klaus Baltzer, *Die Biographie der Propheten* (Neukirchen-Vluyn: Neukirchener Verlag, 1975). See also Charles C. Torrey, *The Lives of the Prophets: Greek Text and Translation* (Philadelphia: Society of Biblical Literature and Exegesis, 1946). *Josephus:* Louis H. Feldman has written several important articles on the Hellenistic tendencies on the biographies in Josephus: "Josephus as an Apologist of the Greco-Roman World: His Portrait of Solomon," in *Aspects of Religious Propaganda in Judaism and Early Christianity,* ed. by Elisabeth Schüssler Fiorenza (University of Notre Dame Press, 1976), pp. 68–98, and "Josephus' Portrait of Saul," *Hebrew Union College Annual* 53 (1982), 45–99. *Philo:* Anton Priessnig, "Die literarische Form der Patriarchen-biographien des Philon von Alexandrien," *Monatschrift für Geschichte und Wissenschaft des Judentums* 37 (1929), 143–155. On the absence of biography in rabbinic literature, see W. S. Green, "What's in a Name?—The Problematic of Rabbinic 'Biography,' " in *Approaches to Ancient Judaism: Theory and Practice,* ed. by W. S. Green (Scholars Press, 1978), pp. 77–96, and Jacob Neusner, *In Search of Talmudic Biography: The Problem of the Attributed Saying* (Scholars Press, 1984).

2

The Gospels as Ancient Biography
and the Growth
of Jesus Literature

The Gospels have no *exact* literary analogues in antiquity. While true, this statement is inconsequential and misleading. It is inconsequential because identical claims can be made for scores of Hellenistic compositions, many biographical in character (e.g., Philostratus' *Life of Apollonius,* Lucian's *Demonax,* the anonymous life of Secundus the Silent Philosopher, and Tacitus' *Agricola*). It is misleading because of the fallacy of holistic comparison. Greco-Roman biography was a continuously developing, complex genre with changing features. An analysis of the constituent literary features of the Gospels situates them comfortably within the parameters of ancient biographical conventions in form and function. They constitute a *subtype* of Greco-Roman biography primarily determined by *content,* reflecting Judeo-Christian assumptions. The Gospels (and other types of early Christian literature) have connections with *both* Jewish and Greco-Roman literary traditions. Hellenistic Jewish and early Christian literature invariably exhibit various degrees of literary syncretism. *Adaptation,* not wholesale borrowing, was the rule.

After considering the form, content, and function of the Gospels in terms of primary and secondary generic features, I will discuss the intrinsic and extrinsic reasons for categorizing the Gospels as a type of ancient biography. Mark is the primary focus of attention. As the first written Gospel, it does not exhibit ancient literary qualities as obviously as the other Gospels. Since the production of literature dealing with the words and deeds of Jesus did not cease with the composition of the canonical Gospels, we will conclude this chapter with a survey of later Jesus literature.

The Form of the Gospels

The *form* of the Gospels includes such matters as language and style, structure, and constituent oral and literary forms.

Language and Style

The type of Greek found in Mark and the other Gospels has been variously assessed as the language of the lower classes (as reflected in the papyri), or a Jewish Greek similar to that spoken by translators of the Greek Septuagint (from the Hebrew Scriptures), or a "ghetto" Greek reflecting the minority group status and outlook of early Christians. Recently Marius Riesner has demonstrated that many so-called "Semitisms" in Mark (i.e., Hebrew or Aramaic idioms awkwardly expressed in Greek) are common in Greek popular literature. The style of Mark, therefore, is a *popular literary style,* even though it does not rise to the literary standards of the highly educated.

Structure

Structurally the Gospels consist of a chronological presentation of Jesus' public career (here form is difficult to distinguish from content). Only once is a story-unit presented out of chronological sequence as a "flashback": the story of John the Baptist's fate in Mark 6:17–29. This Markan "flashback" is essentially a major "digression," in this case a novella, a developed story. None of the Evangelists presents a topical or systematic presentation of Jesus' words or deeds. Of course the modern study of the Gospels has long recognized the artificiality of Mark's time framework, into which he inserted a variety of traditional sayings and deeds of Jesus, and there is temporal vagueness in editorial links between some individual units. While that is true, it is clear that *the Evangelists chose to maintain the appearance of a chronologically ordered narrative.* While some originally oral traditions still exhibit preliterary features, often the Evangelists have given them conventional literary form. Formally the Gospels are indistinguishable from Greco-Roman biographies. That should not be surprising, since discrete biographies occur only very rarely in Judaism (e.g., *Lives of the Prophets;* Philo, *Life of Moses, On Abraham,* and *On Joseph*), and then they tend to combine Jewish and Hellenistic features.

Mark and John begin their narratives with the activity of John the

Baptist and the baptism of Jesus. Some versions of the oral proclamation of Jesus, or kerygma, apparently began this way (cf. Acts
10:37; 13:24f.), and that may have determined Mark's point of departure. Yet there is another reason why this starting point is appropriate in a *biographical* composition within a Jewish ambience. The
baptismal scene (Mark 1:9–11), provides divine legitimation for
Jesus' identity "son of God," or "Messiah," in a manner that functions similarly to the definition provided by ancestry, birth, and
education in Greco-Roman biography. Further, the word "beginning" in Mark 1:1 is virtually a technical term in historical and
biographical writing, based on the notion that the complete explanation of a historical phenomenon must be based on its origins
(Polybius 5.31.1–2; Tacitus, *Histories* 1.1.1; Dionysius of Halicarnassus 1.8.4; Polybius 1.5.1). The phrase "In the beginning" (John 1:1)
is a play on words referring both to Gen. 1:1 and to the proper
beginning for the story of Jesus.

Mark and John both have a dramatic structure that some have too
closely associated with Greek tragedy. Mark does not simply narrate
the story of Jesus by placing various episodes in chronological
order. He imposes a plot that connects individual episodes in a
causal sequence. This imposition of dramatic structure has simplified and stylized the story. Mark, followed by Matthew and Luke,
depicts Jesus as active in Galilee for about one year, followed by a
single fateful trip to Jerusalem where he spends his final week. John,
however, presents Jesus' ministry as lasting two to three years and
punctuated by several trips to Jerusalem (2:13; 5:1; 7:10). The last
trip puts him in Jerusalem for a full half year. The plot is moved by
various degrees of conflict between Jesus and other characters (including disciples) over the issue of his true identity and significance.
These are revealed by words and deeds that disclose his status and
authority (though ambiguously). The plot of Mark (closely followed
by Matthew) includes formal features of Greek tragedy: (1) *Introduction* or *exposition:* The Old Testament predicts the coming of John
the Baptist, who baptizes Jesus, whom a heavenly voice (i.e., God)
identifies as "my beloved Son." Jesus is then driven to the wilderness and tempted by Satan (1:1–13). (2) *Rising action* or *complication:*
After announcing the imminent arrival of the Kingdom of God and
the necessity of believing the gospel, and by implication its proclaimer, Jesus roams about Galilee teaching and performing miracles of healing and exorcism. Though he is generally well received,
increasing conflict with Jewish religious leaders provokes them to
plot his death (1:14–8:21). (3) *Climax* or *crisis:* This central section,
framed by two stories of the healing of blind men (8:22–26; 10:

46–52), is a fateful journey from Bethsaida to Jerusalem signaled by the recurring phrase "on the way" (8:27; 9:33, 34; 10:17, 32, 52). Peter, representing the disciples, identifies Jesus as the Messiah (8:27–30), whereupon Jesus explicitly predicts the passion and resurrection of the Son of Man (8:31; 9:31; 10:33f.). In each case the misunderstanding of the disciples results in lectures on discipleship (8:22–10:52). (4) *Falling action:* Jesus arrives in Jerusalem and by his actions (cleansing the Temple) and teaching antagonizes the religious leaders, who plot his death (11:18) and unsuccessfully try to arrest him (12:12). In chapter 13 he predicts the fall of the Temple and the events of the last days (11:1–13:37). (5) *Catastrophe:* Jesus and the disciples celebrate the Passover, followed by his betrayal and arrest, trial and crucifixion (14:1–15:39). (6) *Denouement:* The empty tomb is discovered and the resurrection is announced (15: 40–16:8). The final resurrection, more appropriate to comedy, makes a "tragicomedy" of Mark and the other Gospels. While Greco-Roman biography rarely exhibits a plot, the "plot" of Mark appears to have been generated by early Christian apologetic explaining the troubling death of the Messiah. The story of Jesus' death, the passion narrative, which probably existed prior to Mark, was cast in the dramatic literary *topos* of the persecution and vindication of an innocent person.

Matthew essentially follows the plot of Mark, though incorporating large sections of teaching material that tend to obscure the clarity of Mark's structure. Matthew has imposed rhetorical "division" on his material of a type wholly absent from Mark by concluding each of five lengthy speeches by Jesus with the phrase "And it came to pass, when Jesus had finished" (7:28; 11:1; 13:53; 19:1; 26:1). Jack Dean Kingsbury suggests the following structure for Matthew: (1) The Person of Jesus the Messiah (1:1–4:16); (2) The Proclamation of Jesus the Messiah (4:17–16:20); (3) The Suffering, Death, and Resurrection of Jesus the Messiah (16:21–28:20). The Gospel of John is arranged in two nearly equal parts, according to C. H. Dodd, the Book of Signs (1:19–12:50), in which Jesus performs seven signs and Jewish opposition to him steadily mounts from chapter 5 through 8 until his death is plotted in 11:53, and the Book of the Passion (13:1–20:31), in which Jesus, rejected by all but his own followers despite the signs, turns from the world, and through a series of discourses prepares the disciples for his departure (13–16), followed by his arrest, trial, execution, and resurrection. This is framed by a prologue (1:1–18) and an epilogue (21: 1–25).

Constituent Oral Forms

The Gospels exhibit an episodic quality recognized earlier in this century as reflecting the incorporation of originally independent units of story and sayings material. The Evangelists apparently functioned as *author-editors,* since they used many originally independent traditions and (without introducing radical modifications) shaped them into coherent compositions reflecting their own perspectives. John is a partial exception, however, since he and his sources reformulated received traditions more thoroughly, forging larger, more coherent panels of material. Form criticism is a method that tries to (1) classify the unit or form, (2) reconstruct the original form, and (3) establish the original setting of the oral forms that were incorporated into the Gospels. The early proponents of form criticism used both Greco-Roman rhetorical terms for different kinds of sayings and direct analysis of the forms found in the Synoptic Gospels. The classification schemes have proven relatively useful, though the second and third tasks are problematic. Likewise it is not the exact words of Jesus which have been preserved, but the basic structure or sense of his words. Folklorists now recognize that the same tradition can be used and reformulated in many different settings. The quest for a *single* "original" setting cannot be successful, since the same form could have had settings in the ministry of Jesus as well as in the early church. The reconstruction of the original setting and function of Gospel traditions has therefore been the least successful aspect of form criticism.

The constituent oral forms of the Gospels can be classified on the basis of whether story (narration) or sayings (discourse) predominates. Narrative types include (1) miracle stories, (2) pronouncement stories, and (3) stories about Jesus, while discourse types include (4) parables (i.e., narrative sayings) and (5) sayings or aphorisms.

Miracle stories often consist of three structural elements: (a) circumstances of the healing, (b) the healing itself, and (c) confirmation of the cure and/or impression on audience (e.g., Mark 1:23–27, 29–31, 40–43; 3:1–6; 5:1–20; 7:24–30; 10:46–52; altogether all four Gospels contain twenty-nine miracles, including five exorcisms, eighteen healings, and six "nature" miracles, not counting Jesus' walking on water, which is an epiphany story).

Pronouncement stories are short narrative frames (often mini-dialogues with a specific setting) that focus on a culminating saying of Jesus (e.g., Mark 2:15–17; 3:22–27; 10:17–22; there are about three dozen in the Gospels).

Stories about Jesus, a blend of history and legend, exhibit great variety in form and have no consistent formal features (e.g., Mark 1:9–11, 12–13; 6:30–44; 8:1–10).

Parables, perhaps the most intensively investigated of all Gospel forms, are metaphorical narrative sayings of Jesus which make one central point. The sixty-five parables of the Synoptic Gospels constitute 35 percent of the teaching of Jesus. The parable (from a Greek term meaning "to place alongside," i.e., a "comparison") is distinguished from the allegory in that the latter has many separate but connected meanings. Four types of parables can be distinguished, though somewhat artificially: (a) the *similitude*, which describes a typical situation or event (e.g., the parables of the sower and the mustard seed in Mark 4; the lost sheep and the lost coin, Luke 15:1–10); (b) the *parable* proper, or analogy, which describes a particular event or incident (Mark 12:1–11; Luke 14:16–24; 16:1–9; Matt. 21:28–32); (c) the *example story* (e.g., the good Samaritan, Luke 10:29–37; the rich fool, Luke 12:16–21; the rich man and Lazarus, Luke 16:19–31); and (d) the *allegory* (e.g., Mark 4:13–20; 12:1–12; Matt. 22:1–14).

Sayings of Jesus, or aphorisms, lack the narrative framework typical of pronouncement stories, though they can be expanded to form pronouncement stories. Sayings can be classified by content as: (a) *wisdom sayings*, or proverbs (e.g., Matt. 6:34; 12:34; 22:14); (b) *prophetic and apocalyptic sayings* (Mark 1:15; Luke 6:20f.; 10:23f.); (c) *laws and church rules* (Mark 3:4; 7:15; Matt. 18:15–17); and (d) *"I" sayings* in which Jesus speaks of himself, his work or destiny (Mark 10:45; Matt. 5:17; 15:24).

The Fourth Gospel contains traditional material recast into a distinctive Johannine idiom and is consequently less amenable to form-critical analysis. John includes seven miracle stories, though unlike their Synoptic counterparts they sometimes become points of departure for lengthy discourses. The first two signs are numbered (2:11; 4:54), an indication that John used a "signs source." John begins by quoting a hymn (1:1–18), with some prose modifications (vs. 6–8). John also contains several relatively long discourses of Jesus, more unified in form and content than anything comparable in the Synoptics. Many Johannine discourses begin as dialogues and develop into monologues (e.g., 3:1–21, 31–36; 13:31–14:31). Typically they begin with a statement of Jesus, followed by a response indicating incomprehension or misunderstanding, which becomes the basis for a monologue (3:1–21; 4:31–38; 9:38–41). The author also uses pure monologues (5:19–47; 12:20–36, 44–50; 15:1–16: 15), monologues framed by dialogue (16:16–30), dramatic dialogues (4:7–27; 6:25–59), and about eight short controversy dialogues (7:14–24, 25–36, 37–44, 45–52; 8:12–20, 21–30, 31–40; 10: 22–39). John often links a narrative section to a discourse by means of a dialogue (chs. 5; 6; 9; 11). The structure and composition of some Johannine discourses have parallels with Hermetic dialogues and Gnostic revelation discourses (particularly the "I am" predications), but others are similar in structure to Jewish synagogue homilies. Many portions of the Johannine discourses may have originated as homiletic elaborations of Jesus traditions.

The irregular, episodic quality of the Synoptic narratives reflects the utilization of existing Jesus traditions with only minor modifications. The material common to Matthew and Luke but not in Mark, called "Q," and the later Gospel of Thomas serialize discourse materials without using Jesus' life as a framework (sayings, parables, and pronouncement stories; Q contains just three narrative units: the temptation in Luke 4:1–13 = Matt. 4:1–11; one healing miracle, Luke 7:1–10 = Matt. 8:5–13; one exorcism, Luke 11:14 = Matt. 12:22f.). The first three Gospels tend either to make use of existing *collections* of Jesus traditions, or to arrange traditions into new literary units.

The identification of pre-Markan collections often turns on how creative Mark is judged to be. Possible pre-Markan collections include 2:1–3:6 (five pronouncement or conflict stories); 4:1–34 (three parables); 4:35–5:43 (four miracle stories); 6:32–52 (two miracle stories); 10:1–45 (three conflict stories); and 13:5–27 (an apocalyptic discourse containing many sayings of Jesus). Though the original settings of these collections remain speculative, they appear to have been formed initially on the basis of similar forms and functions, common themes and catchwords. In themselves, these collections betray no tendency to portray the life of Jesus, and so do not suggest the inevitability of the gospel form.

Constituent Literary Forms

The Evangelists also used earlier traditions to construct conventional literary forms, though insufficient attention has been paid to this literary phenomenon.

The *Passion narrative* in Mark 14–16, perhaps the oldest continuous narrative in the Gospels, exhibits motifs similar to those associated with stories of persecution and vindication of innocent persons in Jewish literature (e.g., Gen. 37ff.; Esther; Dan. 3 and 6; Susanna; Wisd. of Sol. 2–5; 3 Macc.; 2 Macc. 7). The sequence of common motifs in such stories constitutes a literary *topos*. The dramatic structure of this *topos*, which centers on the resolution of conflict between the innocent victim and the authorities, may have generated the basic plot of Mark, supporting the description of Mark as a Passion story with an extended introduction. Similar sequences of motifs also occur in the adventures of the Greek romances. During the late Hellenistic period there was a strong interest in the deaths of famous men. This is reflected in the lives of philosophers by Dionysius Laertius, in the anonymous lives of the Greek poets, and as a subgenre of biography on the deaths of famous men (cf. Pliny, *Letter* 5.5.3). Further, the image of Socrates as a martyr had a powerful impact on Christian literature, including the acts of the martyrs and the apologists. Further the extensive trial scenes in Acts in which Paul is the central figure also reflect this *topos*.

Another literary form, the *temple dialogue,* occurs in the apocalyptic discourse in Mark 13. The introductory framework has two striking features: an introductory peripatetic (strolling) dialogue (vs. 1–2), and a seated dialogue with the Temple in view (vs. 3–4). These conventions were combined in many Greco-Roman dialogues (cf. Plutarch, *On the Cessation of Oracles; On the E at Delphi;* Varro, *On Agriculture*).

Several scholars have proposed that the Synoptic Gospels contain examples of the *homiletic midrash* or sermon. These are explanations, in sermon form, of the Sabbath and festival synagogue readings from the Torah and Prophets. Two patterns are generally distinguished. (1) The "proem" homily consists of the Torah text for the day, a second text as "proem" or opening portion of the homily, an exposition using additional biblical texts, including the *haphtarah* text from the Prophets (often beginning with the phrase "Its interpretation is"), assembled on the basis of catchwords, and a concluding text with links to the appropriate Torah text (e.g., Mark 12:1–12; Matt. 21:33–46). (2) The *"yelammedenu rabbenu"* (literally, "let our master teach us") homily begins with a problem or question answered in the exposition following the "proem" format (e.g., Mark 12:28–31; Luke 10:25–37). There is a danger of anachronism, however, in using Jewish homiletic forms from later centuries, since Jewish scholars place the beginning of these forms in the third century A.D.

Genealogies, like those in Matthew 1 and Luke 3, illustrate a special form of list favored by Near Eastern cultures. Biblical genealogies may function in one of several ways: to establish identity, to legitimate the status of an individual or a series of officeholders, or to account for the character of a descendant.

Mark contains a number of *summary reports,* which are attempts by the author to make general statements about the activities of Jesus that go beyond the specific examples included in the narrative. Their primary literary function is to help the narrative to flow smoothly. Mark 1:39 is a typical example of a summary report: "And he [Jesus] went throughout all Galilee, preaching in their synagogues and casting out demons." Eight summary reports are found in Mark (all used by Matthew): 1:14–15, 32–34, 39; 3:7–12; 6:6b, 34, 53–56; 10:1. Other passages with generalizing character function to introduce pericopes (e.g., 1:4–5; 2:1–2; 4:1–2; 10:1) or to conclude them (1:28, 45; 4:33–34; 6:12–13). The summary reports in the *Life of Apollonius* by Philostratus illuminate the function of the Markan summary reports: (1) independent summary reports (e.g., 3.24; 3.58); (2) generalizing introductions (e.g. 3.41; 4.1; 6.35); (3) generalizing conclusions (3.40; 5.43; 6.43); and (4) generalizing transitions (4.10; 5.18; 7.28). The similarities between these passages and those in Mark reveal a common literary technique in Hellenistic prose narrative writing.

The Content of the Gospels

The content of the Gospels is a stereotyped presentation of the public career of Jesus beginning either with his divine commission mediated through John the Baptist (Mark, John) or with his ancestry and birth (Matthew and Luke), and concluding with his death and resurrection (all the Gospels), his commission to the disciples (Matthew and Luke) and ascension (Luke). Greco-Roman biographies focused on people with such significant social roles as kings, military commanders, philosophers, poets and artists, while Israelite-Jewish biographical writing emphasized charismatic leaders, kings, and prophets. Old Testament figures such as Moses, Elijah, and Elisha (heroized with postbiblical legendary embellishments) served as models for conceptualizing Jesus at both preliterary and literary stages of Gospel tradition. Jewish kingship traditions had, in the absence of national independence and the suppression of native kingship, become idealized and projected into the eagerly expected "end time," the eschatological future. The role into which Jesus is typecast in the Gospels is an amalgam of existing conceptions of the categories eschatological prophet and messianic king.

The ultimate religious claim made for Jesus, which played a special role in the kerygma or proclamation, dominates the literary presentation of his activities and teachings in the four canonical Gospels. Mark's position is clearly stated when he designates the content of his work as "the gospel of Jesus the Messiah, the Son of God" (Mark 1:1). Similarly, Matthew labels the genealogy at the beginning of his Gospel "The book of the genealogy of Jesus Christ, the son of David, the son of Abraham" (Matt. 1:1). The Fourth Evangelist summarizes his purpose in his concluding paragraph: "that you may believe that Jesus is the Messiah, the Son of God" (John 20:30–31). The content of Mark and the other Gospels, then, is dominated by attempts to demonstrate and confirm the supreme significance of the identity of Jesus conceptualized in terms of various types of eschatological deliverers. Terms such as "Messiah" and "Son of God" were ambiguous among Jews of the time, and perhaps for this reason a number of other terms and conceptions are drawn into the narrative. These include Son of David, the prophet, Son of Man, King of Israel, Lord, Son, Word, etc. Because these roles are attributed to Jesus, they are denied to potential competitors (cf. Mark 13:21f.). God identifies Jesus as his "beloved Son" at Jesus' baptism and transfiguration (Mark 1:11; 9:7). Demons call him the "Holy One of God" (Mark 1:24), the "Son of God" (Mark 3:11), and the "Son of the Most High God" (Mark 5:7). Peter, speaking for the disciples, calls him the "Messiah" (Mark 8:29). In Mark 12:6, Jesus designates himself as the "beloved son" but in parabolic speech. At the pivotal trial scene, when asked if he is "the Messiah the Son of the Blessed," Jesus replies positively (Mark 14:61–62). Pilate and his guards ironically identify him as "King of the Jews" (Mark 15:9, 12, 18), a title inscribed on the indictment on the cross (15:26). Finally, after his death a centurion exclaims, "Truly this man was the Son of God!" (Mark 15:39).

This emphasis on the identity of Jesus is strengthened by the use of several supportive literary themes or motifs, including (1) the depiction of the disciples as obtuse, fearful, and misunderstanding; (2) the refutation of the charge that Jesus practiced magic; and (3) the secrecy surrounding Jesus' true identity (the last is missing from John). Each of these requires elaboration.

1. Recently scholars have proposed that the disciples are unfavorably presented in Mark because they represent either a current heresy that Mark wants to refute, or the Jerusalem leadership of the church to which he is opposed. In the ancient world, *misunderstanding* was understood as a characteristic human response to divine revelation. This is evident in Greco-Roman revelatory dialogues, in which the human recipient of divine revelation is usually depicted as obtuse (e.g., *Hermetica* 13; cf. *Shepherd of Hermas*). Even revelation in human language (e.g., oracles and prophecy) was widely assumed to be enigmatical and ambiguous. In the late biographies of holy

men (Philostratus' *Life of Apollonius* and the lives of Pythagoras by Porphyry and Iamblichus), the misunderstanding of disciples and the hostility of authorities are stock themes. In the Gospels, the ignorance and fear of those in contact with Jesus are literary devices emphasizing the revelatory character of his words and the supernatural power evident in his deeds. In Mark, the ignorance of the disciples is often emphasized in editorial or redactional passages contributed by Mark himself (Mark 4:13, 41; 6:52; 8:17–21; 9:10, 19). This blindness often gives rise to questions to which Jesus gives private responses (4:10; 7:17; 9:11, 28; 10:10, 26; 13:3–4). In contrast, Matthew and Luke tend to tone down or eliminate Markan criticism of the disciples (cf. Mark 6:51f. with Matt. 14:32f.; Mark 4:13 with Matt. 13:18 and Luke 8:11; Matthew eliminated Mark 8:17f.). The motif of misunderstanding is more highly developed in John, where it is broadened to include others besides disciples (the Jews, Nicodemus, the crowd and the Samaritan woman). Misunderstandings are the result of ambiguities or double meanings in Jesus' discussions (e.g., 2:19–21; 3:3–5; 4:10–15, 31–34; 6:32–35). Eight of a total of eighteen instances of misunderstanding involve Jesus' death and/or resurrection (e.g., 7:33–36; 8:21–22; 13:36–38).

2. All of the Gospels contain defenses against the charges that Jesus was a magician. Such a charge, if true, would contradict the ultimate claims for Jesus made by the Evangelists. Disproving a negative image reinforces a positive one. This motif is also a stock feature in biographies of holy men. In Mark this surfaces in the Beelzebul pericope, in which Jesus claims to be an instrument of God, not Satan (3:20–30); in the attribution of counterexorcistic language to demons (1:23–28, 32–34; 5:1–20); in Herod's notion that Jesus might be a necromancer (6:14–15). In Matthew and Luke this is broadened to include the temptation story derived from Q (magicians fly and transform matter; Matt. 4:1–11; Luke 4:1–13), and it appears in charges that Jesus is an "impostor," perhaps reflecting Deut. 13:1–11; 18:20 (Matt. 27:63). The antimagical polemic of Acts (8:14–24; 13:4–12; 19:11–20) may be linked to the Lukan emphasis on the physicality of Jesus' resurrection, since those who died violently were thought "available" for facilitating magical feats (such as healings "in the name of Jesus"). In John this antimagical polemic is expressed when Jesus is thrice charged with having a demon (7:20; 8:48–53; 10:20f.).

3. The motif that Jesus concealed his identity, the Messianic secret, is emphasized in Mark, taken over by Luke, slightly attenuated in Matthew, and absent from John. This motif includes the commands of Jesus to demons (1:24–25, 34; 3:11–12) and disciples

(8:29–30; 9:9) and injunctions to those healed to keep silent about the miracle (1:43–44; 5:43; 7:36; 8:26), to keep his true identity secret. The function of the secrecy motif is implied in Mark 9:9: "And as they were coming down the mountain, he charged them to tell no one what they had seen, until the Son of man should have risen from the dead." Only when the mission of Jesus is completed in his suffering, death, and resurrection is a full understanding of his identity possible. Though the secrecy motif is used inconsistently by Mark (occurring in just three healing miracles), it nevertheless complements the motif of misunderstanding and the antimagic apologetic in focusing on the identification of Jesus as the Messiah, the Son of God.

The primary vehicles for biographical characterization in the Gospels, as in Greco-Roman biography, are miracle stories, sayings, and anecdotes (i.e., pronouncement stories and stories about Jesus) that support and demonstrate the appropriateness of the stereotypical role assigned to Jesus. While they do not primarily function as revelations of *character* (as in Greco-Roman biography), they are literary vehicles that legitimate the presentation of Jesus as Messiah, or Son of God. The performance of miracles of healing and casting out evil spirits (exorcism) was never a major feature in popular perceptions of the eschatological roles assigned to Jesus—e.g., Messiah, Son of God, Son of Man, (eschatological) prophet, etc.—but must have arisen for other reasons. Since there is little doubt that the historical Jesus was an exorcist and a healer, this historical factor has helped to shape the components of the stereotypical role he plays in the Gospel presentations. The importance of miracle stories in Mark's story of Jesus is indicated by the author's editorial summaries (1:32; 3:7–12; 6:12–13, 53–56), and by the fact that Mark's sixteen miracle stories (taken together with summary statements about Jesus' wonder-working) constitute more than 25 percent of the narrative. Gerd Theissen has emphasized the relationship between miracles and missionary activity, both in the career of the historical Jesus and in the early church. The task of the apostles was to preach and to heal (Mark 3:14–15; 6:7, 12–13; cf. Matt. 10:7; 2 Cor. 12:12; Heb. 2:4). Reports of Jesus' miracles attracted people from far and wide (1:45; 2:2; 3:7–8; 5:27; 6:13–14; 7:25; cf. 10:47). Those who experienced healing or exorcism presumably became followers of Jesus (1:45; 5:17–20; 10:52), for confidence in Jesus was linked with successful results (6:5–6). The acclamation of onlookers that concludes many miracle stories supports their evangelistic function (1:27; 2:12; 4:41; 5:42; 7:37). Just as the oral reports of miracles mentioned in Mark draw people to Jesus, so Mark's miracle narratives take the place of actual miracles and inculcate belief in the reader. Yet miracles can also be provocative by providing divine legitimation for violating religious customs (2:1–12, 23–28; 3:1–6; 5:17). Mark contains no criticism of miracles as means for arousing faith (Jesus refuses signs only because of unbelief, 8:11–13). For John, faith apart from miracles is commended (John 4:48; 20:29), yet signs reveal the true identity of Jesus (5:36; 20:30–31). Regardless of how miracle stories may have functioned in hypothetical pre-Markan collections, Mark uses them to demonstrate that Jesus is the agent of supernatural powers (4:35–41; 5:25–34; 6:47–52), and to provide divine legitimation for his proclamation. The Spirit came upon Jesus at his baptism (1:10), and Mark implies that the Spirit empowered him to perform exorcisms (3:22–30).

The sayings and anecdotes used by Mark function in two primary ways. First, their *content* provided Christian readers with the teaching and exemplary behavior of Jesus on many important issues and in various situations. Second, they stress the astonishing *wisdom* and authority of Jesus (necessary in light of his critical stance toward conventional Jewish authorities), underscoring the revelatory character of his speech, emphasized by the acclamations or stunned silence with which several anecdotes end (Mark 1:22, 27 and par.; 10:24; 12:17 and par.; 12:34; Matt. 22:33, 46; Luke 20:39–40). Jesus is designated a "teacher" twelve times in Mark (three times as "rabbi," equivalent to the Greek term for "teacher"), an emphasis taken over by the other Evangelists. The followers of Jesus are correspondingly designated "disciples," i.e., "pupils," forty-six times in Mark. For the ancient Mediterranean world, this teaching emphasis is more characteristic of philosophical schools than religious sects. Yet it coheres with the emphases of the New Testament letters, which reveal more about Christian ethics and theology than about religious practices. About 40 percent of Mark's Gospel is devoted to Jesus' *teaching,* emphasizing: (1) Relations with Judaism, including the problem of legitimate association (2:15–17), the practice of fasting (2:18–20), Jewish ritual purity (7:1–23), and discipleship that goes beyond observance of the law (10:17–22). (2) Implications of discipleship, including rewards for perseverance vs. result of failure (4:2–21), the importance of mission (6:7–12; 13:10), discipleship and suffering (8:34–38; 13:9, 11), the importance of humility (9:33–37; 10:43–45), responsibility for others (9:42–50), and rewards for discipleship (10:29–31). (3) Various other matters, such as the indissolubility of marriage (10:2–12), the nature of true piety (12:38–44), the true identity of Jesus (8:27–33 and passim), and God's program for the end of the age (ch. 13).

At the same time, the information assembled by Mark does describe varied aspects of Jesus' professional life: his conduct on the Sabbath (2:23–28), his acquaintance with tax collectors and sinners (2:13–17), his revolutionary attitude toward ritual, rules of purity, and food taboos (2:18–28; 7:1–23); his dignified demeanor before the high priests and Pilate (14:53–15:5), his quick wit in controversies (2:23–28; 3:1–6; 7:1–13; 10:2–9; 11:27–33; 12:13–17), differences with his family (3:21, 31–35), and his love for children (9:36; 10:16). The miracle stories in Mark do not demonstrate the *divinity* of Jesus (a notion foreign to the Evangelist), but rather confirm his status as an emissary of God (i.e., Messiah).

The Function of the Gospels

The *function* of the Gospels has both conscious and unconscious dimensions, though it is not always possible to separate the two.

To Awaken or Strengthen Faith

One conscious function involves the explicit and implicit purpose for which they were written. Rhetorically, the Gospels are primarily persuasive literature, using various strategies to persuade their audiences that the crucified and risen Jesus is the Messiah, the Son of God. The Gospels, then, are fundamentally Christian literary propaganda. This implicit purpose of Matthew and Mark is made explicit in John (20:30–31): "These [signs] are written that you [plural] may believe that Jesus is the Messiah, the Son of God." The Fourth Gospel can thus be viewed as a document for reinforcing Christian faith, or a missionary tractate for Jews and pagans of the Hellenistic world. Neither Mark nor Matthew provides an explicit statement of his literary intentions.

None of the Gospels (or any other New Testament books) can be considered a missionary tractate for evangelizing pagans. Before ca. A.D. 125, early Christian literature was written exclusively for Christian consumption. However, this should not impede recognition that the aggressive conversionist orientation of early Christians profoundly shaped their understanding of the mission and message of Jesus and imprinted itself indelibly on Gospel tradition. To clarify the purpose of the Gospels we must ask who the first Christian readers of the Gospels were, and why the Gospels appear so propagandistic.

The basic social unit of the ancient Mediterranean world was the household (Greek *oikia, oikos;* Latin *familia, domus*), an extended family with slaves, freedmen, hired laborers, and other clients. All were bound together by a network of mutual duties and obligations under the considerable authority of the householder, usually the father. The solidarity of the household and the authoritarian role of its head meant that "conversion" to Christianity often involved households as units (1 Cor. 1:16; Acts 10:2, 48; 11:14; 16:15; 16: 31–34; 18:8; cf. 2 Tim. 1:16). A Christian household could form the nucleus of a church (Rom. 16:5; 1 Cor. 16:19; Philemon 2), providing a meeting place and leadership, and perhaps also the basis for potential rivalry with other household churches (1 Cor. 1:11–16; 3 John 9f.). There were, of course, converts to Christianity who were part of non-Christian households (Phil. 4:22; 1 Cor. 7:13–14; cf. 2 Tim. 1:5), and non-Christian members of Christian households (e.g., the slave Onesimus, Philemon 10–16; cf. Matt. 13:24–30). Furthermore, individual or group conversion to Christianity did not automatically include the Christianization of pagan norms and values. That involved the kind of intensive program of resocialization implicitly pursued by Paul. These social factors suggest that the Gospels were consciously designed both to reinforce the personal and social implications of belief in Jesus as Messiah and Son of God, and to persuade non-Christian members of Christian households (some of which doubtless functioned as church centers) of the ultimate religious significance of Jesus. One could be an "insider" in a social sense, yet an "outsider" in the matter of personal faith.

The Paradigmatic Function of Jesus

One concern of redaction critics, scholars who try to determine the theological viewpoint of the gospel authors (complemented by recent interest in the sociological investigation of early Christianity), has been the description of the Christian communities within which the Gospels arose. This approach presupposes that the Gospels reveal more about the authors' situations than about the historical situation of Jesus. While one cannot assume that each Gospel story exactly mirrors the situation of the Evangelist's community, each Evangelist wrote on *two levels*. One level was the "historical" presentation of the story of Jesus, while the other involved superimposing concerns and circumstances of the author's own day upon the narrative (occasionally with telltale anachronisms). The proclamation of Jesus in Mark 1:14f., for example, is a mixture of Jesus' own terms ("kingdom of God") and those of the early church ("believe," "gospel"). Jesus speaks "the word" (Mark 2:2; 4:33; 8:32) just as Christian missionaries do. He is presented as teaching "in the house" (Mark 2:15; 9:33; 10:10), and houses were the meeting places for early Christian communities. Jewish-Christian debates over ritual purity are reflected in Mark 7. Jesus' teaching in parables (Mark 4:2–9) is expressed in terms of later Christian experience (4:14–20). Yet these are all relatively trivial instances of two-level composition. There have been many more sustained (and sometimes mutually contradictory) attempts to profile the communities reflected in the Gospels. The itinerant charismatic character of the Q community, for example, has been extrapolated from the Q tradition of the sending out of the Twelve (Matt. 10:5–42; Luke 9:1–6). Matthew is widely regarded as having been involved in a dispute with a prophetic faction within his community. Some scholars have argued that Matthew's community is a wandering charismatic group, while others have argued that he represents a sedentary urban church not overly concerned with charismatic activities.

Recently scholars have proposed that Mark wrote to resolve various theological conflicts within his community. Some think that Mark wrote to oppose believers who saw Jesus as a miracle worker in the pattern of Hellenistic wonder-workers called "divine men." For Mark, authentic messiahship is based on suffering that leads to crucifixion. In terms of christological titles, "Son of God" reflects the divine man christology and requires the corrective of the "Son of Man" title, which involves the suffering of the Messiah. Other scholars have proposed that Mark might be countering those who believed that the Jewish revolt against Rome played a key role in God's plan for the "end times." Writing shortly after A.D. 70, Mark represented Galilean Christianity in opposition to an errant Jerusalem-Judean Christianity caught up in the apocalyptic excitement generated by the Jewish revolt of A.D. 66–73. Their prophets mistakenly connected the Parousia to the revolt and to the Jerusalem temple. The Parousia, according to Mark, will occur in Galilee, not Jerusalem, in the generation following the revolt.

The Gospel of John, according to Louis Martyn, is the product of a Christian theologian writing in response to contemporary issues. The Gospel of John, he argues, is a two-level drama, consisting of various historical episodes reflecting Jesus' career influenced in presentation by the experiences of the Johannine community. John 9:1–7 narrates the story of a blind man whose sight is miraculously restored, followed by a dramatic expansion (vs. 8–41) reflecting a contemporary crisis in John's community. This crisis involves the expulsion of members of the community from local synagogues (ca. A.D. 85), anachronistically reflected in the "excommunication" (*aposynagogos*) of the blind man from the synagogue (John 9:22, 34f., cf. 12:42; 16:2). Martyn proposes that this synagogue expulsion reflects the adoption by Judaism (after ca. A.D. 85) of the *birkat ha-minim* (Benediction against the heretics), a revision of Jewish statutory prayer intended to expose Jews who maintained a dual allegiance to Moses and Jesus the Messiah.

Ancient Hellenistic biographers and historians also wrote on two levels, combining ideas from their own time with events from the past. This can be explained in two complementary ways: (1) They lacked the historical imagination to mentally reenact the different experience of those whose actions they were describing, and projected their own cultural experience into the past. (2) Most historians and biographers of the Hellenistic period regarded the past as normative for present conduct, i.e., it provided moral guidance for the present and future (Isocrates, *Nicocles* 35; *To Demonicus* 34; Polybius 1.1.2; Livy 1, preface 10–11; Plutarch, *Aemilius Paulus* 1.1; Lucian, *Demonax* 2). History and biography focused on the past as a source of lessons for the future. Hellenistic history and biography, no less than the Gospels, tended to *merge* the past with the present. If the Gospels and Acts deserve the (exaggerated) designation "theology in narrative form," then Greco-Roman history and biography fully merit the label "ideology in narrative form." Functionally the differences are minimal.

Past and present merge in Gospel narratives because the Evangelists regarded the story of Jesus as an example for Christian faith. Christian values and beliefs were personified, and historically legitimated, in the person of Jesus of Nazareth. This coheres with the significance that ancient Greek and Roman communities attached to their founders. The progenitor or founder was often turned into a myth-image that summed up the qualities and character of his descendants or followers, becoming a corporate personality. While the Synoptic Gospels, particularly Matthew and Luke, have a prominent didactic element sanctioned by attribution to Jesus, they do not explicitly emphasize the *imitation* of Jesus. Similarly, there are very few passages in Plutarch's *Lives*, for example, where he makes his paradigmatic intentions explicit. The reason for this reticence is simply that this use of the past was implicitly understood.

Some Christian literature outside the Gospels points to the paradigmatic role of Jesus in the Gospels. The exemplary character of his suffering and demeanor before his judges is emphasized (1 Peter 2:21–23; 1 Tim. 6:13). His paradigmatic humility is reflected in Paul's use of the Philippians hymn (Phil. 2:5–11). The Letter to the Hebrews reflects great interest in the historical Jesus. The testing which Jesus experienced (possibly referring to the Synoptic temptation story) means that he understands human weakness and can provide help (Heb. 2:18; 4:5). In an injunction reminiscent of the later "stages of the cross," the readers are exhorted to go outside the camp and endure abuse just as Jesus did (13:12–13). Jesus was perfected and learned obedience through suffering just as Christians now can (2:10; 5:8). This exemplary role of the story of Jesus is clearly expressed in Heb. 12:1b–4; Jesus "endured the cross, despising the shame, and is seated at the right hand of the throne of God."

The Gospels as Greco-Roman Biography

Ancient vs. Modern Biography

Modern scholarship often ignores or underestimates the biographical character of the Gospels. The Evangelists, it is true, were uninterested in Jesus' education, appearance, personality, motivations, and development, all typical concerns of modern biography. Yet many of these features were foreign to ancient biography. An emphasis on the personality of Jesus or concern with his motivations and development cannot reasonably be expected in ancient cultures which assumed that personalities were static. Even the concern of Greco-Roman biography with character had no counterpart in ancient Near Eastern cultures. Even such apparently modern biographical concerns as origins and education were closely linked in Greco-Roman biography with character.

The Literary Level of the Gospels

Classical Greek and Latin literature preserves the values and traditions of the educated class. The Greco-Roman biographies surveyed in chapter 1 are primarily products of authors with literary ambitions writing in the setting of a highly structured traditional body of literary and rhetorical conventions. The Gospels (and most New Testament writings) reflect the popular literary culture of the lower classes. The linguistic and rhetorical style and standards of educated authors and orators of antiquity were attenuated and imitated in popular literature. The New Testament itself exhibits various levels of literary quality. Very few examples of popular literature have survived antiquity. Yet we are not completely uninformed about its basic character. Popular biographical literature, such as the *Life of Aesop,* some lives of the Greek poets (many written without literary pretensions, such as the *Life of Homer* and the very similar

Jewish *Lives of the Prophets*), the life of Secundus the Silent Philosopher and the composite "life" of Herakles (Apollodorus, *Library* 2.4.6–2.7.8). These popular lives share a structural feature with the Gospels. They all exhibit a thoroughly *chronological* organization and avoid topical exposition.

Biography as "History"

The notion that the Gospels cannot be biographies is sometimes supported by the contention that biographies (ancient or modern) are intrinsically concerned with *history*. Since the Gospels focus on proclamation, the argument runs, they have no interest in history and cannot be "biographical." This view is often supported by the theological position that, since faith cannot be dependent on contingent historical events (making it superfluous), the truth of the gospel is immune from historical confirmation or disconfirmation. From this perspective kerygma and history are mutually exclusive categories. This view is wrong on two counts: (1) "kerygma" and "history," properly understood, are overlapping conceptions, and (2) it is illegitimate to allow theological assumptions to determine the results of literary criticism.

The view proposed here, that the Gospels are a subtype of Greco-Roman biography, assumes that the Evangelists wrote with historical intentions. Of course, what the ancients regarded as "history" differs considerably from modern historiographical standards (with the exceptions of Thucydides, Polybius, and Ammianus Marcellinus), and "intentions" do not always produce the desired results. For the Greeks, history was the arena in which transcendent values were exemplified in exceptional individuals and states that could serve as models for the present and future. This idealism had an "anti-historical" tendency that valued persons as *types* and *paradigms* rather than as historical individuals. Fiction played a significant role in Hellenistic historiography and biography, whose authors had rhetorical training. Plausibility was the primary means of separating truth from falsehood (rather than the critical analysis of sources), and the main requirement of narrative. Since both historians and biographers were interested in providing incentives to virtue, they often wrote with rhetorical purposes and techniques. Despite the "historical intention" implicit in the biographical task, some ancient biographies are almost completely fictional, such as the life of Heraclitus in Diogenes Laertius (9.1–17), almost entirely based on false inferences from traditional anecdotes about Heraclitus. Fiction also pervades the lives of the Greek poets, the result of flawed inferences made from their works. The emphasis on plausibility rather than truth and a pronounced lack of historical imagination frustrated historical-biographical *intentions*. There was also an indeterminate amount of intentional fiction in ancient biography. Ancient readers recognized, appreciated, and could discount rhetorical exaggeration, while modern readers find that task difficult. Menander Rhetor (third century A.D.) recommended that miraculous signs attending the birth of an emperor be invented for speeches praising him (371.3–14). To claim that the Evangelists wrote biography with historical intentions, then, does not guarantee that they preserved a single historical fact. It does suggest that they restricted the scope of invention to that appropriate to the biographical task as popularly understood.

The Process of "Literaturization"

While educated pagans reacted negatively to Mark, Matthew and Luke responded positively if somewhat ambivalently. They used Mark as a model and major source, but they introduced supplementary material and made numerous linguistic, stylistic, and compositional improvements. While neither Matthew nor Luke is high literature according to Greco-Roman rhetorical standards, these Gospels do reflect popular literary usage, which attenuated the more elevated literary standards. The movement toward greater conformity to elevated literary conventions can be called "literaturization." In Matthew and Luke the process of literaturization is exhibited in many ways. First, Matthew and Luke have followed the conventional ancient approach to biographical and historical composition by making one source the backbone of the narrative, supplemented by other sources. Second, by adding background material, genealogies, and birth narratives at the beginning and resurrection appearances and other materials at the end, Matthew and Luke have moved closer toward the biographical and historiographical expectations of pagan readers. Papias' judgment that Mark was "not in order," i.e., not artistically arranged (Eusebius, *Church History* 3.39.15), is similar to Dionysius of Halicarnassus' criticism that Thucydides' history was not in order because it did not begin and end properly (*On Thucydides* 10; cf. Lucian, *True History* 47f.). Mark does not begin with the recommended topics of birth and ancestry (cf. Theon, *Progymnasmata* 8), and it ends abruptly in 16:8. Third, Matthew and Luke have made many linguistic and stylistic improvements in Mark. Mark has 151 instances of the historic present; Matthew retains 21 of them, and Luke only one. John has 164 instances of the historic present. Luke tends to eliminate Markan parataxis (the tendency to avoid subordinate clauses and connect clauses with "and"), favoring the balancing particles and subordinating participles of periodic style. While Mark transliterates Aramaic words, Matthew retains one phrase (27:46) and Luke eliminates them entirely. Mark's repetitive style is smoothed out (compare Mark 1:32 with Matt. 8:16 and Luke 4:40). Inelegant expressions are replaced (compare Mark 2:4 with Matt. 9:2 and Luke 5:18). Taken together, these factors suggest that the Lukan and Matthean use and modification of Mark, together with other traditions, was a self-conscious literary enterprise.

Ancient Views of the Gospels

Educated pagans, like the second-century philosopher Celsus, were never very impressed with the literary qualities of the Gospels (Origen, *Against Celsus* 6.1–2; cf. Lactantius, *Divine Institutes* 5.1. 15–16). However, two educated Christians of the first half of the second century, Papias of Hierapolis (died ca. A.D. 156) and Justin Martyr (died ca. A.D. 165), understood the Gospels and the traditions they contained in terms of Hellenistic rhetorical categories.

Papias is an enigmatical figure whose works survive only in fragments. In addition to being the bishop of Hierapolis, he was a scholarly historian who avidly collected written and oral traditions about Jesus. About A.D. 125 he wrote a five-volume work entitled "Interpretations of the Logia of the Lord" (*logia* = "the Gospel," i.e., what Jesus said and did). In a fragment revealing a knowledge of technical rhetorical terms and conventions, Papias (quoting the Presbyter) defends the literary character of Mark against unknown detractors (Eusebius, *Church History* 3.39.15; my trans.):

> Mark, who was Peter's interpreter, wrote down accurately, though not in order [*ou mentoi taxei*] what he remembered that the Lord said and did. For he had not heard the Lord or followed him but later, as I mentioned, had followed Peter, who formulated his teachings in the form of anecdotes [*chreiai*], but not as a finished composition [*syntaxis*] of the sayings of the Lord, so that Mark made no errors in writing them down individually as he remembered [*apomnēmoneuein*] them.

Mark's Gospel, in Papias' view, consisted of *apomnēmoneumata* ("reminiscences") previously fashioned into anecdotes or chreiai by Peter. The term *apomnēmoneumata* is roughly synonymous with *hypomnēmata* (meaning "notes," or "rough draft," connoting unfinished form, or "commentary") but in the singular can mean "book."

Clement of Alexandria referred to Mark's *hypomnēmata* (*To Theodore* 1.20), by which he understood the notes that became the basis for his Gospel, while Eusebius (*Church History* 2.15) identified the *hypomnēmata* with the Gospel of Mark itself. Papias, however, regarded the Gospel of Mark as *apomnēmoneumata* (= *hypomnēmata*), in contrast to Matthew, which he considered a finished composition (Eusebius, *Church History* 3.39.16). Paratactic and asyndetic style are characteristic of *hypomnēmata* (cf. Theophrastus, *Characters*), both features of Mark. Papias' assessment of Mark as *apomnēmoneumata*, then, means that he thought of it as unfinished and unpolished. This is also reflected in his claim that Mark is "not in order," a rhetorical term meaning "not artistically arranged." Portions of the historical preface *(prooimion)* of Papias' lost work survive complete with references to sources and method in accordance with historiographical convention (Eusebius, *Church History* 3.39.2–4, 15; note the formal parallels with Luke 1:1–4). This reveals Papias' familiarity with the rhetorical conventions of Hellenistic historiography. His explicit preference for oral over written tradition (Eusebius, *Church History* 3.39.3–4) typifies ancient historians from Herodotus to Plutarch (cf. Plutarch, *Demosthenes* 2.1).

Justin Martyr (writing ca. A.D. 155) described the Gospels as "reminiscences [*apomnēmoneumata*] of the apostles" (*1 Apology* 66.3; 67.3) and "reminiscences of Peter" (*Dialogue with Trypho* 106.3). Thus Justin, like Matthew, Luke, and Papias, prefers to designate the Gospels by a recognized literary term. Though *apomnēmoneumata* are not carefully defined in rhetorical handbooks, they are essentially expanded chreiai, i.e., sayings and/or actions of or about specific individuals, set in a narrative framework and transmitted by *memory* (hence "reliable"). Unlike Papias, Justin does not regard Mark as unfinished, since he uses the term of all the Synoptic Gospels. Justin was a Christian philosopher by profession (at a time when educated Christians began to regard their faith as a philosophy) and an ardent admirer of Socrates. His use of the term "reminiscences," therefore, suggests a connection with Xenophon's *Memorabilia* (in Greek *apomnēmoneumata*), a "biography" of Socrates. For Justin the Gospels are *apomnēmoneumata* because they preserve the authentic teachings of Jesus, the true master of philosophy.

These examples reveal that educated early Christians within two generations after the "publication" of the Gospels understood them within the canons of ancient rhetoric. While this does not prove that Mark shared their view, there are reasons to suspect that Matthew and Luke did.

Later Jesus Literature

The production of Jesus literature was a Christian growth indus-
try during late antiquity. Scores of compositions appeared, many
explicitly labeled "gospels." Some of these "apocryphal" (literally
"secret," but with the connotation "spurious") gospels contain sayings of or stories about Jesus (e.g., the gospels of Thomas and
Peter); others are rambling homilies with little resemblance to the
canonical Gospels (e.g., the gospels of Philip and Truth). "Gospel"
as a literary term in Gnosticism, therefore, can include the achievement of redemption within a cosmic setting. This broadened perspective is already operative in the Fourth Gospel (cf. John 1:1–18),
as well as in the early christological hymns (Phil. 2:5–11; Col. 1:
15–20).

Many ancient Jesus compositions exist only as titles or fragmentary quotations in later Christian authors, with the fortunate exception of the Nag Hammadi library (see below). The task of compiling
or improving biographies of Jesus, however, begun by Mark and
made more literarily respectable by Luke, was of little concern to
educated Christians of the second century and later. Papias and
Tatian were exceptions, yet the work of the former has perished and
the latter's *Diatessaron* (the four Gospels woven into one continuous
narrative) survives only in late translations. Christian literature of
the second through fourth centuries reflects several cultural levels.
Christians with rhetorical training produced an extensive apologetic
or protreptic literature (Quadratus, Aristides, Justin, Tatian,
Athenagoras, and Theophilus). The less educated produced reams
of anonymous or pseudepigraphical imaginative apocryphal gospels
and acts, in which Christian folklore, legend, and romantic fiction
found expression. One significant development was that of the separate directions taken by narrative and discourse. One or the other
tends to dominate particular compositions, rarely both. Perhaps the
most common function of Jesus literature, particularly sayings collections, is to legitimate particular forms of Christianity.

The historical reliability of Jesus traditions has been a prominent
issue in the study of the apocryphal gospels. The widespread view
that the apocryphal gospels are fictional and heretical has driven a
wedge between them and the canonical Gospels. Yet recent insis-
tence on the possibility of late circulation of early and possibly
authentic Jesus traditions (particularly in some Nag Hammadi tractates) has encouraged the evaluation of these writings as potential
sources for earlier developments of Jesus traditions. The analysis of

this literature in its own right, however, is an important though neglected task.

Tatian's Diatessaron

Tatian was a Syrian trained in Greek rhetoric and philosophy. Converted in Rome near the middle of the second century, he became a pupil of Justin Martyr. In the *Oration to the Greeks,* Tatian vilifies Hellenistic civilization and culture, a position that only hardened after his return to Syria in A.D. 172. Early heresiologists regarded him (probably erroneously) as the founder of the ascetic Encratites and (more accurately) as having close ties to Valentinian Gnosticism. Tatian's chief claim to fame lies in his compilation of the *Diatessaron,* a biography of Jesus based on the conflation of the four canonical Gospels, possibly with some apocryphal additions. The *Diatessaron* was widely used in Syrian Christianity until the fifth century, when the Syrian bishop Theodoret (ca. A.D. 393–466) destroyed all available copies, replacing them with the four separate Gospels. The *Diatessaron,* originally written in Greek or Syriac, is partially preserved in one small Greek fragment (dated ca. A.D. 220), several translations (including Arabic, Persian, and Latin), and a fourth-century Syriac commentary on the *Diatessaron* by Ephraem (ca. A.D. 306–373).

In compiling the *Diatessaron* Tatian preserved most of the content of the four Gospels in a single narrative, following Matthew's order before the Passion story, and John's thereafter. He omitted some material, such as the genealogies of Matthew and Luke (an omission criticized as heretically motivated by Theodoret) and the introduction to Luke (1:1–4). He also corrected John by the Synoptics and vice versa. Following the rhetorical practices of ancient historians, Tatian's chief method for determining which conflicting datum was historical was the criterion of *plausibility.* Ancient historians who wrote new versions of existing narratives tended to follow one source more or less exclusively (often by memory) before switching to another. The revered status of the Gospels probably caused Tatian to deviate from this conventional procedure.

What was Tatian's motivation in producing a *single* account of the life of Jesus? Eusebius disapproved of Tatian's attempt to "correct their [i.e., the apostles'] modes of expression" (*Church History* 4. 29.6). Yet Tatian, who admired the unaffected style of Christian literature (*Oration to the Greeks* 29.2), was probably not motivated merely by the desire to improve the language and style of the Gospels. The phenomenon of several biographies of the same person existing side by side and with approximately equal esteem had no parallel in antiquity, a situation potentially disturbing to an educated person in view of the numerous discrepancies in order and content among the Gospels. Since Tatian was highly critical of the contradictions of Greek philosophy and history (*Oration* 4.3; 31.4), it is likely that his Greek education drove him to compile a credible narrative of the life of Jesus free from contradiction and disagreement.

Jesus Narratives

Apocryphal gospels in which sayings of and stories about Jesus were set in an overall narrative framework continued to be composed. These include (1) an unknown gospel (preserved in Papyrus Egerton 2), composed before A.D. 150, containing four pericopes including two previously unknown sayings of Jesus, a fragmentary "Johannine"-style dialogue, and a new miracle story; (2) the Gospel of the Nazaraeans, apparently a rewritten form of Matthew (before A.D. 150), extant only in thirty-six fragmentary quotations in Christian authors; (3) the Gospel of the Ebionites, composed ca. A.D. 180 and extant in just seven quotations of Epiphanius (ca. A.D. 315–403); (4) the Gospel of the Hebrews (between A.D. 120 and 140), used by Jewish Christians in Egypt and extant in only seven fragmentary quotations; (5) the Gospel of the Egyptians (early second century), used by Gentile Christians in Egypt and extant in only about ten fragments.

A more restricted type of Jesus narrative focused on imaginative reconstructions of gaps in the canonical accounts. Among the so-called infancy gospels two can be singled out: (1) the almost entirely fictional *Protevangelium of James*, perhaps originating in Egypt after A.D. 150, which promotes the doctrine of Mary's perpetual virginity, and (2) the *Infancy Story of Thomas* (end of the second century A.D.). The end of Jesus' life is the focus of the *Gospel of Nicodemus*, consisting of the Acts of Pilate (an original form of which existed before A.D. 150), and Christ's Descent Into Hell. Many other gospels written in the names of Old Testament figures, apostles, and prominent early Christian women were written from the second through fifth centuries and later.

The *Gospel of Peter* is the most important and earliest noncanonical gospel narrative. Composed ca. A.D. 125 in Greek, it briefly narrates the passion and resurrection of Jesus; both the beginning and ending are lost. The fragment begins just after Pilate has washed his hands, and concludes just short of a resurrection appearance with Peter and his brother Andrew going fishing. While the canonical Gospels (except Mark) contain traditions of Jesus' appearances to his followers, the *Gospel of Peter* mentions only the experience of the guards who see Jesus emerging from the tomb, assisted by two mysterious figures (a possible allusion to the transfiguration story). Although obviously dependent on the canonical Gospels, *Peter* may also preserve early extracanonical traditions. Eusebius regarded the *Gospel of Peter* as unacceptable, and he quotes from a book of Serapion of Antioch (written ca. A.D. 200) refuting it (*Church History* 3.3.2; 3.25.6; 6.12).

Sayings Collections

At the end of the first century, sayings of Jesus circulated in both oral and written forms. When isolated sayings are quoted or alluded to in early Christian literature (as in the heterogeneous collection of second-century Apostolic Fathers or in Justin Martyr), the casual mode of citation makes it difficult to determine whether the authors were using (1) written sources no longer extant, (2) written texts imperfectly quoted, or (3) oral tradition. Sayings of Jesus not preserved in the Gospels (called *agrapha*) continued to be incorporated into Christian texts throughout the second century. Occasionally such sayings were inserted into Gospel manuscripts (e.g., John 7: 53–8:11, and additions before Luke 23:34 and after Luke 9:55). Codex Beza, for example, has this chreia in place of Luke 6:5: "On that day, when he [Jesus] saw a man working on the Sabbath, [he] said to him, 'Good man, if you know what you are doing you are blessed; but if you do not know, you are accursed and a transgressor of the law.' " The authenticity of such sayings is impossible to determine.

Four "gospels" were part of a cache of fifty-two tractates in thirteen codices discovered at Nag Hammadi, Egypt, in 1945. Buried in the latter half of the fourth century A.D., this very diverse Coptic library included the Gospels of Truth, Philip, the Egyptians, and Thomas. The *Gospel of Truth* (written ca. A.D. 140) is a rambling homily of Valentinian Gnosticism containing no explicit Jesus traditions. The *Gospel of Philip* is a collection of about a hundred loosely connected "sayings" or meditations, most dependent on the canonical Gospels. While most "sayings" in Philip are unattributed, one is attributed to Philip (II,73.8–19), and thirteen are attributed to Jesus (e.g., 64.3). Quoted Gospel sayings are often embedded in commentary (e.g., 55.24–36; 56.26–57.22; 63.30–64.9; 68.26–29).

The Coptic *Gospel of the Egyptians* is preserved in two versions. The title is given at the conclusion (III,69.6), though the treatise is introduced and concluded by what appears to be an earlier title ("The Holy Book of the Great Invisible Spirit"). The term "gospel" is probably a christianizing addition (equating "gospel" with "holy book"), for the work is only marginally Christian. The composition, attributed to Seth, narrates a mythic cosmogony including the origin and preservation of Seth's line and his redemptive work in the form of the earthly Jesus.

The *Gospel of Thomas*, a collection of 114 sayings usually introduced with the phrase "Jesus said," is the most extensive non-canonical collection of sayings of Jesus extant. Thomas was probably translated from a Greek original (ca. A.D. 140; some argue for a first-century date) and composed in Syria where other Thomas literature originated. A major problem is the relationship of the *Gospel of Thomas* to the Synoptic tradition, since nearly half the sayings have Synoptic parallels. Some sayings may reflect authentic extracanonical Jesus traditions (as the parables in logia 8, 9, 64, 65). Others are reformulated Synoptic sayings (72, 79, 99, 100, 104, 113), while still others are entirely new (7, 10, 15, 30, 52). Apart from the occasional use of catchwords (cf. logia 28 and 29), there is no obvious arrangement to the sayings. There is no mention in Thomas of the cross or the resurrection, nor is the eschatological future the subject of any sayings (consonant with the Gnostic character of the work), and the title "Son of Man" never occurs. Jesus is implicitly presented (as in Q) as a teacher of wisdom and revealer. Thomas contains about twenty-two *pronouncement stories* (e.g., 6, 12, 37, 51–53), as many as twenty-four *parables* (e.g., 8, 20, 63–65, 96–98, 109), eleven *beatitudes* (e.g., 7, 19, 54, 68, 79, 103), two *woes* (102, 112), more than a dozen *proverbs* introduced by the proverbial formulations "whoever" or "the one who" (e.g., 1, 24, 41, 80, 94, 105), and six "I" sayings (e.g., 10, 23, 71).

Dialogues with the Risen Jesus

The most innovative use of Jesus traditions after the canonical Gospels was the development of the *Gnostic revelatory dialogue* in which sayings of Jesus were framed by a conversation between the risen Jesus and his disciples. These dialogues were modeled, not on philosophical dialogues, but on pedagogical *erōtapokriseis* ("questions-and-answers"), which were vehicles for esoteric religious instruction. The canonical Gospels, with the exception of Mark (apart from the apocryphal ending 16:9–20), narrate encounters between the risen Jesus and his followers. While only brief statements are attributed to Jesus in Matthew (28:9–10, 18–20), lengthier conversations characterize Luke 24 (cf. Acts 1:3–9) and John 20–21. Acts 1:3 cryptically mentions a series of appearances over forty days in which conversation centered on the Kingdom of God. Gnostic Christians used the period between Jesus' resurrection and ascension (expanded to 550 days in the *Apocryphon of James* I,2.19–20, and eleven years in *Pistis Sophia* 1.1!) as the setting for fictional seminars chaired by Jesus (*Concept of Our Great Power* VI,42.18–31). The revelatory dialogue was a popular Gnostic form of Jesus literature ostensibly conveying Jesus' true intentions, sometimes presented as reinterpretations of his earthly sayings (*Letter of Peter to Philip* VIII,135.5–8). Gnostic Jesus literature emphasized the postresurrection period, in contrast to the preresurrection focus of mainstream Christianity.

Gnostic dialogues were never entirely improvised. They often preserved and modified earlier traditions, and thus have a very complicated literary history. Three compositional practices are evident: (1) Some dialogues began as treatises which were modified into a conversational format (the *Sophia of Jesus Christ*). (2) Individual sayings could be connected to form dialogues (the *Apocryphon of James* V,2.21–35; 4.22–37; 5.31–6.1). (3) Dialogues were also constructed out of what were originally collections of interpreted parables or sayings of Jesus (*Dialogue of the Savior; Book of Thomas the Contender* II,142.26–145.23). Of the eleven dialogues found in the Nag Hammadi collection, two are non-Christian: *Zostrianos* (VIII,1) and *Hypostasis of the Archons* (II,2). The content of the Christian Gnostic dialogues centers on postmortem salvation through the ascent of the soul, and on a defense of gnosis. *Constituent literary forms* of the dialogues include various short liturgical forms (theological formulas, hymns, and creeds); exegetical and doctrinal instructions *(erōtapokriseis);* and paraenetic sermons. The *content* of the dialogues centers on teaching about the Sophia myth, the necessity of revealed knowledge (gnosis), asceticism, baptism, the ascent of the soul, and exegesis of the New Testament.

One important treatise, recently analyzed by Ron Cameron (1984), is the Coptic-Gnostic *Apocryphon of James,* a dialogue between the risen Jesus and James and Peter, introduced as a letter. The tractate contains ten sayings complexes, several with components strikingly similar to canonical sayings. Three parables are unattested elsewhere: (1) the date shoot that withered (I,7.22–35), (2) the grain of wheat (8.16–27), and (3) the ear of grain (12.22–30).

Two kingdom sayings are found in 2.29–33 and 13.17–19, a prophecy of judgment in 9.24–10.6, and some wisdom and prophetic sayings in 12.31–13.1.

For Further Study

General: For a general bibliography in English, see David E. Aune, *Jesus and the Synoptic Gospels: A Bibliographical Study Guide* (Theological Students Fellowship, 1980). For an important collection of essays reflecting recent research on the Gospels, see W. O. Walker, Jr., ed., *The Relationships Among the Gospels: An Interdisciplinary Dialogue* (Trinity University Press, 1978). See also Howard Clark Kee, *Jesus in History: An Approach to the Study of the Gospels*, 2nd ed. (Harcourt Brace Jovanovich, 1977); John Reumann, *Jesus in the Church's Gospels: Modern Scholarship and the Earliest Sources* (Fortress Press, 1968).

On Individual Gospels: *Mark:* For a balanced approach that interacts with the last decade of scholarship, see Ernest Best, *Mark: The Gospel as Story* (Edinburgh: T. & T. Clark, 1983). Earlier research is surveyed by Ralph Martin, *Mark: Evangelist and Theologian* (Zondervan Publishing House, 1973). The best commentary on Mark is Rudolf Pesch, *Das Markus Evangelium*, 2 vols. (Freiburg, Basel, and Vienna: Herder, 1976–77). See also Howard Clark Kee, *Community of the New Age: Studies in Mark's Gospel* (Westminster Press, 1977). Two studies of the function of Mark are T. J. Weeden, *Mark: Traditions in Conflict* (Fortress Press, 1971), and Werner Kelber, *The Kingdom in Mark* (Fortress Press, 1974). *Matthew:* Jack Dean Kingsbury, *Matthew: Structure, Christology, Kingdom* (Fortress Press, 1975). *John:* One of the better introductions is Stephen S. Smalley, *John: Evangelist and Interpreter* (Thomas Nelson & Sons, 1984). The indispensable commentary is Raymond Brown, *The Gospel According to John*, 2 vols. (Doubleday & Co., 1966–70). See also C. H. Dodd, *The Interpretation of the Fourth Gospel* (Cambridge: University Press, 1965), and R. Alan Culpepper, *Anatomy of the Fourth Gospel: A Study in Literary Design* (Fortress Press, 1983). Two studies of the function of John are Raymond E. Brown, *The Community of the Beloved Disciple* (Paulist Press, 1979), and J. Louis Martyn, *History and Theology in the Fourth Gospel*, rev. ed. (Abingdon Press, 1979).

On Language and Style: Abraham J. Malherbe, *Social Aspects of Early Christianity* (Louisiana State University Press, 1977), has a survey of the problems in evaluating New Testament Greek on pp. 29–59. See also Marius Reiser, *Syntax und Stil des Markusevangeliums* (Tübingen: J. C. B. Mohr [Paul Siebeck], 1984), and Nigel Turner, *Style*, vol. 4 of *A Grammar of New Testament Greek*, by J. H. Moulton et al. (Edinburgh: T. & T. Clark, 1976).

On Oral Forms: *General:* Jan Harold Brunvand, ed., *Folklore: A Study and Research Guide* (St. Martin's Press, 1976). The two most important early treatments of form criticism are Rudolf Bultmann, *History of the Synoptic Tradition,* tr. by John Marsh (Harper & Row, 1963; 2nd ed., Oxford: Basil Blackwell, 1968), and Martin Dibelius, *From Tradition to Gospel* (Charles Scribner's Sons, 1935). See also Vincent Taylor, *The Formation of the Gospel Tradition* (London: Macmillan & Co., 1953). **Miracle Stories:** Robert W. Funk, ed., *Early Christian Miracle Stories, Semeia* 11 (1978); Gerd Theissen, *The Miracle Stories of the Early Christian Tradition,* tr. by F. McDonagh (Fortress Press, 1983). **Parables:** Joachim Jeremias, *The Parables of Jesus,* rev. ed. (Charles Scribner's Sons, 1963); Eta Linnemann, *Parables of Jesus: Introduction and Exposition* (London: S.P.C.K., 1966). **Pronouncement Stories:** John Dominic Crossan, *In Fragments: The Aphorisms of Jesus* (Harper & Row, 1983); Arland J. Hultgren, *Jesus and His Adversaries: The Form and Function of the Conflict Stories in the Synoptic Tradition* (Augsburg Publishing House, 1979); R. C. Tannehill, ed., *Pronouncement Stories, Semeia* 20 (1981); R. C. Tannehill, "Types and Functions of Apophthegms in the Synoptic Gospels," *ANRW* II.25.2, 1792–1829; R. F. Hock and E. N. O'Neil, *The Chreia in Ancient Rhetoric,* I (Scholars Press, 1986).

On Literary Forms: Hans Dieter Betz, "The Sermon on the Mount (Matt. 5:3–7:27): Its Literary Genre and Function," *Essays on the Sermon on the Mount,* tr. L. L. Welborn (Fortress Press, 1985), pp. 1–16. **Sermons or Homilies:** Peter Borgen, *Bread from Heaven: An Exegetical Study of the Concept of Manna in the Gospel of John and the Writings of Philo* (Leiden: E. J. Brill, 1965); Morton Smith, *Tannaitic Parallels to the Gospels* (Society of Biblical Literature, 1951). *Johannine Discourses:* George W. MacRae, "Discourses of the Gnostic Revealer," *Proceedings of the International Colloquium on Gnosticism* (Stockholm: Almqvist & Wiksell; Leiden: E. J. Brill, 1977), pp. 111–122. **Genealogies:** W. S. Kurz, "Luke 3:23–38 and Greco-Roman Biblical Genealogies," in *Luke-Acts: New Perspectives from the Society of Biblical Literature Seminar,* ed. by C. H. Talbert (Crossroad Publishing Co., 1984), pp. 169–187; Robert R. Wilson, *Genealogy and History in the Biblical World* (Yale University Press, 1977). **Dialogue:** C. H. Dodd, "The Dialogue Form in the Gospels," *BJRL* 37 (1954). **Passion Narrative:** Donald Senior, *The Passion of Jesus in the Gospel of Mark* (Michael Glazier, 1984). **Summaries:** W. Egger, *Frohbotschaft und Lehre: Die Sammelberichte des Wirkens Jesu im Markusevangelium* (Frankfurt: Knecht, 1976); C. H. Hedrick, "The Role of 'Summary Statements' in the Composition of the Gospel of Mark: A Dialog with Karl Schmidt and Norman Perrin," *NovT* 26 (1984), 289–311.

On Ancient Views of the Gospels: Robert M. Grant, *The Earliest Lives of Jesus* (Harper & Brothers, 1961), is an important study discussing the relationship between the Gospels and ancient rhetoric. Ulrich H. J. Körtner, *Papias von Hierapolis: Ein Beitrag zur Geschichte des frühen Christentums* (Göttingen: Vandenhoeck & Ruprecht, 1983). R. O. P. Taylor, *The Groundwork of the Gospels* (Oxford: Basil Blackwell, 1946), takes seriously the constituent Gospel forms as chreiai (pp. 75–90) and includes translations of relevant sections of Theon, Hermogenes, and Nicolas the Sophist.

Later Jesus Literature: Ron Cameron, ed., *The Other Gospels: Non-Canonical Gospel Texts* (Westminster Press, 1982). Marvin W. Meyer, *The Secret Teachings of Jesus: Four Gnostic Gospels* (Random House, 1984), includes translations and notes on the *Apocryphon of James,* the *Gospel of Thomas,* the *Book of Thomas the Contender,* and the *Apocryphon of John.* See also Elaine Pagels, *The Gnostic Gospels* (Random House, 1979).

Sayings Collections: On the *Gospel of Thomas* see William A. Beardslee, "Proverbs in the Gospel of Thomas," in *Studies in New Testament and Early Christian Literature: Essays in Honor of Allen P. Wikgren,* ed. by D. E. Aune (Leiden: E. J. Brill, 1972), pp. 92–102; Steven L. Davies, *The Gospel of Thomas and Christian Wisdom* (Seabury Press, 1983); Joseph A. Fitzmyer, "The Oxyrhynchus Logoi of Jesus and the Coptic Gospel According to Thomas," in idem, *Essays on the Semitic Background of the New Testament* (Scholars Press, 1974), pp. 355–433. See also Robert M. Grant and David Noel Freedman, *The Secret Sayings of Jesus* (Doubleday & Co., 1960); Ron Cameron, *Sayings Traditions in the Apocryphon of James* (Fortress Press, 1984).

On Gnostic Dialogues: Pheme Perkins, *The Gnostic Dialogue: The Early Church and the Crisis of Gnosticism* (Paulist Press, 1980).

3

Luke-Acts
and Ancient Historiography

Luke-Acts is a popular "general history" written by an amateur Hellenistic historian with credentials in Greek rhetoric. Historians were trained in rhetoric, not historiography, and supported their hobby through independent means or were stipended clients of wealthy patrons. Luke's patron was Theophilus, though we know only his name (Luke 1:3; Acts 1:1). Luke was also a convert to Christianity. This combination of Greco-Roman literary skill and Christian faith resulted in a novel literary work. Using his rhetorical skills, Luke adapted the genre of general history, one of the more eclectic genres of antiquity, as an appropriate literary vehicle for depicting the origins and development of Christianity.

The Problem of Genre

The Gospel of Luke and the Acts of the Apostles originally constituted a two-volume work by a single author. Early in the second century, Luke was separated from Acts and combined with the other Gospels to form the *Tetraevangelium* (fourfold Gospel). This separation was facilitated by the fact that Luke and Acts were written on separate papyrus rolls (however, the author could, like some ancient historians, have published each book separately). Luke is commonly regarded as a "gospel" because of obvious similarities to the other Gospels, and Acts is widely categorized as "history," though lacking exact Hellenistic or Israelite-Jewish literary analogues. By itself, Luke could (like Mark, Matthew, and John) be classified as a type of ancient biography. But Luke, though it might have circulated separately, was subordinated to a larger literary structure. Luke does not belong to a type of ancient biography for it belongs with Acts, and Acts cannot be forced into a biographical mold.

More than fifty years ago Henry J. Cadbury compared Luke-Acts with both biography and history. He concluded it was probably closer to history in form but did not fit the formal features of either category. Yet the fact that no historical work is *exactly* like Luke-Acts does not mean that Luke did not work within the accepted parameters of ancient historiographical conventions, for Greco-Roman historiography exhibits great variety. Luke also exhibits familiarity with the conventions of Israelite and Jewish historiography.

Acts and Ancient Praxeis ("Acts") Literature

The Greek title *praxeis apostolōn* ("Acts of the Apostles") was attached to Acts by A.D. 150. Thereafter it is increasingly referred to with this title (Muratorian Canon, line 34; Irenaeus, *Against Heresies* 3.12.11; 3.13.3), or the shortened form "Acts" (*Acta,* often in Tertullian). Though not original, this title stuck because it appropriately characterized the work for ancient readers. Luke described his first book as dealing with "all that Jesus began to *do* and teach" (Acts 1:1). The second book deals with the deeds and teachings of the apostles. *Praxeis* ("deeds" or "achievements") was a term applied to entire historical works (Polybius 1.1.1; 9.1.5–6; Diodorus Siculus 1.1.1) or to portions of them (Xenophon, *Education of Cyrus* 1.2.16; Polybius 4.1.3; Josephus, *Antiquities* 14.68; Diodorus Siculus 3.1.1; 16.1.1; Dio Cassius 62.29). The emperor Augustus wrote his own obituary summarizing his public achievements, called *Res Gestae Divi Augusti,* "the acts of the deified Augustus." The Latin phrase *res gestae* ("achievements") is translated *praxeis* in an ancient Greek translation of the inscription. The term is also used as a title of three or four ancient works, including Callisthenes' *Acts of Alexander* (fourth century B.C.) and Sosylus' *Acts of Hannibal* (second century B.C.). Some scholars have maintained that *Praxeis* were an established literary form. *Praxeis* literature, unlike biography, does not treat character and development, but rather depicts the outstanding deeds of a prominent person, such as a king, general, or hero. *Praxeis* is a nontechnical, descriptive term for narratives of the accomplishments of noteworthy individuals or cities (whether mythical, historical, or fictional). The term offers little help in determining the genre of Acts.

Luke-Acts as Biographical Succession Narrative

Charles Talbert has proposed that Luke-Acts is a *succession narrative,* a type of Greco-Roman biography. Talbert proposes a threefold pattern in this biographical genre: (1) the life of the founder,

(2) a list or narrative about disciples and successors, and (3) a summary of the teaching of the school. The genre originated, he suggests, when later adherents found it necessary to legitimate their ties to the founder. The only examples of this genre are Diogenes Laertius' *Lives of Philosophers,* a lengthy compendium of the lives and teachings of eighty-two ancient philosophers from Thales to Epicurus, written ca. A.D. 250 at the earliest. Talbert regards the similarities between Diogenes' *Lives* and Luke-Acts as remarkable, for both contain the life of a founder of a religious community, a list or narrative of successors, and a summary of the community's teaching.

Talbert's analysis of Diogenes Laertius is unsatisfactory for several reasons: (1) Although he claims that Diogenes' lives "usually" consist of three elements (life + successor + teachings), in fact only six of eighty-two lives have this pattern (Aristippus, Plato, Zeno, Pythagoras, Pyrrho, Epicurus). (2) Talbert's contention that a succession list or narrative reveals where authentic tradition is located finds no confirmation in Diogenes, who is concerned only with who studied with whom and who succeeded whom, not with the legitimacy of their views. (3) Talbert's use of the phrase "succession *narrative*" is an inappropriate description of brief *lists* of students or successors. Yet Talbert's proposal has the merit of attempting to find an analogy in genre to Luke-Acts as a whole.

Acts and the Greco-Roman Novel

Hellenistic *histories* are vehicles for narrating events worthy of record. Hellenistic *biographies* focus on the lives of prominent people worth remembering and emulating. Hellenistic *novels* narrate stories worth telling. Historians and biographers treated events that actually happened and people who really lived; they had *historical* intentions. Novelists narrated imaginary events that could have happened but did not; they had *fictional* intentions. Neat distinctions, however, can be misleading. Dramatic historians manipulated and embroidered historical events to an extent unacceptable to modern historiography, while ancient novels (like modern historical fiction) treated the adventures of imaginary or real people in known or at least plausible historical settings.

Many scholars have proposed a generic relationship between Acts and ancient novels, but none have argued the case more thoroughly than Richard Pervo. Since Acts lacks factual accuracy, he claims, it should be classified as a *historical novel,* not as history. The primary purpose of Acts is *edification* (the empirical demonstration that virtue is superior to vice) in an *entertaining* form (a purpose the canonical book of Acts shares with the novels and the five earliest apocryphal acts). Luke achieves this using the same themes and motifs as the novelists. Pervo finds 33 episodes in Acts (23 in Acts 13–28) that feature miraculous and exciting last-minute escapes from various perils (e.g., 14:2–6; 16:16–40; 22:22–24). These episodes, with close analogies in ancient novels, fall into five categories: (1) arrests and imprisonments (3:1–4:31; 5:12–42); (2) persecution and martyrdom (21:27–22:29); (3) mob scenes (eleven, including 16:19–23; 18: 12–17; 19:23–41); (4) trial stories (nine, including 4:5–22; 18:12–17; 25:6–12); (5) travel and shipwreck (e.g., 27:1–28:16). Pervo focuses on the *fictional* features of these and other elements in Acts and the links which they have with novelistic themes and motifs.

Pervo's main contention is correct: Acts *is* entertaining and edifying. That Acts should be categorized as a *historical novel* with closer links to fiction than history, however, is doubtful. His arguments have several weaknesses: (1) Though ancient historians wrote to entertain, they did not think truth and usefulness had to be sacrificed. (2) The term "historical novel" should be reserved for novels that follow a historical sequence of events (like Xenophon's *Education of Cyrus* or Pseudo-Callisthenes' *Alexander Romance*), rather than applied to fictional narratives set in the real world. (3) The factual accuracy of Acts (variously assessed) is irrelevant to generic classification if Luke *intended* to narrate actual events. Luke's use of historical prefaces and his mention of sources are not found in novels. (4) Luke-Acts *must* be treated as affiliated with *one* genre, but Pervo treats Acts in isolation. (5) Many of the episodes he discusses, with their constituent themes and motifs, far from being unique to novels and Acts, are found in both factual and fictional narratives in the Hellenistic world.

Hellenistic Historiography

The diversity of Hellenistic historical writing suggests that it consists of not one but many interrelated yet individually distinct generic forms. Lucian of Samosata, a second-century A.D. Greek satirist, claimed that "there is no one who isn't writing history" (*How to Write History* 2). Though he obviously exaggerated, evidence suggests that Greeks and Romans were very interested in historical literature during the Hellenistic period and that an extremely large number of histories were produced, though few have survived.

"History" (Greek: *historia,* "inquiry") is a term that originally was used of any type of research but eventually was restricted to the study of the past. As a designation for a type of writing, "history" emphasizes a *method* that describes a main feature of this type of literature. *"Historia,"* therefore, included not only "history" as we understand it, but the reporting of all aspects of the world and its inhabitants based on inquiry or discovery.

Historical Methods and Sources

From Herodotus (died ca. 420 B.C.) to Ammianus Marcellinus (ca. A.D. 330–395), ancient historians preferred oral over written sources. Access to sources was through the eyes and ears, for "eyes are surer witnesses than ears," meaning that direct experience is preferable to hearsay (Heraclitus, quoted in Polybius 12.27.1). Ancient writers often claimed to be eyewitnesses of the events they described. Personal visual knowledge, i.e., eyewitness evidence *(autopsia)*, was thought the most reliable historical source (Herodotus 2.99; Polybius 12.27.1–6; 20.12.8; Lucian, *History* 47). Polybius thought that historians should be "men of affairs" who actually participated in the events they narrated (3.4.13; 12.25g.1; 12.28. 1–5). Roman historians from Q. Fabius Pictor (late third century B.C.) to Dio Cassius (ca. A.D. 40–112) were either senators or their clients. The study of history was one of the better ways of acquiring experience in war and politics.

The requirement of personal visual experience resulted in several restrictions. First, the historian was limited to contemporary history. Historians who restricted themselves to contemporary or near-contemporary events include Thucydides, Xenophon, Polybius, Sallust, and Tacitus. Livy is the only "major" ancient historian who is an exception. Second, historians could not be everywhere, necessitating other ways of collecting evidence. Third, an important dimension of eyewitness evidence was familiarity with regions where historical events had taken place. Herodotus (following the example of Hecataeus of Miletus) was one of the most widely traveled ancient historians, visiting important places from Greece to Babylon. Travel (requiring leisure and means) was thus a necessity for the accomplished historian (Appian, preface 12).

Hearing was also indispensable for historical research. First, the historian could hear about events through interviewing eyewitnesses (Polybius 4.2.2). Second, he could obtain oral information from reliable authorities, usually by traveling to the scene (Herodotus 2.52; Polybius 3.48.12; 4.38.11; 10.11.4). Third, he could listen to and evaluate popular traditions. Fourth, he could read and compare accounts written by those who were eyewitnesses (since ancients read aloud, written accounts were "heard"; cf. Polybius 28. 4.8; 38.4.8).

The way in which historians composed their works can be understood from ancient historiographical theorists (e.g., Dionysius of Halicarnassus and Lucian of Samosata), from digressions on methodology in ancient historians (e.g., Polybius), and by comparing finished works with their sources when both survive. The first stage in writing history involved the preparation of a preliminary sketch of events *(hypomnēma)* in chronological order (Josephus, *Against Apion* 1.47–50; Lucian, *History* 16, 48). *Hypomnēmata* characteristically lacked speeches, dramatic episodes, digressions, and topical organization, all composed and inserted later. The narrative must also have appropriate diction, periodic style (the use of complex sentences), and smooth links between narrative units (Lucian, *History* 48, 55).

"Without adding or deleting anything" is a motto some ancient historians applied to the accurate use of sources or facts (Dionysius of Halicarnassus, *Roman Antiquities* 5, 8; Lucian, *History* 47; Josephus, *Antiquities* 1.17). This meant sticking to the general sense of the sources, not transcribing them verbatim (cf. Porphyry in Eusebius, *Preparation for the Gospel* 4.7.1). Ancient historians freely abridged, omitted, or expanded material, made substitutions from other sources, shaped and colored the narrative and invented minor improvements in detail. The use of published inscriptions is instructive. Decrees, edicts, and letters inscribed on stone represented the gist of the originals (deposited in archives such as the Tabularium in Rome or the Metroon in Athens) and were not exact copies. If public inscriptions of official documents conveyed only the general substance, why should historians aim at slavish imitation? The speech of Claudius reported by Tacitus *(Annals* 11.23–25) is half the length of the inscribed version. Similarly, when Josephus copied the text of a treaty from 1 Macc. 8:23–32, he boiled the Greek text down from 154 to 81 words *(Antiquities* 12.417f.). Tacitus and Josephus were typical. When Greek and Roman authors "quoted" inscriptions, they never checked originals in archives.

If historians preferred a topical arrangement to the chronological one in the sources, they freely made the necessary changes (Josephus, *Antiquities* 4.197; *Wars* 7.42). Shaye Cohen argues convincingly that both the *Life* and the *Wars* of Josephus are based on an earlier sketch *(hypomnēma)* made in Palestine. *Wars* is a well-written, thematic account of events, while the *Vita* is considerably less polished and in chronological order. The speeches in Dionysius, *Roman Antiquities* 8.1.1–63.4, were omitted or radically abstracted by Plutarch in his *Life of Coriolanus.* Generally ancient historians followed one source at a time, though they often supplemented their primary source by inserting material from other sources where amplification or more detail was desirable.

History and Rhetoric

History was not in the curriculum of Greek and Roman schools. Most historians had formal rhetorical education, however, and used that training to write history. According to the rhetorical handbooks, narratives ought to be *veri similis,* "like the truth." Rhetoricians (particularly Sophists) were more concerned with plausibility than truth, and plausibility (a combination of logic and common sense) was the ancient historian's only method for determining historical reliability. Given this kind of formal training it was inevitable that the standards of oratory would profoundly influence historiography. Historians were often concerned to convince their readers that *their* account of events was more reliable than that of others—a purpose similar to that of legal and advisory oratory. Hellenistic historians tried to influence the attitude and behavior of readers by depicting particular individuals as examples of virtue or vice. That task was essentially one of persuasion. Rhetorical theory distinguished three categories of narration: (1) history *(historia),* for narrating actual events; (2) fiction *(plasma* or *argumentum),* for narrating events similar to actual events; (3) myth or legend *(mythos* or *fabula),* for narrating events that could not happen (Quintilian 2.42; Cicero, *On Rhetorical Invention* 1.27; Sextus Empiricus, *Against the Professors* 1.263f.). In practice these categories merged (Strabo 1. 2.17, 35).

Dionysius of Halicarnassus was a rhetorical historian who used rhetorical exaggerations in battle accounts (*Roman Antiquities* 8. 89.1–2: the number of spears in a shield weighed them down), introduced hypothetical situations to contrast with reality (2.3.7; 8.86.2; 9.45.1), and used antitheses (not . . . but) in describing inspiring and emotional scenes like Brutus punishing his sons (5. 8.5). An important use of rhetoric in historiography was the composition of fabricated speeches or declamations. Dionysius of Halicarnassus and Livy may have published the speeches included in their histories separately. These sometimes read more like classroom exercises than speeches appropriate to actual situations (Polybius 12.25a.5; 25b.4; 25k.8; 26.9).

Another influence of rhetoric on historiography took the form of dramatic episodes enabling the reader to participate emotionally in the events and situations of the story. Many scholars regard "tragic history" or "dramatic history" as a separate literary genre or a product of a particular school of thought. Polybius, who coined the phrase "tragic history" (for him it improperly combined fictional drama with factual history), criticized the historians who used such techniques excessively (2.2.56–63; 3.47.6–48.12). Polybius argues against *excess,* not elimination, as his own use of "tragic" episodes suggests (15.25–33; 16.30–34; 23.10–11). Lucian too complained of the wholesale use of tragic features in history, but approved of their moderate use (*History* 7–10). F. W. Walbank has argued convincingly that tragic history is a *style* originating with Herodotus rather than a historiographical genre or school.

The Form and Content of History

There are five major genres of Hellenistic "historical" writing in antiquity, each distinguished by a special content correlated with a complementary structural form: (1) genealogy or mythography, (2) travel descriptions (ethnography and geography), (3) local history, (4) chronography, and (5) history. They are all *prose* genres that attempt to distinguish fact from fiction.

The five types of historical writing can be subdivided into types that are *chronologically* arranged (history in the modern sense), and those which are *systematically* arranged (learned research on the past or antiquarian studies). Chronological types of historical writing include *local history, chronography,* and *political and military history.* Genealogy, mythology, ethnology, and geography, and related concerns were the primary concern of ancient antiquarian tradition (Greek: *archaiologiai;* Latin: *antiquitates*), subjects best presented systematically. Antiquarians were interested in the social, cultural, legal, economic, and religious institutions of antiquity, in language and customs; in short, everything subject to rational inquiry. Polybius first designated historical narratives of political and military events *pragmatikē historia,* i.e., "politico-military history" (6.5.2), which he distinguished from antiquarian research (9.1–2). In modern terms, antiquarians were social and cultural historians, whose studies frequently invaded histories in the form of digressions.

Genealogy or Mythography

Genealogy or mythography was an early type of "historical" writing which attempted to integrate heroes of myth and legend into historical families and clans, often to link descendants with the virtues and qualities of important progenitors. Inspired by Hesiod's epic lists of gods and heroes, this type of history reflects Greek interest in the heroic past. It served the purpose of separating "prehistory" from "history," and it survived most frequently as a short literary form included in larger compositions.

Travel Descriptions

Travel descriptions (ethnography) were written from the early fifth century B.C. to late antiquity, and usually focused on a particular ethnic group in its native habitat. Four types of information were characteristically included: (a) geography, i.e., a description of a region, (b) dynastic history, or a description of the succession of native rulers, (c) the marvels or wonders of the region, and (d) the customs of the inhabitants. Ethnography was characteristically more tolerant of exaggerated reports and improbabilities than other forms of history. Since ancients assumed that environmental determines group character traits (cf. Hippocrates, *Airs, Waters, Places*), geography was a presupposition for historiography.

Local History

Local history (or horography, "annalistic writing"), which originated during the late fifth century B.C. in Athens, narrated the parochial annual events of a city-state in chronological sequence. While the Greeks themselves maintained a distinction between history proper and horography (local history), the Romans blended them. In Rome the practice of compiling "Great Annals" *(annales maximi)* by the chief priest, the Pontifex Maximus, had a decisive influence on Roman historiography (e.g., Q. Fabius Pictor, Livy, Dio Cassius). Annalistic historiography dealt with events in annual segments, a technique that tended to interrupt historical continuity.

Chronography

Chronography, or the chronicle, in its simplest form consisted of chronologically ordered lists of priests, priestesses, kings, magistrates, officials, and Olympic victors. These were used for dating by years; a year was identified by officials who held office in that year (e.g., archons in Athens, ephors in Sparta, stephanephoroi in Miletus). By the fifth century the Greeks used numerical dating by Olympiads (four-year periods starting with 776 B.C). In the absence of a universally recognized chronological scheme, "chronicles" (which, unlike histories, do not *explain* the facts) were indispensable for writing local histories. When these were coordinated with chronographies from other cities and regions, the writing of general history became possible. The dating of John the Baptist's ministry in Luke 3:1-2 (the resultant date is A.D. 28 or 29) is an example of the coordination of chronographic lists.

Scientific measurement of time began in Alexandria with the lost *Chronographiai* of Eratosthenes of Cyrene (third century B.C.), covering Greek history from the Trojan war to Alexander the Great and using Olympiads as a chronological yardstick. He and later chronographers were chiefly interested in games, treaties, lives of great men, destruction of cities, great battles and victories, political events, and such natural phenomena as comets and earthquakes. In the cultural conflicts of the Hellenistic and Roman periods chronography became a propaganda tool. The Hellenistic historians Berossus and Manetho (both third century B.C.) argued that Greek culture was secondary and derivative, using arguments based on the chronological priority of their native cultures. Judaism also claimed cultural and religious superiority by arguing the antiquity of Moses over Plato. Christian apologists used the apologetic chronology of Judaism to argue the priority and superiority of biblical revelation over Greek philosophy and religion (Justin, *1 Apology* 54–59; Tatian, *Oration to the Greeks* 31–42; Theophilus, *To Autolycus* 3.16–29). The Christian world *Chronicle* by Eusebius of Caesarea (ca. A.D. 260–340) combined classical and nativistic chronologies in a form and style that influenced Christian scholarship for centuries.

History

History proper is a unique historiographical genre since it is *mimetic*, i.e., it attempts to dramatize and interpret the memorable actions of people in time. The other four types described above collected and reported data without interpretation or dramatization. The historian, on the other hand, created the illusion that he was an observer of the events he depicts. Since the collective actions of people are most significant, *war* (strife between states) and *politics* (factional conflicts within states) came to occupy a place of central concern in Greco-Roman historiography through the influence of Herodotus and Thucydides. History was subdivided into two subgenres by Polybius and other ancient critics: (1) *kata meros*, "historical monographs," and (2) *katholou*, "general history" (Polybius 2. 37.4; 12.23.7; 29.12.2–5; Dionysius of Halicarnassus, *On Thucydides* 5). To these we add a third subgenre: (3) antiquarian history. While straight chronological schemes were appropriate for historical monographs, general and antiquarian history usually dealt with several historical theaters, using separate chronologies for each region (e.g., Appian's *Romaika*).

Historical Monographs

Historical monographs focused on an important sequence of events (typically a war) during a restricted period of time. Herodotus and Thucydides (ca. 455–400 B.C.) wrote *historical monographs* about war under the conviction that the most significant type of human change was political and military in nature. Herodotus treated the single memorable theme of the conflict between East and West, culminating in the wars between Persia and Greece. Herodotus was concerned with the problem of causation (etiology), based on the ancient notion that the key to understanding individual and group behavior is tied to the question of origins. In 430 B.C. he completed a history of the wars between the Greek and the Persians later published posthumously. In it he focused on the period from the Ionian revolt (499 B.C.; 5.28ff.) through the final Greek victories at the battles of Plataea and Mycale (479 B.C.; 9.1–106), combining constitutional history and ethnography (which dominate the first half of his work) with military history in an attempt to describe and explain events. His work has an episodic quality both because he uses a folkloristic technique of composition, linking discrete episodes together in a chain, and because he designed his work to be read publicly in manageable segments.

Thucydides, unlike his predecessors, chose the innovative subject of the contemporary war between Athens and Sparta (431–404 B.C.). He focused on political and military affairs and their interrelationship. His work is incomplete, ending in the winter of 411, though the author intended to end with the cessation of hostilities in 404 (5.26.1). Thucydides was criticized in antiquity both for rhetorical infelicities and for not giving proper attention to proper "beginnings," i.e., historical causation (Dionysius, *On Thucydides* 9–20).

The anonymous author of the *Hellenika Oxyrhynchia* imitated Thucydides and continued his history by covering the period 411–386 B.C. This history, reconstructed from papyrus fragments discovered in this century, is (aside from Thucydides) the only Greek historical work to use the chronological "divisions" *(diaireseis)* of "summer and winter" to structure his narrative. Other successors and imitators of Thucydides, such as Theopompus and Xenophon, wrote

Greek histories (*Hellēnika,* literally "Greek Affairs") that emphasized political and military affairs as central and yet focused on the deeds of a single great individual, such as Alexander the Great. This was in effect a movement in the direction of biographical history, with an emphasis on personality traits, emotions, attire, virtues, vices, dreams, and portents, all of which became regular and appropriate subjects for narration. This kind of history tended to be laudatory or encomiastic. The *Wars of the Jews* by Josephus is the only historical monograph to survive from the early Empire.

General History

General histories narrated the important historical experiences of a single national group from their origin to the recent past. This usually involved contacts with other nations (mostly through warfare). General history is a genre that first appeared in the Hellenistic period. In one sense, Herodotus anticipated general history because of the scope of his undertaking (Dionysius, *On Thucydides* 5). Yet for the ancients, general history began with the *Historiai* of Ephorus (ca. 405–330 B.C.), a work in thirty books surviving only in later authors (epitomized in Diodorus 11–16). This work was "general" in the sense that it dealt with Greek history from earliest times including contacts with barbarian nations. "General history" translates such phrases as *koinai historiai, koinai praxeis* (Diodorus Siculus 1.1.1; 1.4.6; 4.1.3; 5.1.4), and *katholou praxeis* (Polybius 12.23.7; 29.12.2–5). These expressions are often misleadingly translated *"universal* history." While some late historians did treat "the inhabited world" *(oikoumenē),* others focused on the history of a single national group in relation to neighboring nations. Polybius (ca. 200–118 B.C.) was the first general historian whose work has partially survived. His history was continued down to ca. 60 B.C. by Posidonius (135–50 B.C.), whose work was in turn continued to ca. 30 B.C. by Strabo (ca. 64 B.C. to A.D. 21). Other Greek writers of general history include Diodorus Siculus (first century B.C.) and Nicolaus of Damascus (born 64 B.C.), who wrote perhaps the largest such history in 144 books. Of the many general histories written in Latin only part of the work of Ammianus Marcellinus (late fourth century A.D.) has survived.

In the Hellenistic period many general histories were written by "barbarian" intellectuals who wished to communicate to the Greeks the achievements (and superiority) of their native lands. The writing of such histories reflects a national consciousness of a people united (particularly in opposition to Greeks and then Romans) by language, geography, and customs. The model for such apologetic and propagandistic histories was the *History of Egypt* by Hecataeus of Abdera (ca. 300 B.C.). He was followed by a host of imitators, including Manetho (*History of Egypt,* ca. 280 B.C.), Berossus (*History of Babylonia*), and several Hellenistic Jewish historians (Artapanus, Eupolemus, and Pseudo-Eupolemus). The Jewish historian Josephus wrote *Antiquities of the Jews* using both these nativistic general histories and the eclectic antiquarian history of Dionysius of Halicarnassus as models.

Antiquarian History

Antiquarian history is really a more eclectic form of general history, combining the concerns of antiquarian studies (mythology, genealogy, local history, ethnology, geography) with a chronological survey of states in terms of conflicts both internal (politics) and external (military), from mythical times to the recent past. Dionysius of Halicarnassus (late first century B.C.), who taught rhetoric in Rome after 30 B.C. and wrote *Roman Antiquities,* describes the inclusive character of his history at length (1.7.1–4). He wants to begin with the oldest myths (avoided by many historians) and bring the narrative *(diēgēsis)* down to the First Punic War (264 B.C.). He includes foreign wars and civil strife during that period, showing their causes and the actions and arguments (speeches) that brought them to an end. He also discusses the various types of constitutions that evolved along with characteristic Roman laws and customs, i.e., the whole corporate life of the ancient Romans. He does not want to limit his treatment either to wars or forms of government or to annalistic accounts, but consciously presents a "combination [*miktos*] of every kind, forensic, speculative, and narrative" to provide satisfaction and entertainment to all types of readers. Dionysius, in short, was consciously writing a *mixed* history by including features that normally characterized a variety of historical and antiquarian genres.

Constituent Literary Forms

Historical Prefaces

History was the first type of prose writing to develop a distinctive type of preface *(prooimion).* Themes in the prefaces of Herodotus and Thucydides became conventional *topoi* for subsequent historians: the praise of history, the claim of impartiality and the permanent value of the subject. The use of introductory chapters prefacing individual books became a historiographical convention (Polybius 11.1 knows, but rejects, this practice). In such prefaces the author could reveal his views and prejudices (e.g., by praising or condemning important figures, or drawing moral lessons), discuss aims and methods, criticize earlier historians, and demonstrate rhetorical skill. One use of prefaces in books of lengthy works was to recapitulate the previous book and summarize the next (e.g., Diodorus 1.42; 2.1.1–3; 3.1.1–3; 18.1.1–6).

Lucian emphasizes three functions of *rhetorical* prefaces: (1) to secure the goodwill of the audience, and (2) to gain their attentiveness; (3) to dispose them to receive instruction (*History* 53). Several *topoi,* or stock themes, came to be associated with the prefaces of Hellenistic historiography: (1) requests and dedications (Isocrates' *To Nicocles* contains the first extant dedication in a prose preface); (2) apology for defective style; (3) comments on the value and utility of history; (4) mention of predecessors (often critical); (5) assurance of impartiality; (6) use of appropriate methodology; and (7) reason(s) for choice of subject.

The Use of Episodes

The success of extended narrative fiction (epics, novels) and nonfiction (histories) depends on how well individual episodes are connected to form a unified composition. The three primary historical genres (historical monographs, general history, and antiquarian history) are all complex genres constructed of individual episodes. History involves events that occur within a given period no matter how disconnected they appear (cf. Aristotle, *Poetics* 1459a). Historians often treated subjects that lent themselves to unified presentation (e.g., on cities or kings; cf. Diodorus 16.1), often coincident with the division of a work into books (Diodorus 5.1.6). Lucian recommended that historians link episodes together like a chain to avoid breaks and disjunctions (*History* 55; cf. Quintilian 7.1.1). Polybius, on the other hand, recognized and defended his "incomplete and disconnected" narratives, arguing that variety was indispensable (38.5.1–8). The *dramatic* episodes lack extraneous detail and emphasize the mounting tension just before the resolution or denouement.

Speeches

History for the ancients consisted of actions *(praxeis)* and speeches *(logoi);* Homer was the model for both. Direct speech in the Homeric epics (one half of the *Iliad* and three fifths of the *Odyssey*) plays an important dramatic role by presenting past events as if present. In this and other respects, Homer exerted a lasting influence on Greek historiography. In content, Homeric single and paired speeches (all obviously fictional) involve *commands* (e.g., *Iliad* 1.321–325; 4.192–197), *advice* (2.23–34; 5.347–351), *appeals,* including prayers (1.36–42; 3.250–258), and *announcements* (1.442–445; 5.102–105). Speeches not only dramatize relationships but show how and why people act as they do. Speeches of command, advice, and appeal usually function to *motivate* action, i.e., to show why people did what they did. Speeches of announcement, on the other hand, usually *explain* the speaker's actions or foreshadow coming events. In epic, tragedy, comedy, and Herodotean history, characterization does not include linguistic individualization; direct speech uniformly reflects the author's style (note the "inappropriately" elegant speech of the savage cannibal giant Polyphemus in *Odyssey* 9.447–460).

Discourse plays a significant role in Herodotus, the first historian to use direct speech for dramatization. According to Mabel L. Lang, his history contains 861 speeches in both direct discourse (The general said, "I won") and indirect discourse (The general said that he won). Less than half (47.5 percent) are direct discourse. The important role of indirect discourse in Herodotus contrasts with the preference for direct discourse in Homer (as in Old Testament narrative). The ninety-two single direct speeches in Herodotus are similar in content and function to those in Homer. Herodotus, who found discourse combined with events in his oral sources, treated words differently from actions. While he occasionally gives different versions of events *(erga),* he never gives different versions of speeches *(logoi).* This suggests his creativity in composing and using them as narrative devices, not only for dramatization but also to provide motivations and explanations for behavior.

The use of discourse in historiography reached a new and significant level of development in Thucydides, at a time when oratory began to make important strides in classical Athens. By earlier reckoning there are forty-one speeches in direct discourse in Thucydides (24 percent of the narrative), uniformly reflecting his own language and style. According to the recent assessment of W. C. West, there are fifty-two speeches in direct discourse, eighty-five in indirect discourse (three combining direct with indirect discourse), and the Melian dialogue, comprising 141 speeches, forty-four of which are paired. In an endlessly debated passage, Thucydides comments on his use of speeches (1.22.1; trans. by J. H. Finley, Jr.):

> With reference to the speeches in this history, some were delivered before the war began, others while it was going on; some I heard myself, others I got from various quarters; it was in all cases difficult to carry them word for word in one's memory, so my habit has been to make the speakers say what was in my opinion demanded of them [*ta deonta epein*] by the various occasions, of course adhering as closely as possible to the general sense [*hē xympasa gnōmē*] of what they really said.

The ambiguity of this statement centers on two phrases *ta deonta epein* and *hē xympasa gnōmē*. The first can mean either "what the speakers needed to say" (i.e., actually said). The second phrase can mean "the general intention" of what was said, or "the overall opinion" expressed. In both cases the second alternative is preferable. Thucydides proposes to give a reliable account of what the original speakers needed to say to accomplish their objectives with particular audiences in particular situations. There is little doubt, however, that he did not fully carry out his intentions. The language of the speeches is uniformly Thucydidean. The analysis of the speeches themselves, some of which are clearly anachronistic or inappropriate, suggests that they are neither historical nor authentic, but are vehicles for analyzing historical situations from various perspectives.

During the fourth and third centuries there was a reaction to the rational historicism of Thucydides. Historians like Ephorus wrote more *inclusive* histories following Herodotus. Speeches were inventions displaying the writer's rhetorical ability rather than the actual or epitomized remarks of the speakers. They also served as oratorical models. Polybius reacted against this feature of dramatic history and revived what he *thought* was the Thucydidean standard of accuracy. Like all ancient historians, he used speeches frequently (about fifty in the surviving parts of his history). In 12.25a.5–25b.1, he comments on the proper use of speeches in a polemic against Timaeus (modified LCL trans.):

> For he [Timaeus] has not set down the words spoken nor the sense of what was really said, but having made up his mind as to what ought to have been said, he recounts all these speeches and all else that follows upon events like a man in a school of rhetoric attempting to speak on a given subject, and shows off his oratorical power, but gives

no report of what was actually spoken. The peculiar function of history is to discover, in the first place, the words actually spoken, whatever they were, and next to ascertain the reason why what was done or spoken led to failure or success.

Here Polybius faults Timaeus for freely composing speeches based on situational probability rather than setting down the substance of the actual speeches themselves. For Polybius the difference is between the possibility of tragedy, "what *could* happen," and the actuality of history, "what *did* happen" (2.56.10; cf. Aristotle, *Poetics* 1451a–b). Elsewhere Polybius seems to say that the historian must *choose* the arguments appropriate to a speaker in a given situation, apparently contradicting the view quoted above (12.25i.3–9). Yet in 12.25i.3–9, Polybius is probably concerned with the editing or epitomizing of actual speeches, i.e., with selected arguments in the actual speeches (or epitomes of them) for inclusion in his narrative. Since Polybius apparently avoided presenting speeches as rhetorical models (like the so-called tragic historians), many of his speeches lack appropriate rhetorical structure and focus on one point.

Apart from Thucydides and Polybius, speeches composed for historical works were not based on actual speeches but were rhetorical compositions judged "suitable" *(to prepon)* for the person to whom they were ascribed in the particular situation envisaged. Hellenistic armchair historians found speeches in their sources and freely adapted them for their own compositions. Dionysius was a practicing rhetorician and historian who favored the use of speeches (they constitute 30 percent of his *Roman Antiquities*). He criticized Thucydides' speeches as rhetorically "unsuitable" (*On Thucydides* 37–41). Diodorus Siculus criticized the *excessive* use of rhetoric in framing speeches, but thought that rhetorical embellishment did have a place in historiography (20.1–2). Lucian suggests that speeches should first fit the person and subject, and only then be shaped to reflect the historian's rhetorical abilities (*History* 58). It is clear that both Lucian and Dionysius understood the problematic phrase in Thucydides *ta deonta epein* to mean "what the situation demanded," i.e., speeches should be appropriate for speaker and situation.

Digressions

In Greco-Roman historiography, narrative is reserved for describing people's deeds, while speeches provided explanation and analysis. Yet Greek historians also included personal editorial comments and inserted parenthetical material of descriptive or expository nature in the form of "digressions" of varying length (from one line to one book, e.g., Herodotus 2; Polybius 6, 12, 34). A "digression" (Greek: *parekbasis, ekbolē;* Latin: *egressus, digressio*) is not a literary form, but a technique for temporarily suspending the narrative to include extraneous topical material of various types. Yet literary forms, like the many novellas in Herodotus, could be inserted as digressions.

Digressions function in various ways: (1) They are ancient counterparts to the footnotes, appendices, and excursuses of modern scholarship. Thus they correct erroneous views, as Thucydides' digressions on Themistocles (6.2–5) and the Peisistratids (6:54–59), or criticize earlier historians, as Polybius' debates with Philinus (1.15), Phylarchus (2.56–63), Theopompus (8.9–11), and Timaeus (the entire twelfth book). (2) They can supply important background necessary for understanding the narrative (e.g., geographical information, descriptions of institutions and customs, surveys of conditions), or for understanding the causes of events, as Thucydides' digression on the Pentecontaetis ("Fifty Years"), dealing with the causes of the Peloponnesian war (1.89–118). (3) They can have a didactic function, emphasizing the moral and political lessons to be drawn from the narrative, a major function of Polybian digressions (4.31; 4.74). (4) Digressions can provide variety and enjoyment, both by relieving a long and tedious narrative (Polybius 38. 5–6; cf. Diodorus 20.2.1)—Dionysius calls them "rests" (*anapauseis;* *To Pompeius* 3)—and by inclusion of entertaining stories (Polybius 38.6.2). Herodotus must hold the record for number (about 200) and length of digressions (all of book 2 is a digression on Egypt, which itself contains digressions like the novella about the clever thief, 2.121). Plutarch, critical of Herodotus, thought historical digression should be limited to myths and encomia, i.e., flattering biographical sketches (*On the Malignity of Herodotus* 855D; cf. Polybius 38.6.2). Lucian recommended that both be avoided (*History* 8). Digressions provided myth with a port of entry into history.

There was a tendency among some educated readers to resent detours from the main narrative (Polybius 38.5.1–3), though Dionysius criticized Thucydides for not including more (*To Pompeius* 3). Thus some Hellenistic historians avoided (or made a pretense of avoiding) digressions. Dio Cassius expressly intends to avoid them, but includes scores of them anyway. Josephus tried to avoid breaks in the narrative (*Wars* 4.496), and for that reason sometimes avoids digressions (*Antiquities* 11.68). Livy's preference for "indirect narration" is reflected in his omission of Polybian digressions (Polybius

18.35; cf. Livy 33.11.8ff.; Polybius 29.8–9; cf. Livy 44.24.7–26.2). Historians often carefully identified digressions (Thucydides 1. 97.1; Polybius 2.36.1; 3.2.7; 4.9.1; Dionysius of Halicarnassus 1.53; Diodorus Siculus 1.37). Digressions were an important and entertaining rhetorical device in oratory, where the trick was to make a neat resumption *(epanodos)* enabling the reader or listener to take up the threads of the main narrative (Cicero, *On Oratory* 3.53.203; Lucian, *Demonax* 6). Such resumptions were often accomplished by repeating at the end of the digression the last few lines preceding the digression, forming a kind of "ring composition" (cf. Arrian, *Anabasis,* where, after the digression in 5.1.1–5.3.4, the narrative interrupted at 4.30.9 is resumed in 5.3.5).

The Function of History

In general, every Greco-Roman historian wrote with three combined purposes, though the emphasis could vary greatly. History ought to be *truthful, useful,* and *entertaining,* but it should not be entertaining at the expense of truth or utility. That, at least, was the opinion of many ancient historians. Lucian of Samosata (born ca. A.D. 120) was a great second-century satirist who wrote a short manual entitled *How to Write History.* The Second Parthian war (A.D. 162–165) attracted the attention of many petty historians anxious to chronicle an important contemporary event. Writing shortly before the end of the war (*History* 31), Lucian satirizes these historians, mocking their methodological and stylistic shortcomings. Lucian particularly emphasizes the impropriety of encomium in history, since it involves the kind of exaggeration and falsehood more appropriate to poetry (7–8). Contemporary historians, he observes, provide enjoyment for their audience, a function they divorce from the potential usefulness of history. Lucian claims that history has one purpose: usefulness or practicality, which is the product of truth alone (9). If a truthful historical narrative incidentally provides enjoyment as well as usefulness, so much the better.

Lucian's emphasis on the usefulness of truthful historical accounts of the past was axiomatic among ancient historians, though it could be understood in several ways. Thucydides thought history written by a man of affairs for other men of affairs could provide them with an analysis of historical events to give them the kind of insight needed to deal with similar situations in the future (1.22.4). Dionysius of Halicarnassus also emphasized the usefulness of history (*Roman Antiquities* 1.2.1), as well as the necessity that statesmen understand the causes of events (1.6.4; 5.56.1; 11.1.1, 4). Dio

Chrysostom also regarded the reading of history as beneficial for statesmen (*Oration* 18.9). These historians all wrote to benefit statesmen because they themselves were statesmen or former statesmen, or wrote as their clients.

The usefulness of historical war monographs for statesmen is a central concern of Polybius, who thought that historians should really be participants in the events they narrate (3.31.1–13; 9.9. 9–10; 12.25b.3). It was primarily through the influence of the rhetorician Isocrates (436–338 B.C.) that the value of Hellenistic historiography was understood in terms of moral values. Isocrates wrote *Evagoras,* the first biographical encomium explicitly providing a moral paradigm for emulation (*Oration* 9.77). This program was continued by two influential students, Ephorus and Theopompus. Earlier Herodotus had found ethical meaning in dramatic reversals of fortune. Polybius drew many moral lessons in the requital of evil and the fall of the proud. Similarly Appian editorialized about the disastrous consequences of haughtiness (*Samnite History* 3.4.2), and impiety (3.12.1–2), as well as about divine jealousy of human prosperity (*Macedonian History* 9.19.1).

Israelite Historiography

The remains of ancient Israelite historiography are found exclusively in the Bible. The three major historical compositions in the Old Testament are the Pentateuch, or Torah (Genesis through Deuteronomy, given final form in the fifth century B.C.), the Deuteronomic History (abbreviated DH), or Former Prophets (Joshua through 2 Kings, completed by 550 B.C.), and the Chronistic History, abbreviated CH (1–2 Chronicles and Ezra-Nehemiah, completed by ca. 350 B.C.). The Torah and the Former Prophets present a selectively continuous account of Israelite history from Creation to 561 B.C.

Structure and Content

Nearly fifty years ago Gerhard von Rad, a prominent Old Testament scholar, proposed that the narratives that underlie Genesis through Joshua (the Hexateuch) were expansions of an old confessional pattern now found in Deuteronomy 26:5–9:

> And you shall make response before the LORD your God, "A wandering Aramean was my father; and he went down into Egypt and sojourned there, few in number; and there he became a nation, great,

mighty, and populous. And the Egyptians treated us harshly, and afflicted us, and laid upon us hard bondage. Then we cried to the LORD, the God of our fathers, and the LORD heard our voice, and saw our affliction, our toil, and our oppression; and the LORD brought us out of Egypt with a mighty hand and an outstretched arm, with great terror, with signs and wonders; and he brought us into this place and gave us this land, a land flowing with milk and honey.

This credo recites events that Israel regarded as acts of God: (1) the promise of many descendants and the Land, (2) oppression in Egypt and divine deliverance through the exodus, (3) the realization of the promise in the possession of Canaan. To these should be added (4) the covenant entrusted to Israel at Sinai, and (5) the Davidic covenant (2 Sam. 7:4–16). Despite some objections to the theory, its central idea, the recital of major stages in the past relationship between God and Israel, was certainly a special feature of the Israelite-Jewish religious perspective. These five events, regarded by Israel as constitutive of its national existence and identity, provided a paradigm for understanding the meaning of history. Faithfulness to the covenant results in national blessing (peace and prosperity); unfaithfulness results in national disaster (plagues, famines, conquest).

The structure and content of historiography, therefore, is determined by the view that history is shaped by the vicissitudes of Israel's relationship to God. In *form,* this historiography uses a chronological narrative focusing on the administrations of Israelite leaders (judges, prophets, kings) and events of national importance. A strong biographical tendency is also evident. Topical organization is found largely in works influenced by Hellenism. In *content,* events in Israel (centering in Jerusalem) occupy center stage. This is due to the religious significance of Israel's possession of the Land. It is not surprising, therefore, that in spite of Israel's extensive experience in exile after 721 B.C., *no historical work seriously treats experience outside of Palestine.*

The Pentateuch

Although incorporating earlier sources and traditions, the Pentateuch is a product of the postexilic period (late fifth century B.C.). Three conflated strands of tradition run through Genesis–Numbers: the J (Yahwist) document (ca. 950 B.C.), the E (Elohist) document (ca. 750 B.C.), and the P (Priestly) document (ca. 515 B.C.). All were originally independent narrative histories. J and E were combined before 700 B.C., with J providing the basic framework. This composite narrative, with the addition of the D (Deuteronomist) document, Deuteronomy (ca. 620 B.C.), was in turn both edited and set within the more encompassing P document, the present framework for Genesis–Deuteronomy. Deuteronomy functions as a transition from the Torah to the Former Prophets; while set in the Mosaic period it contains many themes of central concern in the DH.

The Deuteronomic History

The Deuteronomic History (Joshua–2 Kings) is the product of the Deuteronomic "school," which brought a distinctive theological perspective to bear on the interpretation of Israelite history. This "school," which began ca. 650 B.C., was composed either of rural Levites (priests), Jerusalem clergy, or official scribal circles in Jerusalem. This redaction brought together a variety of historical genres such as king lists (never quoted but important for chronology), genealogies, royal annals (lists of officials, letters) and chronicles. Also included were various types of folk traditions, prophetic oracles, and prophetic stories. The author-editors linked these materials together into a comprehensive chronological framework informed by a distinctive theological understanding of history.

The DH used a theological theory of divine retribution to explain the history of Israel. This perspective, expressed in repeated cycles of disobedience, oppression, repentance, and deliverance (particularly in Judges), is summarized in two "digressions" written for the reader (Judg. 2:11–3:6 and 2 Kings 17:7–23). Obedience to the commandments found in the book of the law results in blessing (Deut. 28:1–14), while disobedience produces judgment (Deut. 27: 15–26; 28:15–68). This theological perspective became part of the fabric of Jewish theological thought. The capture of Samaria in 721 B.C. was understood as the consequence of persistent idolatry and the failure to heed prophetic warnings (2 Kings 17:7–23). The capture of Jerusalem in 597 B.C. was similarly understood (2 Kings 24:3; cf. 21:11–15). The corporate effects of sin are often stressed; the people can be punished for the sins of the king (2 Sam. 21:1–9; 2 Kings 23:26–27), descendants for the sin of an ancestor (1 Sam. 3:12–14; 1 Kings 21:29; 2 Kings 5:27). Occasionally divine punishment occurs in accordance with the principle of *lex talionis,* or retaliation in kind (Judg. 9:56f.; 1 Kings 21:17–19; 2 Kings 5:27).

Major themes running through the work include Israel's obligation to be faithful and obedient to God, the disastrous consequences of unfaithfulness (primarily idolatry), and the mitigating role of repentance (1 Kings 8:46–53). Another central theme is God's permanent commitment to Israel based on the unconditional Davidic covenant (Judg. 2:1; 1 Sam. 12:22; 2 Sam. 7:16). The role of prophecy is also important. Some oracles are sought for guidance in particular situations (2 Sam. 2:1; 5:19; 24:12). Others are vehicles for the author-editors' view that divine retribution awaits those who are unfaithful to Israel's covenant with God (Judg. 6:8–10; 1 Sam. 2:27–36). First and Second Kings emphasize the fulfillment of earlier prophecies (2 Kings 1:17; 7:17–20; 9:36–37; 15:12).

Many of the speeches of the Deuteronomist interpret Israel's history from the theological perspective of the obedience/disobedience cycle (Josh. 1:2–9; 22:1–6; 23:2–16; 24:2–27; 1 Sam. 12:1–25; 1 Kings 8:54–61). They are expressions of the theological purpose of the author-editors attributed to historical figures rather than actual speeches. The same is true of the lengthy prayers of Solomon (1 Kings 8:22–53) and Hezekiah (2 Kings 19:15–19), and the prophetic speeches of Isaiah (2 Kings 19:20–34) and Huldah (2 Kings 22:15–20).

The narrative of 1–2 Kings is regularly punctuated with regnal summaries which introduce (1 Kings 14:21–24; 2 Kings 14:1–4) or conclude a reign (1 Kings 21:41–44; 2 Kings 13:8–9). Occasionally uneventful reigns are reported only through a merged introductory and concluding regnal summary (2 Kings 13:10–13; 15:1–7). Theological judgments about the character of particular kings are regularly expressed with the formula "he did what was evil [or good] in the sight of the LORD." When a king's administration is judged evil, a punitive event (typically enemy invasion or assassination) is often narrated (2 Kings 16:1–5; 17:2–3; 23:31–33).

Though miracles play a subordinate role in the DH, many are narrated in the Elijah-Elisha cycle (1 Kings 17–2 Kings 13). These prophets are depicted as working miracles by virtue of the powers they possess as holy men. Four miracles performed by Elijah relate to the drought during the reign of Ahab (1 Kings 17:3–7, 8–16, 17–24; 18:1–46). Many miracle stories are told of Elisha, including the parting of Jordan's waters (2 Kings 2:14), the foul water made potable (2:19–22), the resurrection of the Shunammite's son (4: 18–37), the cleansing of Naaman the leper (5:1–14), and the revival of a dead man who touched Elisha's bones (13:21).

The Chronistic History

The anonymous Chronistic History (1–2 Chronicles and Ezra-Nehemiah) was completed by the end of the Persian period (331

B.C.). Differences between Chronicles and Ezra-Nehemiah suggest the existence of a Chronistic "school" active ca. 515–300 B.C., perhaps composed of Second Temple cult personnel, since the work promotes their interests. The history covers the period from Saul to Ezra, with a long introductory genealogy beginning with Adam and concluding with the Jewish repatriates from Babylon (1 Chron. 1:1–9:34). Though the Chronicler cites sixteen separate sources, his primary source for the preexilic period was Samuel and Kings, which he alters and supplements, revealing his historical and theological perspective. The CH idealizes David (depicted as the real founder of the Temple cult) and Solomon, emphasizes the reforms of Hezekiah and Josiah, exhibits a special interest in the role of the Levites, and focuses exclusively on the southern kingdom of Judah (which he calls "Israel"), treating the northern kingdom of Israel with benign neglect. The emphases on the interrelationship of the Israelite kingship, the Davidic covenant, and the sovereignty of Yahweh intertwine politics with religion. Judgments of the past are viewed as divine retribution meted out to *individuals* responsible for violating God's laws (2 Chron. 25:4). The corporate effects of sin are ignored. In the DH, the capture of Jerusalem in 597 B.C. is the consequence of Manasseh's sins (2 Kings 24:3f.), whereas in the CH Manasseh is punished for his own sins (2 Chron. 33:10–13).

Direct discourse in 1–2 Chronicles occupies about 20 percent of the narrative. There are few examples of indirect discourse (1 Chron. 15:16; 21:18; 2 Chron. 15:12f.; 30:1, 5; 31:4, 11). Most direct discourse consists of brief statements or dialogues. Longer speeches include a psalm (1 Chron. 16:7–36), a revelatory message to David (17:3–14), with his responsory prayer (17:16–27), a prayer of Solomon (2 Chron. 6:14–42), and a speech of Abijah (13:4–12). Shorter examples of direct discourse include several prophetic oracles: messages to a prophet by God (2 Chron. 11:2–4; 12:7f.), messages delivered by a prophet (2 Chron. 12:5; 15:1–7; 18:18–22), and a prophetic letter (2 Chron. 21:12–15). Direct speech is also presented in the form of letters (e.g., 2 Chron. 2:11–16) and prayers (e.g., 2 Chron. 6:14–42).

Regnal summaries play an important role in introducing (2 Chron. 33:1–9; 34:1–7) and concluding (1 Chron. 29:26–30; 2 Chron. 13:18–20) narrative accounts of reigns. There are also many generalizing summaries like 1 Chron. 14:17: "And the fame of David went out into all lands, and the LORD brought the fear of him upon all nations" (cf. 1 Chron. 6:31f., 49; 12:21f.; 18:14–17). Theological summaries often evaluate events like deaths, plagues, and invasions in terms of the principle of divine retribution (e.g., 1

Chron. 10:13: "Saul died for his unfaithfulness," or 1 Chron. 9:1: "Judah was taken into exile in Babylon because of their unfaithfulness").

The CH makes frequent allusion to the influence of God upon historical events, particularly in terms of the principle of divine retribution. Though miracles occur rarely (2 Chron. 7:1; 32:21), the Chronicler often mentions God as the one who grants victory and causes defeat (e.g., 2 Chron. 13:15f.; 14:12; 25:20; 26:7). Prophecy plays an important part in the narrative. Divinely inspired prophets point out instances of unfaithfulness to God (usually idolatry or pride) for which divine chastisement will follow unless repentance ensues (e.g., 1 Chron. 7:3–14; 2 Chron. 11:2–4).

The books of Ezra and Nehemiah, which conclude the CH, have several special features. These books contain fragments of first-person singular autobiographical narratives ("memoirs") of Nehemiah (1:1–2:20; 4:1–7:5; 11:1–2; 12:27–13:31) and Ezra (7:11–9:15). Possible literary parallels are Near Eastern inscriptions of kings narrating their accomplishments in the first person, and Egyptian autobiographical inscriptions. Remarkably, both Nehemiah and Ezra wrote about contemporary events as eyewitness participants at approximately the same time as Thucydides experimented with the same approach in Greece. The postexilic reforms reflected in Ezra-Nehemiah produced a climate for the worship of God fully acceptable to the Chronistic school and superior to the preexilic situation.

Constituent Literary Forms

Many of the literary forms found in Israelite histories compiled after 539 B.C. are in fact documentary and literary sources from an earlier period (like the Song of Deborah in Judges 5). Yet the study of literary forms in Israelite historiography need not be limited to source analysis or form criticism. Without discussing the complex problem of sources, then, we will highlight major types of literary forms in Israelite historiography.

Discourse plays a very important role in Israelite historical narratives. Narration, in fact, is subordinated to speech, frequently in the form of dialogue. Further, third-person narration often repeats what the participants in the dialogue have already said (e.g., 1 Sam. 21:2–11), thus underscoring the central significance of discourse. Even thought tends to be presented as direct speech (e.g., 1 Sam. 20:26; 27:1; 1 Kings 12:26f.; 2 Kings 20:19). Dialogue is important in historical narrative because of the impulse to dramatize scenes using only two characters (occasionally three). Private conversations were literary devices used by the Israelite historian to "reconstruct" historical events. Direct discourse often has an obviously stylized and fictitious character (cf. Judg. 10:10; 2 Chron. 22:9).

Documents quoted extensively in Ezra-Nehemiah, 1–2 Maccabees, and Josephus reflect the existence of official archives maintained by the highly bureaucratic Persian state, eventually taken over by the Greeks (cf. Ezra 5:6–6:2). The documents in Ezra-Nehemiah, which are probably authentic ("authentic" does not mean verbatim copies), include four letters (Ezra 4:7–16, 17–22; 5:6–17; 7:11–26) and two decrees (Ezra 1:2–4; 6:2–12). The use of public records not only presupposed the existence of archives and a state bureaucracy; it also shows a concern for historically reliable sources.

Digressions, though never designated as such, occur occasionally. They can range from brief parenthetical remarks to explanations directed to the reader. Examples include the explanation of why Joshua circumcised the people (Josh. 5:4–7), the use of the terms "seer" and "prophet" (1 Sam. 9:9), and why Amaziah did not kill the children of his father's assassins (2 Kings 14:6–7). Occasionally explanations take the form of flashbacks (2 Kings 7:6–7), interrupting the chronology of the narrative. Among the longer digressions is one on the pagan practices of the Samaritans (2 Kings 17:23–41 and a thumbnail sketch of the Romans in 1 Maccabees 8:1–16 presented as information in indirect discourse given to Judas.

Summary reports are frequently used to link events together and to present material not narrated. In the Deuteronomic History monarchs are often introduced with general summary of the character and achievements of their reigns. Apart from regnal summaries there are other general summaries used to connect or conclude episodes or clusters of episodes.

Theological summaries and comments by the author-editors are one of the major ways in which historical events are given an explicit religious interpretation. One of the more extensive examples is found in Judg. 2:11–3:6, which gives a synopsis of Israel's experience during the period of the judges in terms of the cycle of disobedience, oppression, repentance, and deliverance, words that occur with some frequency.

Dramatic episodes occur frequently in historical narratives, partly because of the basic episodic quality of Hebrew paratactic style and partly because of the tendency to dramatize scenes by fabricating extensive dialogues. Dramatic episodes have a plot consisting of a tension that moves toward resolution. Examples include the dowry of Caleb's daughter (Judg. 1:11–15), Ehud's assassination of Eglon

(Judg. 3:15–30), the story of Tamar (2 Sam. 13:1–39), and the execution of the house of Saul (2 Sam. 21:1–14).

Descriptions of the lavish furnishings of the Temple and the building itself are given because of the central importance of the Temple (1 Kings 6:14–36; 7:15–50). The Deuteronomist also includes a description of Solomon's residence (1 Kings 7:2–12). These correspond to *ekphraseis* ("descriptions") in Greek literature beginning with Homer's digression describing the shield of Achilles (*Iliad* 18.478–607). The *Letter of Aristeas* 51–82 contains a lengthy description of the gifts Ptolemy Philadelphus sent to Jerusalem, an *ekphrasis* copied by Josephus (*Ant.* 12.60–84). He also embellished the descriptions in 1 Kings of the Temple and its furnishings (*Ant.* 8. 63–98) and Solomon's residence (8.133–140).

Function

While Greco-Roman historians often made their purpose explicit through prefaces and digressions, Israelite-Jewish historians rarely reveal their purposes directly. One of the basic purposes of the Deuteronomic History is hortatory, to present the past in terms of positive and negative examples of *national* religious behavior. Idolatry is the primary form of Israel's unfaithfulness in the Deuteronomic History. This corporate emphasis fits the use to which the Deuteronomic History was put as national sacred literature read on a cyclical basis in synagogues. This group emphasis is largely absent from Greco-Roman historiography, which is concerned with the exemplary behavior of *individuals*. In the Jewish tradition this emphasis changed with Hellenistic influence. The Chronicler emphasized the fact that *individuals* who sin are punished. The list of courageous Israelite heroes of the past attributed to Mattathias on his deathbed (1 Macc. 2:50–68) is intended to encourage similar heroic behavior in his sons.

The frequency with which summaries of Israel's historical relationship to Yahweh are recited suggests a function for the longer reports which take the form of historical narrative. The recitation of one or more of the events constitutive of Israel's national existence is often used in prayer to persuade God to act in a particular way, or in speeches intended to persuade people to follow a particular course of action.

Israelite historiography also has the latent function of providing definition for the Jewish people through the many changes in national fortune. That definition, in which religious and political factors are enmeshed, centers on the theme of the consequences of faithfulness and unfaithfulness to Yahweh and Yahweh's covenant. Possession of Jerusalem and the Land is the reward, while domination by enemies, persecution, and dispersion are the costs of disobedience.

Hellenistic Jewish Historiography

The development of Hellenistic Jewish historiography (third century B.C. through second century A.D.) reflects the increasing dominance of Hellenistic rhetorical and literary culture, which gradually replaced most of the distinctive features of Israelite historiography. Important representative works include 1 Maccabees, 2 Maccabees, and the *Wars* and *Antiquities* of Josephus. The *Seder Olam Rabbah,* the oldest Jewish chronological work, was written ca. A.D. 150, and one of the last histories by early Judaism was the *Seder Olam* (ca. A.D. 225), a historical synopsis from Adam to Alexander the Great. Thereafter Jewish historiography disappeared for centuries.

The direct political control of Palestine by the Greeks began in 331 B.C. when Alexander the Great occupied the region, ending two centuries of Persian rule. After Alexander's death in 323 B.C., his empire was sliced up by his Greek successors, each of whom wanted the whole pie. Palestine fell under the control of the Ptolemaic dynasty of Egypt. In 200 B.C., Palestine passed into the hands of the Seleucid empire. The Palestinian Jews, however, were just one of many small nations subject to Greek monarchies. All subject peoples were profoundly affected by Hellenistic culture, a potent Greek device for pacifying and unifying the many diverse nationalities, languages, and cultures of the former Persian empire.

Propaganda was a central means by which the new Greek dynasties consolidated and legitimated their Near Eastern territories. Hecataeus of Abdera, commissioned by Ptolemy I, wrote *Aegyptiaka* ("History of Egypt"), an influential apologetic and flattering history of Egypt (ca. 300 B.C.) popularizing the view that Egypt was the birthplace of civilization. This popular history (partially preserved in Diodorus 1.10–98) became a model for oriental intellectuals who popularized native history and culture for Greek consumption. The Hellenistic Jewish historians Artapanus, Eupolemus, and Pseudo-Eupolemus tried to demonstrate the antiquity and superiority of Jewish culture and civilization within a cosmopolitan Hellenistic framework. Like many contemporary Hellenistic historians they manipulated data for parochial national interests and propagandistic motives.

1 Maccabees

First Maccabees is an anonymous historical monograph written about 100 B.C. by a Palestinian Jew, possibly as a sequel to the Chronistic History. Originally composed in Hebrew in an intentionally archaizing biblical style, yet exhibiting Hellenistic influence, the work survives only in translations, of which the Greek version is particularly important. The narrative focuses on the causes of the Maccabean revolt (the accession and repressive policies of Antiochus IV, 175–164 B.C.), how Mattathias and his sons Judas, Jonathan, and Simon (called Hasmoneans) delivered the Jews, and it concludes with the death of the last surviving son, Simon (134 B.C.), a period of about forty years. A central purpose of the author is to support and defend the legitimacy of the Hasmonean dynasty.

Direct discourse is found in two forms: (1) statements, conversations, speeches, and prayers, and (2) quoted documents such as letters, inscriptions, and poems. Many of the shorter statements, following Hebrew narrative style, are created by the author for dramatic purposes, e.g., 1 Macc. 5:57: "So they said, 'Let us also make a name for ourselves; let us go and make war on the Gentiles around us.'" Yet the author avoids the biblical convention of using dialogue as a dramatic device. Also unbiblical is the occasional use of indirect discourse.

The extensive use of public documents is a heritage from the Persian period, probably in imitation of the CH. The author quotes twelve letters (e.g., 1 Macc. 10:3–5, 25–45; 11:30–37; 12:6–18; 15:2–9), two inscriptions (8:22–32; 14:27–45), three messages, or orally transmitted letters (10:3–5, 52–54, 55–56), and six poems (1:24–28, 36–40; 2:7–13; 3:3–9, 45; 14:4–15).

2 Maccabees

It is likely that 2 Maccabees was originally written in five books by Jason of Cyrene but later subjected to anonymous abridgment and embellishment between 124 and 63 B.C. (2 Macc. 2:23). The work narrates Jewish history from the high priest Onias III (ca. 180 B.C.) to the defeat of the Syrian general Nicanor (161 B.C.), combining Jewish content with Hellenistic form. The language and style of the epitomizer reflects formal rhetorical training, and 2 Maccabees is an example of dramatic history. The introductory letters encourage the observance of the Jewish festival of Hanukkah among Egyptian Jews. The central theme is the Hellenistic one of the deity who defends his temple. According to Robert Doran, the work has three structural parts, all involving attacks against the Temple: (1) The attack against the Temple by Heliodorus fails because the Jews observe God's law (3:1–40). (2) In 4:1–10:9, the wickedness of the Jewish people results in the successful capture of the Temple by Antiochus IV. (3) In 10:10–15:36, God responds with compassion to Jewish suffering by granting the Jews victory over the Syrian army; the death of Antiochus IV and the restoration of the Temple quickly follow. Direct and indirect forms of discourse together constitute about 40 percent of the text, fairly high for a Greco-Roman history.

The epitomizer introduces his work with two extensive letters, followed by a typical Hellenistic preface (2:19–32); he also appends a conclusion (15:38–39). He uses summary reports, usually to conclude a section (4:50; 5:27; 6:3–6; 7:42), but once as a transition (8:5–7). Digressions are relatively few. One provides background information (13:5–6), another explains that divine punishment of the Jews is for the purpose of discipline, not destruction (6:12–17), and a third explains why Antiochus was not immediately punished for profaning the Temple (5:17–20; his punishment is finally meted out in chapter 9). The author delights in pointing out instances of *lex talionis*, i.e., retaliation in kind: "The Lord thus repaid him with the punishment he deserved" (4:38b; cf. 5:10; 8:33; 9:5–6; 13:8), providing moral lessons from previously narrated behavior.

Josephus

Josephus (ca. A.D. 37–100) was a prolific Jewish historian whose works have nearly all survived. A member of an aristocratic priestly family, he sampled the three Jewish "philosophies" before becoming a Pharisee (*Life* 10–12). At the begining of the first Jewish revolt (A.D. 66–73), he was reluctantly (he claims later) placed in command of Galilee, but was captured by the Romans in Jotapata in 67. Freed by Vespasian in 69, he accompanied Titus and witnessed the final siege and conquest of Jerusalem (*Life* 414–421). He received a pension from the Flavian emperors and settled down in Rome to write history (*Life* 422–430).

Josephus wrote two major historical works, *Wars of the Jews*, on the Jewish rebellion of A.D. 66–73, and *Antiquities of the Jews*, on Jewish history and culture from Creation to the eve of the revolt of A.D. 66.

Josephus was a dramatic historian like most of his contemporaries and immediate predecessors. He used rhetorical exaggeration (*Ant.* 2.324; 5.64; 6.129; *Wars* 2.598) and included many purple passages (*Wars* 3.248–249; *Ant.* 14.168, 354–358). He makes extensive use of dramatic episodes, e.g., the sacrifice of Isaac (*Ant.* 1.222–236) and the story of Joseph (2.39–167). In the Joseph story, the episode of Potiphar's wife (*Ant.* 2.41–59, based on Gen. 39:7–20) has been embellished with folktale motifs also found in the Greek stories of Phaedra and Hippolytus, Hippolyte and Peleus, and earliest of all in Homer under the names of Anteia and Bellerophon (*Illiad* 6. 156–205). There are also many dramatic episodes set in the period after 300 B.C., such as the Pauline story (*Ant.* 18.66–80) and the Fulvia story (18.81–84).

Wars of the Jews was Josephus' earliest work (written between 75 and 79; the plural "Wars" reflects its Greek title). It is the only war monograph in the Thucydidean tradition to survive from the early Empire. Like Thucydides, Josephus narrated a contemporary war of great significance, first as a participant and later an observer (*Wars* 1.1–30; *Against Apion* 1.47–56). The comparison of their historical prefaces suggests that Josephus consciously imitated Thucydides (*Wars* 1.13–15; Thucydides 1.21). Josephus refers to notes he made while observing the Jewish revolt (*Against Apion* 1.49f.). Such *hypo-mnēmata* probably excluded dramatic episodes or speeches. Those were added later. Josephus followed Hellenistic practice by improving the language of his sources (*Wars* 1.15). He took certain liberties in reworking narratives, but in general was faithful to the content and order of his sources.

Josephus included 109 speeches in *Wars* (excluding very short statements and conversations). All are uniformly cast in the author's language and style, all are deliberative or advisory, and all are vehicles for his personal viewpoint. He tries to show, for example, that most Jews did not wish rebellion but were forced into it by a relatively small fanatical group of rebels. He uses several lengthy speeches to accuse the rebels of cruelty, sin, and tyranny (4.162–192; 4.239–269; 6.99–112). Further, he held that internal dissension rather than external opposition led to the defeat of Jerusalem (*Wars* 1.10). Several speeches emphasize the folly of resisting Rome (2. 345–401; 5.362–419), and one theme running through the work is the necessity of reconciliation to Roman rule. Reconciling Greeks to Roman rule was also of concern to Dionysius of Halicarnassus; one way he sought to accomplish this was by showing that the founders of Rome were actually Greeks (*Roman Antiquities* 1.2.1–2; 5.1–2). Purely rhetorical are the pro and con speeches on suicide.

Josephus argues against suicide (*Wars* 3.362–382) and the rebel
leader Eleazar argues for it (*Wars* 7.341–388); such speeches are a
technique practiced in rhetorical school drills (Polybius 36.1–5).
The Agrippa speech is an example of pro-Roman propaganda, as is
the speech of Titus (6.328–350). The high percentage of speeches
in indirect discourse (55 percent) is significant, for they are used to
convey content rather than to display the author's rhetorical skills.

Josephus' largest work, *Antiquities of the Jews,* in twenty books (published in 93–94; cf. *Ant.* 20.267), was modeled after the twenty-book
Roman Antiquities of Dionysius of Halicarnassus (late first century
B.C.), a dramatic historian who in turn emulated Herodotus. Josephus was a Hellenized oriental who interpreted the history of his
people for the Greeks. At the same time he tried to demonstrate the
antiquity and superiority of Jewish civilization and culture (*Against
Apion* 1.1–46, 69–160). In the *Antiquities,* Josephus relied heavily on
the Bible, probably some form of the Greek Septuagint (*Ant.* 1–11),
filling gaps in the Hebrew Bible with 1 Maccabees and 1 Esdras,
supplemented by other historians (e.g., Nicolaus of Damascus, in
Ant. 14–17; Alexander Polyhistor) and quasihistorical literature
(e.g., the *Letter of Aristeas* in *Ant.* 12.12–118). The moral lesson which
Josephus sees in history is that those who are obedient to the will
of God prosper, while disaster follows disobedience (*Ant.* 1.14, 20).
He holds up particular individuals as examples of virtue or vice (*Ant.*
17.60; 18.128f.).

Josephus was very familiar with the conventions of Hellenistic
historiography. This is clear from the historical prefaces to *Wars*
(1.1–30) and *Antiquities* (1.1–26), both riddled with Hellenistic conventions and clichés. He promises not to add or omit anything from
his biblical sources (*Ant.* 1.17; 4.196; 8.56; 10.218), using a formula
often applied to historical accuracy. Yet he adds the fantastic story
of Moses' Ethiopian wife (*Ant.* 2.238–253) and leaves out the embar-
rassing story of the golden calf. Like other Hellenistic historians,
Josephus claims to be concerned with truth and literary style (*Ant.*
14.1–3). He takes great pains to describe Jewish culture in Greek
categories. The Jewish sectarian groups (Pharisees, Sadducees, Essenes) are described as three "philosophies." Major biblical heroes
like Abraham, Joseph, Moses, David, and Solomon are presented
as examples of Hellenistic virtues. Josephus used the concept of
tychē, "fortune," from Hellenistic historiography as a way of conceptualizing the will of God in history. He was convinced that "fortune
had been transferred to the Romans" (*Wars* 3.354; cf. 2.360), but
only *temporarily* (5.367). He knew this from the prophecy of Daniel
(cf. *Ant.* 10.206–210). In addition to the speeches discussed above,

he also used numerous historiographical techniques and devices such as the *ekphrasis,* or description of a work of art (*Ant.* 12.60–84, taken from Aristeas 51–82). He also included several chreiai, revealing the extent to which biography and history had merged (*Wars* 1.91–92, 272, 651–653; 3.207–210; 6.409–411; *Ant.* 11.300f.; 12. 210–214; 18.174–175).

One of Josephus' main contributions was to introduce into Hellenistic historiography the role played by God in Israelite historiography (*Ant.* 1.14–17). Josephus narrates miracles found in the Bible, but followed the practice of Hellenistic historians by affixing a consumer warning label urging the readers to decide the truth for themselves (*Ant.* 1.108; 2.348; 3.81, 322; 4.158).

Comparing Ancient Historiographies

Considering ancient nations generally, comparable literary forms of historiography arose only in Greece and Israel. These were nearly contemporaneous developments in Israel (sixth and fifth centuries B.C.), and in Greece (fifth century B.C.). They occurred without benefit of direct cultural contact. Historians in both cultures, however, were profoundly affected by Persian influence (539–331 B.C.). Some of the more important similarities and differences between these two historiographical traditions require comment.

1. The episodic narrative style of the Pentateuch and the *Deuteronomic History* are organized *paratactically* in a way very similar to the history of Herodotus. Herodotus used archaic parataxis ("placing side by side") as a compositional technique in which short literary units of various types are strung together in sequences that form larger compositions. External structure is provided by introductory and concluding sentences that frame the larger unit. This composition technique produces the effect of discontinuity, since dramatic unity is usually lacking. In the Greek world the development of the periodic ("knit-together") style in rhetoric provided standardized schemes of organization that rejected paratactic style. Using this style, Greek historians preferred to narrate limited sequences of contemporary events that could be portrayed in a unified way. Nevertheless general and antiquarian histories continued to use paratactic style to connect larger literary units often coextensive with "books." In Israelite-Jewish historiography, paratactic style (reflecting the paratactic character of Hebrew syntax) continued to characterize narrative style into the Hellenistic period.

2. In both cultures there was a tendency for historians to continue previous histories. Among the Greeks such serial works usually

retained separate identity, though many fell victim to epitomizers. The author of the *Hellenika Oxyrhynchia* and Theopompus both continued Thucydides, and Polybius was continued by Posidonius and then Strabo. The practice of continuing previous histories reveals an increasing preference for *general* history. In Judaism anonymous earlier works were incorporated into increasingly more comprehensive compositions including the Pentateuch and the Deuteronomic History, which in final form present a continuous account from Creation to the early postexilic period. Josephus included subsequent sources and covered the period from Creation to the first Jewish revolt. The author of 1 Maccabees, more in the Greek tradition, wrote a separate continuation of the Chronistic History. Yet differences are evident in that while the historical works in the Bible are anonymous and also give evidence of having undergone numerous redactions, Greek histories are attributed to specific authors and, while avoiding radical editing, often suffered epitomization.

3. Discourse was indispensable for both Greco-Roman and Israelite historiography. In both, dialogue was an important device for dramatizing individual episodes and for revealing the character of the persons portrayed. Speeches (in contrast to dialogue) occur in Hebrew historiography, but they are far less important for revealing why people act as they do compared with Greco-Roman historiography. Greek historians used both direct and indirect discourse, which they favored about equally. Israelite historiography shows a marked preference for direct discourse.

4. Unlike their Greek counterparts, Israelite historians never discussed historiographical conventions, and only rarely and indirectly dropped hints on the scope, purpose, and methods of historical research and writing. Twice in the Deuteronomic History the author's theological perspective on God's control of historical events is summarized in "digressions" (Judg. 2:11–3:6; 2 Kings 17:7–23). This means that modern scholars must inductively examine ancient Israelite history in order to make theoretically explicit what to the ancient authors was reflexive and implicit.

5. Another difference lies in the views of myth, legend, and history held by Israelite and Greek historians. While Greek historians and intellectuals distinguished the mythical period (for which sources were spotty and unreliable) from the historical period (for which accurate sources were available), Israelite historians made no such distinction. Greek historians sometimes expressed opinions of the reliability of conflicting sources or recorded several conflicting accounts to let the reader decide, but no such hesitation fogs the

narratives of Israelite historians. Concern for reliable sources led Greek historians to focus on contemporary events, though Israelite historians confidently wrote about the distant past like Greek and Roman antiquarians.

6. Are the three biblical historical works, the Pentateuch, the Deuteronomic History, and the Chronistic History, fact or fiction? Or are they a combination dominated by one element or the other, i.e., fictionalized history or historicized fiction? There are really two questions involved. First, did the Israelite historians intend to narrate events that actually happened? Second, if they did, what value do their works have as sources for modern historians? Scholars often point to the account of David's rise to power (1 Sam. 17–2 Sam. 5), and to the court history of David (2 Sam. 9–20; 1 Kings 1–2), as high points of Israelite historiography. The Deuteronomic historian's use of such sources, like the Chronicler's use of autobiographical sources in Ezra-Nehemiah, suggests a basic concern for narrating actual events, for the final product is only as reliable as the sources used. Whether they succeeded or not must be judged by historical criticism. Recently the emphasis on the narrative art of the biblical historical works has led to their being treated as fiction. Yet the literary styles and structures associated with fiction by modern scholars cannot exclude the use of narrative art in ancient cultures to mediate a historical view of reality.

7. Biblical scholars have often contrasted Israelite with pagan ideas of history. The Israelites, they claim, held a "linear" view of history and understood time as the progression of events moving in a straight (or inclined) line with a start (creation) and finish (eschatology). Revelation occurs within history through divine acts that bring the plan of God to ultimate fulfillment. Biblical theologians have labeled this combination of faith and history as "salvation history." Pagan historical thought (whether Greek or Near Eastern), in contrast, is thought "cyclical," i.e., time was regarded as an eternal series of purposeless cycles. For Near Eastern nations particularly, myth rather than history is the supposed medium for narrating divine activity. However, historical thought in Israel was not fundamentally different from that of ancient Near Eastern nations and Greece. Old Testament historiography also used patterns of recurrence, and history among the Hittites and Mesopotamians was seen in terms of divine responses to human actions.

For Further Study

On Greco-Roman Historiography: The basic bibliography on the study of ancient history and historiography is Hermann Bengtson, *Introduction to Ancient History*, tr. by R. I. Frank and F. D. Gilliard (University of California Press, 1970), which should be supplemented with Michael Crawford, ed., *Sources for Ancient History* (Cambridge: University Press, 1983). The best general introduction to Greco-Roman historiography is C. W. Fornara, *The Nature of History in Ancient Greece and Rome* (University of California Press, 1983). Still indispensable is Ulrich von Wilamowitz-Moellendorff, "Hellenische Geschichtsschreibung," in idem, *Reden und Vorträge*, 4th ed., vol. 2 (Berlin: Weidmannsche Buchhandlung, 1926). A popular but scholarly survey is available in Michael Grant, *The Ancient Historians* (London: George Weidenfeld & Nicolson, 1970). A useful older work (1909) in reprint is J. B. Bury, *The Ancient Greek Historians* (Dover Publications, 1958). An important collection of articles dealing with the fourth century A.D. is found in B. Croke and A. M. Emmett, eds., *History and Historians in Late Antiquity* (Sydney: Pergamon Press, 1983). For an excellent discussion of Alexandrian historiography and geographical writing see P. M. Fraser, *Ptolemaic Alexandria* (Oxford: Clarendon Press, 1972), I, 495–553. On Homeric influence see Hermann Strasburger, *Homer und die Geschichtsschreibung* (Heidelberg: Carl Winter, 1971). On the connection between Greek political developments and the beginnings of historiography, see Christian Meier, *Die Entstehung des Politischen bei den Griechen* (Frankfurt: Suhrkamp Verlag, 1980), pp. 326–499.

On Greco-Roman Historians: *Arrian:* Philip A. Stadter, *Arrian of Nicomedia* (University of North Carolina Press, 1980). *Dio Cassius:* Fergus Millar, *A Study of Cassius Dio* (Oxford: Clarendon Press, 1964). *Ephorus:* G. L. Barber, *The Historian Ephorus* (Cambridge: University Press, 1935). *Hellenika Oxyrhynchia:* I. A. F. Bruce, *An Historical Commentary on the Hellenica Oxyrhynchia* (Cambridge: University Press, 1967). *Herodotus:* The best introduction with extensive bibliography is now K. H. Waters, *Herodotus the Historian: His Problems, Methods and Originality* (University of Oklahoma Press, 1985). For literary analyses see H. R. Immerwahr, *Form and Thought in Herodotus* (American Philological Association, 1966), and Charles W. Fornara, *Herodotus: An Interpretive Essay* (Oxford: Clarendon Press, 1971). *Livy:* T. J. Luce, *Livy: The Composition of His History* (Princeton University Press, 1977). *Philo of Byblos:* R. A. Oden, "Philo of Byblos and Hellenistic Historiography," *Palestine Exploration Quarterly* 110 (1978), 115–126. *Polybius:* Kenneth Sacks, *Polybius on the Writing of History*, Classical Studies, 24 (University of California Press, 1981); F. W. Walbank, *Polybius* (University of California Press, 1972). *Tacitus:* Ronald Martin, *Tacitus* (University of California Press, 1981); Ronald Syme, *Tacitus*, 2 vols. (Oxford: Clarendon Press, 1958). *Thucydides:* A. W. Gomme et al., *A Historical Commentary on Thucydides*, 5 vols. (Oxford: Clarendon Press, 1945–81), contains important essays in Appendices 1 and 2 of volume 5 on "Indications of Incompleteness" (pp. 361–383) and "Strata of Composition" (pp. 384–444). On Thucydides' political perspective, see David Grene, *Greek Political Theory: The Image of Man in Thucydides and Plato* (University of Chicago Press, 1965), pp. 3–92 (first published 1950 under the title *Man in His Pride*). **Xenophon:** W. P. Henry, *Greek Historical Writing: A Historiographical Essay Based on Xenophon's Hellenica* (Argonaut, 1966).

On Universal History: S. Accame, "De l'histoire universelle," *Cahiers d'histoire mondiale* 4 (1958), 464–470; Arnaldo Momigliano, "The Origins of Universal History," in *Settimo contributo alla storia degli studi classici e del mondo antico*, Storia e Letteratura, 161 (Rome: Edizioni di Storia e Letteratura, 1984), pp. 77–103 (extensive bibliography).

On Antiquarian Research: Arnaldo Momigliano, "Ancient History and the Antiquarian," in idem, *Studies in Historiography* (London: George Weidenfeld & Nicholson, 1966), pp. 1–39; G. Maslakov, "The Roman Antiquarian Tradition in Late Antiquity," in *History and Historians in Late Antiquity*, ed. by B. Croke and A. M. Emmett (Sydney: Pergamon Press, 1983), pp. 100–106.

On Historical Methods: Gert Avenarius, *Lukians Schrift zur Geschichtsschreibung* (Meisenheim: Verlag Anton Hain, 1956); Arnaldo Momigliano, "Historiography on Written Tradition and Historiography on Oral Tradition," in idem, *Studies in Historiography* (London: George Weidenfeld & Nicholson, 1966), pp. 211–220.

On History and Rhetoric: D. A. Russell, *Greek Declamation* (Cambridge: University Press, 1983); K. Sacks, *Polybius on the Writing of History* (University of California Press, 1981), pp. 144–170 (on "Tragic History"); B. L. Ullmann, "History and Tragedy," *Transactions and Proceedings of the American Philological Association* 73 (1942), 25–53; F. W. Walbank, "History and Tragedy," *Historia* 9 (1960), 216–234. A particularly excellent and comprehensive discussion is found in T. P. Wiseman, *Clio's Cosmetics: Three Studies in Greco-Roman Literature* (Leicester: Leicester University Press, 1979).

On Constituent Literary Forms: *Prefaces:* Donald Earl, "Prologue-form in Ancient Historiography," *ANRW* I.2 (1972), 842–856; Georg Engel, *De antiquorum epicorum didacticorum historicorum prooemis* (Marburg: Koch, 1910); Tore Janson, *Latin Prose Prefaces: Studies in Literary Convention* (Stockholm: Almqvist & Wiksell, 1964). *Speeches:* C. W. Fornara, *The Nature of History in Ancient Greece and Rome* (University of California Press, 1983), pp. 142–168 ("The Speech in Greek and Roman Historiography"), insists that the ancients unanimously adopted the Thucydidean principle of accurate reporting of speeches. See also A. W. Gomme, "The Speeches in Thucydides," in idem, *Essays in Greek History and Literature* (Oxford: Basil Blackwell, 1937), pp. 156–189; idem, *A Historical Commentary on Thucydides*, I (Oxford: Clarendon Press, 1945), pp. 139–150; A. W. Gomme, A. Andrewes, and K. J. Dover, *A Historical Commentary on Thucydides*, V (Oxford: Clarendon Press, 1981), pp. 393–399. For a careful analysis of speeches in Herodotus, with

Homeric comparisons, see Mabel L. Lang, *Herodotean Narrative and Discourse* (Harvard University Press, 1984). See also Kenneth S. Sacks, "Rhetorical Approaches to Greek History Writing in the Hellenistic Period," in *Society of Biblical Literature: 1984 Seminar Papers,* ed. by Kent H. Richards (Scholars Press, 1984), pp. 123–133. A very important collection of essays with an extensive bibliography is Philip A. Stadter, ed., *The Speeches in Thucydides* (University of North Carolina Press, 1973). See also F. W. Walbank, *Speeches in Greek Historians* (The Third J. L. Myres Memorial Lecture, 1965).

On Israelite Historiography: B. Albrektson, *History and the Gods: An Essay on the Idea of Historical Events as Divine Manifestations in the Ancient Near East and in Israel* (Lund: Gleerup, 1967); R. C. Dentan, ed., *The Idea of History in the Ancient Near East* (Yale University Press, 1955), particularly Millar Burrows, "Ancient Israel," pp. 99–131. A good introduction to the Deuteronomic History is T. E. Fretheim, *Deuteronomic History* (Abingdon Press, 1983). See also H. Gese, "The Idea of History in the Ancient Near East and the Old Testament," *Journal for Theology and the Church* 1 (1965), 49–64; A. Momigliano, "Eastern Elements in Post-Exilic Jewish, and Greek, Historiography," and "Time in Ancient Historiography," in idem, *Essays in Ancient and Modern Historiography* (Wesleyan University Press, 1977), pp. 25–35, 179–204; M. Noth, *The Deuteronomistic History* (Sheffield: JSOT Press, 1981); J. R. Porter, "Old Testament Historiography," in *Tradition and Interpretation: Essays by Members of the Society for Old Testament Study,* ed. by G. W. Anderson (Oxford: Clarendon Press, 1979), pp. 125–165, a survey of research since 1950; J. J. M. Roberts, "Myth *versus* History: Relaying the Comparative Foundations," *CBQ* 38 (1976), 1–13. In *In Search of History: Historiography in the Ancient World and the Origins of Biblical History* (Yale University Press, 1983), John Van Seters compares Greek, Israelite, Mesopotamian, Hittite, and Egyptian historiography and includes an extensive bibliography. See also G. W. Trompf, *The Idea of Historical Recurrence in Western Thought from Antiquity to the Reformation* (University of California Press, 1979). For the ancient period Trompf compares Polybius with Luke and biblical historiography very carefully and convincingly.

On Jewish Historiography: H. W. Attridge, "Historiography," and "Josephus and His Works," in *Jewish Writings of the Second Temple Period,* vol. 2 of sec. 2, *CRINT* (1984), pp. 157–184, 185–232; Elias Bickerman, *From Ezra to the Last of the Maccabees* (Schocken Books 1962); John J. Collins, *Between Athens and Jerusalem: Jewish Identity in the Hellenistic Diaspora* (Crossroad Publishing Co., 1983), pp. 23–59; Robert Doran, *Temple Propaganda: The Purpose and Character of 2 Maccabees, CBQ* Monographs, 9 (Catholic Biblical Association of America, 1981); Martin Hengel, *Judaism and Hellenism,* tr. by John Bowden (Fortress Press, 1974). For a very recent edition of historians surviving only fragmentarily with a commentary, see Carl R. Holladay, *Fragments from Hellenistic Jewish Authors,* vol. 1: *Historians* (Scholars Press, 1983); Greek texts with English translation accompanied by excellent introductions and commentaries. See also Peter Schäfer, "Zur Geschichtsauffassung des rabbinischen Judentums," *JJS* 6 (1975), 177–188; Emil Schürer, *The History of the Jewish People in the Age of Jesus Christ (175 B.C. –A.D. 135)*, rev. by G. Vermes et al., I (Edinburgh: T. & T. Clark, 1973), pp. 17–122 (extensive bibliography and discussion of sources for the period).

On Literary Forms: Robert Alter, *The Art of Biblical Narrative* (Basic Books, 1981); George W. Coats, *Genesis, with an Introduction to Narrative Literature*, The Forms of the Old Testament Literature, 1 (Wm. B. Eerdmans Publishing Co., 1983); J. P. Fokkelman, *Narrative Art in Genesis* (Assen: Van Gorcum, 1975); Leonard Greenspoon, "The Pronouncement Story in Philo and Josephus," *Semeia* 20 (1981), 73–80; Burke O. Long, *1 Kings, with an Introduction to Historical Literature*, The Forms of the Old Testament Literature, 9 (Wm. B. Eerdmans Publishing Co., 1984); Horst R. Moehring, "Novelistic Elements in the Writings of Flavius Josephus" (Ph.D. dissertation, University of Chicago, 1957).

On Jewish Historians: *Artapanus:* Carl H. Holladay, *Theios Aner in Hellenistic Judaism* (Scholars Press, 1977), pp. 199–232. **Demetrius the Chronographer:** E. J. Bickerman, "The Jewish Historian Demetrios," in *Christianity, Judaism and Other Greco-Roman Cults*, ed. by J. Neusner (Leiden: E. J. Brill, 1975), III, pp. 72–84. *Eupolemus:* Ben Zion Wacholder, *Eupolemus: A Study of Judaeo-Greek Literature* (Hebrew Union College Press, 1974). *Josephus:* The best recent introduction to Josephus is Tessa Rajak, *Josephus: The Historian and His Society* (Fortress Press, 1983). Still valuable is H. St. John Thackeray, *Josephus, the Man and the Historian* (Ktav Publishing House, 1967; originally published 1929). Three indispensable works are Richard Laqueur, *Der jüdische Historiker Flavius Josephus* (Giessen, 1920); H. W. Attridge, *The Interpretation of Biblical History in the Antiquitates Judaicae of Flavius Josephus* (Scholars Press, 1976); and Shaye J. D. Cohen, *Josephus in Galilee and Rome: His Vita and Development as a Historian* (Leiden: E. J. Brill, 1979). For an enormous annotated and classified bibliography, see Louis H. Feldman, *Josephus and Modern Scholarship (1937–1980)* (Berlin: Walter de Gruyter, 1984). See also Willem Cornelis van Unnik, *Flavius Josephus als historischer Schriftsteller* (Heidelberg: Verlag Lambert Schneider, 1978), and Helgo Lindner, *Die Geschichtsauffassung des Flavius Josephus im Bellum Judaicum* (Leiden: E. J. Brill, 1972).

4

The Generic Features
of Luke-Acts and the Growth
# of Apostle Literature

The historical preface introducing his work (Luke 1:1–4) is a clear signal that Luke consciously follows Hellenistic literary models. He labels his composition a *diēgēsis,* "narrative" (Luke 1:1), a term used of both fiction and nonfiction. Theon defines the *diēgēsis* as "an expository treatise of events which happened or could have happened" (*Progymnasmata* 4; cf. Cicero, *On Rhetorical Invention* 1.19.27; Quintilian 4.21.31). Later rhetoricians distinguished between a *diēgēma,* a narrative of a single event, and a *diēgēsis,* a narrative account of many events, for which Herodotus and Thucydides were examples (Hermogenes, *Progymnasmata* 2; Aphthonius, *Progymnasmata* 2). By substituting the term "narrative" for Mark's "gospel," Luke indicated his intention to write history.

The Form of Luke-Acts

After Luke had become part of the fourfold Gospel (ca. A.D. 125), it was entitled "According to [i.e., by] Luke," a title later expanded to "The *Gospel* According to Luke." Acts, as part of a larger work, probably had no title originally (unless it was published separately). Its independent literary status after ca. A.D. 125, however, made a separate title necessary, and it was labeled "The Acts of the Apostles" ca. A.D. 150.

Language and Style

Jerome (ca. A.D. 327–420) described Luke as the Evangelist most learned in the Greek language (*Letter* 20.4). Luke's mastery of Greek style is evident in the very first sentence. Luke 1:1–4 is a single balanced periodic sentence carefully structured in two parts with three matching phrases couched in formal literary language (Luke 3:1–2 and Acts 15:24–26 are the only other periodic sentences in Luke-Acts). Since it is the most literary sentence in his entire work, Luke obviously wanted to elicit a favorable initial impression. The remainder of his composition is more colloquial. In Luke 1–2, and Acts 1–12, the author uses a form of linguistic archaism by using "Septuagintal" Greek as a conscious equivalent to the Atticizing tendency of contemporary Greek writers. The rest of Luke-Acts is written in the literary Koine Greek widely used in the Hellenistic period. In rewriting his sources (Mark and Q), Luke makes stylistic improvements reflecting elevated literary standards.

Arrangement in Two Books

Luke regarded the two parts of his composition as "books," since he refers to the first part as a *logos,* "book" (Acts 1:1). An ancient "book" was identical with the content of one papyrus roll. This convention is preserved in the English word "volume," derived from the Latin term *volumen* ("papyrus roll"). Luke used *two* "books" because papyrus rolls came in stock sizes with maximum lengths of 35 to 40 feet (an average thirty-foot roll could contain about 100 columns of writing with 30 to 40 lines per column and 20 letters per line). The dimensions of papyrus sheets varied considerably (8 to 12 inches high: 4⅓ to 9½ inches wide; cf. Pliny, *Natural History* 13.77–78). Thus the length of the rolls Luke used cannot be determined—though, using average sizes, 35 and 32 feet would have sufficed for Luke and Acts respectively. Ancient historians occasionally published books separately (Dionysius, *Roman Antiquities* 7.70.2), particularly if the work was very long.

Following an optional convention, Luke introduced Acts with a secondary preface (1:1–5). Many historians simply began the next book where the last one ended (e.g., Arrian, *Anabasis;* Josephus, *Wars*). Others used various literary devices to begin and end books. To knit Luke-Acts together, Luke used the literary techniques of *recapitulation* and *resumption,* also used by Polybius, Strabo, Diodorus, Josephus, and Herodian. The opening sentence of Acts contains a brief *recapitulation* of the content of the previous book: "In the first book, O Theophilus, I have dealt with *all that Jesus began to do and teach.*" Luke combines this recapitulation with the technique of resumption by paraphrasing the conclusion of Luke (24:36–53) in Acts 1:2–5.

Luke (19,404 words; 2,900 stichoi) and Acts (18,374 words; 2,600 stichoi), the longest and second longest compositions in the New

Testament, were originally written on papyrus rolls of nearly equal length. Greco-Roman authors often tried to keep the size of books roughly symmetrical (Diodorus 1.29.6; 1.41.10; Josephus, *Against Apion* 1.320). Diodorus thought historians should include complete actions of cities or kings within single books or rolls, though their length might vary (16.1). He therefore devoted book 16 to Philip and book 17 to Alexander the Great. Luke, of course, presents an account of the life of Jesus "from beginning to end" in his first book, and a description of the spread of Christianity from Jerusalem to Rome in the second, with more than half the narrative devoted to Paul. Judging from the literary parallels between Luke and Acts, the author attempted to provide his second book with the unity exhibited in his first book. The symmetries within Acts and between Luke and Acts attest the author's intention to provide a "complete" narrative structure.

The Ending of Luke-Acts

Luke-Acts has an apparently unsuitable conclusion. Paul is in Rome under house arrest for two years, awaiting trial. Eusebius thought this ending abrupt, and concluded that Luke ended his narrative there because that was how matters stood when he stopped writing (*Church History* 2.22.6). Eusebius then rounded out the story by relating the tradition that Paul was released, went on another mission of preaching, and then came to Rome a second time and there suffered martyrdom (2.22.2–8). The Deuteronomic History ends in a way analogous to Luke-Acts (2 Kings 24:27–30). The *Life of Apollonius* of Philostratus also ends unsatisfactorily because the sources followed by the author ended unsatisfactorily.

These texts suggest two possible reasons for the abrupt ending of Luke-Acts: (1) The author completed his account when Paul had been under house arrest for two years. (2) The author ended his narrative where his source ended, but unlike Philostratus he did not complete the narrative. Neither possibility is likely. Luke twice relates two revelations to Paul to the effect that he will "bear witness at Rome" (Acts 23:11), and "stand before Caesar" (27:24). This must have occurred after the "two years" mentioned in 28:30. The outcome of that trial was probably the condemnation and execution of Paul, since he is earlier made to say to the Ephesians that they will never see him again (20:25, 38). This ending indicates that it is not the author's purpose to present a life of Paul but to emphasize the worldwide proclamation of the Pauline gospel.

Literary Patterns

The recurrence of similar events or patterns of events in historical narratives can function in several ways. An obvious *literary* function of schemes of correspondence is to unify the composition. A *historical* function of such schemes is to demonstrate that history itself has a pattern. For both these reasons, ancient historians often sought to elicit patterns of historical recurrence in their narratives. Appian (ca. A.D. 95–165) saw historical parallels between the Roman defeat at Cannae and the defeat of Hasdrubal the Carthaginian (*The Hannibalic Wars* 7.8.53).

Since Luke-Acts deals with several important personalities, parallels are often implicitly elaborated between, for example, Jesus and Paul, Jesus and Peter, and Peter and Paul. G. W. Trompf has proposed five cases in which significant events are reenacted in Luke-Acts: (1) the deaths of Jesus and Stephen, (2) the resurrection appearance of Jesus and Peter's miraculous release from prison, (3) the farewell speeches of Jesus and Paul, (4) the journeys of Jesus to Jerusalem and Paul to Jerusalem and Rome, complete with passion predictions, and (5) the trials of Jesus and Paul, each with four hearings. Within Acts there are striking parallels between two healings of men born lame, one by Peter (3:1–10), and one by Paul (14:8–18), and the healings effected by Peter's shadow (5:14–16), and handkerchiefs or aprons touched by Paul (19:11–12). Much more elaborate schemes have been proposed, but the more elaborate they are, the less convincing. Whereas Greco-Roman historians often paused to note the recurring pattern of events, Luke leaves that task to the reader.

The proportionality of Luke-Acts requires some comment. Each book narrates a thirty-year period. Luke's presentation of the events of Jesus' last days, from Jesus' arrival in Jerusalem (Luke 19:28) through his ascension constitutes about 23 percent of his first book. Acts 21:27 through 28:31, which deals with Paul's arrest (ca. A.D. 56), trials, arrival in Rome (ca. A.D. 60) is a four-year period constituting about 24 percent of the narrative. While the heavy emphasis on Jesus' last days in Jerusalem was taken over from Mark, Luke himself has placed nearly equal emphasis on the last days of Paul.

Constituent Oral Forms

For all his literary sophistication, the author of Luke made much the same use of the written sources Mark and Q as Matthew. The oral forms behind Mark and Q are still visible in Luke. Further, even the use of traditional material found only in Luke exhibits the same pericopal structure. Joseph Fitzmyer, in his 1979 commentary on Luke, counts sixty-six pericopes, parts of pericopes, or phrases that belong to "L." These include *parables* (e.g., the Good Samaritan, 10:29–37; the Rich Fool, 12:13–21; the Prodigal Son, 15:11–32; the Unjust Judge, 18:1–8), *miracle stories* (e.g., the Widow of Nain's Son, 7:11–17; the Ten Lepers, 17:11–19), *pronouncement stories* (e.g., 10: 38–42; 11:27–28; 13:1–5, 31–33; 16:14–15; 19:1–10, 39–44; 22: 35–38), and *sayings of Jesus* (6:24–26; 21:34–36). Luke also includes several longer compositions such as the infancy stories (1:5–2:52), the genealogy (3:23–38), parts of the rejection at Nazareth (4: 16–30), and the Road to Emmaus story (24:13–35).

The isolating of oral forms incorporated into the text of Acts is a complex task. Several miracle stories are found in Acts. Five involve Peter (3:1–10; 5:1–11; 5:12–16; 9:32–35; 9:36–43). Seven are associated with Paul (13:6–12; 14:8–18; 16:16–18; 19:11–12; 20: 7–12; 28:1–6; 28:7–11). There are also two miraculous jailbreaks (5:17–21; 12:1–17; cf. 16:25–34) and the punitive death of Herod Agrippa brought about by the angel of the Lord (12:20–23).

Constituent Literary Forms

Complex literary forms like general history tend to frame a variety of shorter literary forms. The episodic character of lengthy narrative structures makes such insertion relatively easy. Parallels for each of the following forms frequently occur in Greco-Roman histories and novels, since the narrative techniques of both nonfictional and fictional narratives overlap considerably.

Historical Prefaces

Conforming to the conventions of Hellenistic historiography, Luke begins his work with a primary preface describing the entire work (Luke 1:1–4), and he prefixes a secondary preface to Acts briefly recapitulating the content of Luke (Acts 1:1–5). Luke 1:1–4 constitutes a single periodic sentence:

> Inasmuch as many have undertaken to compile a narrative of the events completed among us, just as they were delivered to us by those who from the beginning were eyewitnesses and then became ministers of the word, it seemed good to me also, having followed all things closely for some time past, to write an account in logical order for you, most excellent Theophilus, that you may know the truth concerning the instruction you have received.

Historical prefaces allowed an author to display his rhetorical skill, and this carefully crafted sentence does that for Luke. In fact, the phrase "the *events* completed among us," the subject of Luke's composition, indicates a *historical* rather than biographical focus, even though (following Hellenistic historical practice) prominent personalities dominate both books. Prefaces had long been conventional features of Greco-Roman historiography with a distinctive constellation of traditional *topoi* or motifs (Lucian, *History* 23, 52–55). The *topoi* which Luke uses include the dedication to Theophilus, the exaggerated mention of "many" predecessors (i.e., Mark and Q; the sources for Acts are neither extant nor capable of reconstruction), mention of eyewitness sources, emphasis on proper historical method and accuracy, and concern with usefulness. Among the closest parallels to Luke 1:1–4 is Josephus, *Against Apion* 1.1–5 and 2.1–2, a two-volume work with primary and secondary prefaces very similar to those of Luke-Acts. The striking similarities between Papias' historical preface(s) (Eusebius, *Church History* 3.39.2–4, 15) and Luke 1:1–4 suggest that he imitated Luke. The conventionality of such prefaces makes it difficult to determine just how literally Luke means what he says.

Genealogy

The genealogy in Luke 3:23–38, which goes back to Adam, "the son of God," is fully appropriate in general or antiquarian history. Extraordinarily long for a Hellenistic genealogy (77 names, 36 unknown in biblical tradition), it occurs in a *digression*. The author uses the resumptive technique to frame the digression between Luke 3:22 and 4:1. The genealogy reflects both biblical and Hellenistic traditions. Luke keeps the Semitic form of names, avoiding Greek endings (Lucian, *History* 21, derided Attic purists who changed Latin names to Greek counterparts). Most biblical genealogies are arranged in *descending* order (earliest ancestor to latest descendant). Matthew 1:1–17 exhibits a descending order, like an occasional Hellenistic genealogy (cf. Plutarch, *Pyrrhus* 1; *Lycurgus* 1.4). Luke 3:23–38, however, is arranged in *ascending* order (latest descendant to earliest ancestor), typical of Greco-Roman genealogies but sometimes found in late Jewish literature (cf. Ezra 7:1–5; Judith 1:8; Tobit 1:1; Josephus, *Ant.* 1.3.2 [Noah]; 2.9.6 [Moses]). The Lukan genealogy goes back to Adam "the son of God" (Luke 3:38), a phenomenon unparalleled in biblical or postbiblical Jewish genealogies. Greco-Roman genealogies not infrequently go back to the gods (for example, Hecataeus of Miletus reportedly traced his genealogy back sixteen generations to a god; Herodotus 2.143).

Symposia

The symposium in Greco-Roman antiquity was both a social custom and a loosely structured literary form. As a *social custom* symposia were drinking parties following the main evening meal (*symposion* literally means "drink together"). As a *literary genre* the symposium could frame dialogues ("table talks"), discourses, and other short literary forms (cf. Plutarch, *Table Talks*).

While the Gospels occasionally mention meals which Jesus ate with associates, only Luke and John use the symposium as a literary device. Luke has three examples of the symposium used as a framing device: (1) In Luke 7:36–50, a dinner (with the *topos* of the uninvited guest; cf. Plutarch, *Table Talk* 707A) is the occasion for a pronouncement story (the parallels in Mark 14:3–9 and Matt. 26: 6–13 indicate that Luke expanded the material in the meal setting). (2) In Luke 11:37–54, several sayings of Jesus are framed by a dinner and a dialogue which Luke adds to Q, including a pronouncement story (vs. 38–41), a series of woes against the Pharisees (vs. 42–48, 52), and a saying (vs. 49–51). (3) Finally, in Luke 14:1–24 a dinner frames four literary units: (a) the healing of the man with edema (vs. 1–6), (b) the parable of the wedding feast (vs. 7–11), (c) Jesus' teaching on humility (vs. 12–14), and (d) the parable of the Great Supper (vs. 15–24). Luke may have chosen the symposium setting since the second and third units deal with banquet etiquette and the fourth uses a banquet as the setting for a parable. While these three passages are structured as symposia by Luke, it must be observed that the symposium was ordinarily an independent literary form.

Travel Narratives and "We" Passages

One of the formal structural similarities between Luke and Acts is that both are dominated by extensive travel reports (Luke 9: 51–19:44: 37 percent of Luke; Acts 12:25–21:16; 27:1–28:16: 38 percent of Acts). Luke probably used the briefer travel narrative of Mark 10:1–52 as a model. Throughout Luke 9:51–19:44 the reader is often reminded that Jerusalem, where prophets must die, is the goal of Jesus' journey (9:51, 53; 13:22, 33; 17:11; 18:31; 19:11, 28, 41). The reminders are necessary since references to the itinerary are vague (Luke 9:57; 10:38; 11:53; 13:22; 14:25; 17:11b; 18:35;

19:1, 29). Unlike the travel section in Luke, those in Acts (21: 25–28:16) are well organized and essential to the story. The three missionary tours of Paul and his companions are narrated in Acts 12:25–21:16, and Paul's sea voyage to Rome is described in 27: 1–28:16. In contrast to the paucity of geographical references in Luke, there are many *travel notices* in Acts, both by land (nineteen notices) and sea (ten notices); the two longest are 20:3–6, 13–16. There is, however, just one sustained *travel report*, Acts 27: 1–28:16, about a sea voyage and shipwreck.

Literary travel accounts took several forms. The march (*anabasis*, "expedition inland") was an appropriate narrative structure for military campaigns described by Herodotus (his longest march section is 7.26–130, the march of Xerxes to Greece), Xenophon *(Anabasis)*, Caesar *(Commentaries)*, and Arrian *(Anabasis)*. Most of the Pentateuch is also structured as a march (from Ex. 13:17 on). The "travel description," *(periēgēsis)* described land travel, taking an interest in geography and ethnography (cf. the travel descriptions in Philostratus, *Life of Apollonius* 2.1–20; 2.42–3.12; 3.50–58; 4.47–5. 10; 6.1–6, 23–27). The "sea travel account" *(periplous)* focused on coastal voyages (surviving accounts include those by Hanno, Arrian, and Scylax). All three types could exist independently or as forms within more complex genres. In many accounts travel was accomplished by both land and sea (as in Acts). These literary accounts vary in character from historical descriptions (Arrian, *Indica* 18–42), and historicized myth (Dionysius, *Roman Antiquities* 1.49–53) to pure fiction (*Odyssey* 9–12; Lucian, *True History*).

The second half of Acts contains three sections where the narrator suddenly switches from the third-person to the first-person plural: (1) 16:10–17; (2) 20:3–15; 21:1–18; (3) 27:1–28:16. Nowhere else in Luke-Acts does the narrator use the first person, except in the prefaces. Several explanations have been suggested: (1) The author wants to emphasize his participation in the events narrated (Irenaeus, *Against Heresies* 3.14.1). (2) The author used a written source (travel itinerary, or traveler's memoirs, *hypomnēmata*) composed by himself or another. (3) The author uses the "we" passages as a stylistic device to dramatize the narrative. In language and style, the "we" passages do not differ from the rest of Acts. Proposals that the "we" passages reflect the author's use of a "travel diary" founder on the fact that they contained only a detailed itinerary, not a narrative.

The "we" passages all combine *sea travel* (Acts 16:11–12a; 20:6, 13–15; 21:1–3, 7; 27:1–44; 28:11–13) with *land travel* (20:1–3a; 21: 15–17; 28:14–16), punctuated by *layovers* (16:12b; 20:6b–12, 17;

21:4–6, 7b–8; 28:1–2, 7, 14). Vernon Robbins has shown that literary accounts of sea voyages (and storms) often used first-person narration. There are, however, many exceptions: Lucian, *Dependent Scholars* 1–2; Philostratus, *Life of Apollonius* 3.52–58; 8.15; Acts 13: 13; 14:26; 15:39; 18:18, 21–22. Two influential accounts of storms, *Odyssey* 5.291–473 and Vergil, *Aeneid* 1.34–179, are third-person narratives. Yet in first-person narratives of adventures, the first person is naturally used of voyages also (*Odyssey* 12.402–425). Robbins gives many examples of first-person (singular and plural) narratives of sea voyages (Dio Chrysostom, *Oration* 7.2, 10; Petronius 114; Josephus, *Life* 3.14–16; Lucian, *True History* 1.5–6; Achilles Tatius 2.31.6; 3.1.1; 4.9.6). Historians preferred third-person narration, though occasionally the first person occurs in narratives of sea voyages and battles. Robbins finds just two examples from *historical* literature to confirm his contention that first-person narration was stylistically appropriate for accounts of sea voyages. An observation of Polybius is relevant at this point. In a digression on style, *after using the first-person plural in a historical narrative* (36.11), Polybius discusses his use of first- and third-person singular and plural in historical narration (36.12; LCL trans. with modifications):

> It should cause no surprise if at times I use my proper name in speaking of myself, and elsewhere use general expressions such as "after *I* had said this" or again, "and when *we* agreed to this." For as I was personally much involved in the events we are now about to chronicle, it is necessary to change the phrases when alluding to myself, that *we* may neither offend by the frequent repetition of my name, nor again by constantly saying "when *I*" or "for *me*" fall unintentionally into an ill-mannered habit of speech.

While Polybius' use of the first-person singular and plural signals personal participation in the events narrated, his switch to the third person is stylistically motivated and does not indicate a lack of personal involvement. We conclude that the occurrence of the "we" passages in Acts constitutes an implicit claim that the author is not an armchair historian, but one who had personally visited the regions he describes (cf. Polybius 12.27.1–6; 12.28.6; 20.12.8; Lucian, *History* 47). In fact the "we" passages suggest that the author either personally experienced the events narrated (cf. Luke 1:2–3) or at least intended to foster that impression.

Speeches

Speeches played an important part in Hellenistic historiography, often constituting 20 to 35 percent of the narrative. The thirty-two speeches of Acts (excluding short statements) make up 25 percent of the narrative. Eight speeches are attributed to Peter, eleven to Paul, and one each to Stephen, James, and James with the elders. Six are attributed to non-Christians: Gamaliel, Demetrius, the town clerk in Ephesus, Tertullus, and Festus. In addition are two prayers, two letters, and about sixteen short dialogue sections. While speeches occupy 24 percent of Thucydides, and 25 percent of Acts, they function in different ways. The narrative settings of Thucydides' speeches are very brief; speeches and settings make up 25 percent of the narrative. In Acts the narrative frameworks are more important; with the speeches, they constitute 74 percent of the narrative. In Thucydides speeches function as a commentary on events. In Luke-Acts, speeches are an essential feature of the action itself, which is the spread of the word of God.

Do the speeches of Acts represent approximations of what was actually said or were they freely composed by the author? If Luke was a typical Hellenistic historian, we could not expect the speeches to be verbatim reports, epitomes, or even approximations of what was actually said, but rather inventions restrained only by the necessity of suitability to speaker, audience, and occasion. Yet it is difficult if not impossible to prove that particular speeches could not have been spoken by those to whom they are attributed, particularly if the author is skilled in *prosōpopoiia,* the art of composing speeches in character. Luke probably faced the same problem as Thucydides, or any historian of recent events. In Thucydides' day, speeches were not usually transcribed and published. Hellenistic historians, however, found a wealth of discourse material in their sources and were faced with several options. They could omit them (usually unthinkable), faithfully transcribe them (almost unthinkable), or modify them. Most (like Dionysius of Halicarnassus) chose the last option. Since Luke wrote about events of the previous generation, it is unlikely that he found speeches in written sources. His options were three: (1) to interview those present or (if he was present) to recall the substance of what was actually spoken, (2) to freely improvise speeches according to the principle of appropriateness, or (3) to combine research and memory with free composition. Luke followed the last route.

The speeches of Luke-Acts can be examined from two perspectives, historical criticism (are they historical?) and literary criticism (are they contextually appropriate?). There are several important questions which must be considered in order to answer these questions.

1. Although the style of the speeches is not uniform, it is consist-

ent with the author's general style. While most historians imposed their own style on speeches (e.g., Thucydides, Polybius, and Dionysius of Halicarnassus), there are important exceptions (e.g., Herodotus). Writing speeches in styles appropriate to various speakers was widely practiced by Hellenistic writers (Lucian, *History* 58; Theon, *Progymnasmata* 10). If one argued that speeches reflecting the historian's style are not authentic, the speeches of Thucydides would fail the test (dubious), but if one argued that speeches exhibiting stylistic variety are authentic, the speeches of Herodotus could be judged historical (equally dubious). Luke's speeches stand between these two extremes, and no historical judgment is possible based on stylistic criteria alone.

2. The speeches of Acts exhibit considerable variety in form and content: (a) six are evangelistic speeches to Jews and Gentile sympathizers, (b) two are evangelistic speeches to pagans, (c) five are forensic speeches, four by Paul and one by Tertullus. Several observations can be made about each type: (a) According to Eduard Schweizer, the six evangelistic speeches to Jews exhibit a uniform structure: direct address, appeal for attention, mention of the problem of misunderstanding, initial quotation from Scripture, the crucifixion and resurrection of Jesus, proof from Scripture, the proclamation of salvation, and the call to repentance. These similarities suggest that the author has composed the speeches, though there is no way of affirming or denying the antiquity of the core elements. (b) The two speeches to pagan audiences appropriately omit proofs from Scripture and instead quote a Greek poet (17:28). (c) None of the forensic speeches exhibit a complete traditional rhetorical structure (three are interrupted). The speech in Acts 22:1–21 begins with a short introduction, and consists of an autobiographical *narratio* (which also functions as an *argumentatio*) until it is interrupted. The speech of Tertullus (24:2–8) begins with a *captatio benevolentiae* (i.e., an exordium aimed at securing goodwill by flattering the governor) in vs. 2–4, followed by a twofold accusation (vs. 5–8): Paul is a ringleader of the troublesome Nazarenes, and has desecrated the Temple. Paul's response (24:10–21) begins with a *captatio benevolentiae* (v. 10) and continues with a brief *narratio* ("statement of the facts"; v. 11) and *propositio* ("proposition"; v. 12). Paul's defense speech in 26:2–23 also begins with a *captatio benevolentiae* (26:2–3), continues with a *narratio* (vs. 4–18), followed by the *argumentatio* ("proof"), which is interrupted (vs. 19–23). All of these speeches suggest that Luke is familiar with the structures of judicial rhetoric.

3. Some of the speeches are contextually inappropriate. Stephen's outline of Israelite history in Acts 7:2–53 does not fit the

charge in 6:13–14. The apologetic elements in Paul's farewell speech in Acts 20:18–35 (i.e., vs. 20–21, 27, 33–34) do not fit the setting. In Paul's Areopagus speech (Acts 17:22–31), v. 22 is in tension with the context (v. 16). Paul's speech to the crew in 27: 21–26 belongs to the literary convention of a storm at sea (*Odyssey* 5.299–312; Vergil, *Aeneid* 1.92–101) and is appropriate literarily rather than historically. This tension between some speeches and their context may be due to the fact that the speeches were inserted at a final stage in composition or to the fact that the author has focused on the speeches, giving less care to their narrative settings. Historians typically compiled a rough draft (*hypomnēma*), later rewriting the whole according to accepted literary standards (Lucian, *History* 47–48; Josephus, *Against Apion* 1.49–50). Dramatic episodes and speeches were usually inserted at a final stage of composition, judging by their absence from "unfinished" portions of histories (speeches are entirely absent from Thucydides 5.10–83 and all of book 8; Herodian 5–8 contains just six speeches). This was probably Luke's procedure in Acts.

Greek historians often reported speeches using indirect discourse. Indirect discourse is a more accurate way of reporting speeches, while direct discourse is a more vivid and potentially dramatic medium. Some historians (e.g., Herodian) and most novelists preferred direct discourse almost exclusively, probably for its dramatic value. Indirect discourse is largely absent from the New Testament, though it occurs occasionally in Luke-Acts. The speeches of Acts, however, are almost entirely in direct discourse. Luke begins some speeches with indirect discourse and then switches to direct discourse (Luke 5:14; Acts 1:4; 17:3; 23:22–24; 25:4–5). The same phenomenon is found in classical authors such as Herodotus (1.118, 125, 153; 3.156.2–3; 5.31, 39; 6.1; 9.2) and Thucydides (only three speeches combine direct with indirect discourse, 1.137.4; 3.113; 8.53). Josephus also slides from indirect to direct discourse within single speeches (*Wars* 4.40–48; 4.238–269; 4.272–282), as do Herodian (8.3.4–6) and Arrian (*Anabasis* 5.11.4).

Luke uses two distinctive literary techniques in the speeches. First is *intentional interruption,* frequently because of anger or dissension (Luke 4:28; Acts 2:36; 4:1; 7:53; 10:44; 17:32; 19:28; 22:22; 23:7; 26:34). Such interruptions are literary devices common to historians and novelists. They heighten the drama of particular episodes (Josephus, *Wars* 1.629; 2.605; 3.485; 7.389; Herodian, 2.5.8; Achilles Tatius 8.1.2; 8.7.1; 8.11.1). Second, Luke concludes some speeches by suggesting that further remarks were made (Luke 24:27; Acts 2:40; 13:43; 15:12; cf. 28:23). This too is a literary device that shortens the length of a speech and suggests the transcriptional character of the part "quoted." Similar conclusions are found in speeches of Hellenistic historians (Arrian, *Anabasis* 3.9.8; Josephus, *Wars* 1.638; 2.33; 3.383) and novelists (Longus 1.16).

Letters

In historical narratives, quoted letters function much like speeches. They also provide authenticity and verisimilitude to the narrative. Acts contains two embedded letters (15:23–29; 23:26–30). Acts 15:23–29 is an official encyclical letter written by the apostles and elders; the prescript and postscript are more typically Hellenistic than any other New Testament letter except Acts 23:26–30 and James. In form, the body of the letter is a Hellenistic decree for promulgating the decisions of councils and assemblies of provincial cities. Here the council *(boulē)* and the assembly *(ekklēsia)* or people *(dēmos)* consists of the apostles and elders with the people. The literary importance of this letter for Acts is signaled by the very first sentence (vs. 24–26), the only periodic sentence in Acts. The letter employs several technical terms. The phrase "it seemed good" *(edoxe,* 15:22, 28) could be better rendered "resolved," a Hellenistic "mark of approval" formula occurring in decrees. The term *epeidē* ("since") in 15:24 should be translated "whereas," to correspond to legal parlance. Just as provincial assemblies could write to other assemblies, so the church in Jerusalem is presented by Luke as sending envoys with a "decree" for other Christian communities. The Hellenistic conventions reflected in Acts 15 appear to be Luke's way of conceptualizing the corporate deliberations of the Jerusalem church.

Dramatic Episodes

Lengthy Hellenistic narratives, whether fictional or factual, tended to be collections of relatively independent episodes. Historical narratives, at least in first-draft form *(hypomnēmata)*, were linear rather than organic; events were placed in sequence rather than arranged in relation to action. Historians used rhetorical conventions to reorganize linear sequences to capitalize on their dramatic possibilities. Dramatic episodes heighten the dramatic conflict just before a resolution, often exhibiting the structural unity of short stories (novellas). Luke was a dramatic historian who framed his first book with two dramatic episodes, the Sermon at Nazareth (Luke 4:16–30), prefiguring Jesus' rejection, execution, and resurrection, and the story of Jesus' resurrection appearance on the road to Emmaus (Luke 24:13–35). Luke included many more dramatic episodes in Acts, where he was less constrained by his sources. According to Eckhard Plümacher, several dramatic episodes in Acts make programmatic statements: (1) Acts 25:13–26:32, with two dramatic scenes, demonstrates that the state cannot understand or decide religious questions. In the first scene (25:13–22), the Roman procurator Festus consults the Jewish king Agrippa, mentioning Paul's innocence (v. 18), and in the second (25:23–26:32) Paul defends himself. His innocence is twice affirmed by Agrippa and Festus (25:25; 26:30–32). (2) Acts 10:1–11:18, the Cornelius episode, proves that the Gentile mission is part of God's plan through dramatic narrative rather than theological argumentation. (3) In Acts 18:12–17, Gallio affirms Paul's innocence and drives the Jews from the tribunal. (4) Acts 22:17–21 narrates a vision of Paul that traces the conversion of the Gentiles to God's providence. (5) In Acts 8:26–40, the conversion and baptism of the Ethiopian eunuch is traced to divine revelation.

Acts 27:1–28:16 is a dramatic storm scene framing three brief statements and a speech by Paul. Ancient authors often described typical situations in terms of traditional literary conventions. The sea storm and shipwreck was a scene with long and complex tradition. Sea storms in Homer became models for later narrative descriptions (*Odyssey* 5.291–473; 12.402–425): hurricane winds, rough seas with one wave larger than the rest, darkness, clouds, lightning and thunder, destruction of the vessel, despair of the crew, and the loss of almost all hands. The storm scene in Vergil's *Aeneid* (1. 34–179; consciously modeled on Homer) became the model for sea storms in Roman literature (Livy 21.58.3–11; Seneca, *Agamemnon* 465–578; Lucan 4.48–120). Storm scenes also occur in ancient novels (Chariton 3.3.10–18; Xenophon of Ephesus 3.2.11–15; Heliodorus 1.22.3–5; Achilles Tatius 3.1–5). At one point in the diary of the Sophist Aelius Aristides (ca. A.D. 117–181), he narrates an *actual* sea storm using language from Homer's *Odyssey* (*Oration* 48. 65–68). Thus ancients could conceptualize real experiences with traditional literary *topoi*. In Acts 27:41, the author pairs the obsolete term *naus* ("ship") with the poetic verb *epikellein* ("to run aground"). These words occur together in *Odyssey* 9.148, 546, suggesting that Luke followed the Homeric storm scene tradition.

One of the themes of Acts is Paul's innocence (18:12–17; 25:18, 25; 26:30–32). Ancient historians used the theme of divine retribution as exemplified in the fates of various individuals; the good are rewarded and the wicked punished. The ancients were anxious about the risks involved in seafaring, particularly the danger of being thrown in with ritually polluted fellow passengers with whom the gods are angry (Jonah 1:7–15). Shipwreck was thought caused by impiety (Aeschylus, *Seven Against Thebes* 602–604), injustice (*Odyssey* 3.133), and pollution (Antiphon 5.82; Euripides, *Electra* 1350). Pollution was thought incurred through manslaughter (Antiphon 5.82), sacrilege (*Odyssey* 11.110–113; 12.374–449), or perjury (Euripides, *Electra* 1355). From this perspective, had Paul been polluted or guilty of impiety, he would certainly have gone down with the ship. The fact that he survived, and was also unhurt when bitten by a viper (Acts 28:3–6), underscored his innocence for ancient readers.

Digressions

Luke, like Livy and Old Testament historians, prefers the technique of indirect narration and therefore avoids digressions. When he uses them, he never labels them digressions. Examples include the genealogy of Jesus (Luke 3:23–38), the mini-digressions on Athenian curiosity (Acts 17:21), Apollos' identity (Acts 18:24f.), why Paul was mobbed in the Temple (Acts 21:29), and Sadducean beliefs (Acts 23:8). This avoidance of digressions is reflected in the awkward insertion of a list of nations and nationalities into a speech attributed to Diaspora Jews on Pentecost (Acts 2:7–11), or in a clumsy mini-digression on Judas in Peter's speech (Acts 1:18f.). Luke omits Mark's digressive novella on the fate of John the Baptist (Mark 6:17–29). The broader role played by speeches in Luke-Acts in comparison with most Hellenistic histories enables Luke to insert much parenthetic expository material into his narrative in the guise of speeches. Further, Luke never uses a digression to theorize about historical methods or values as many Hellenistic historians did. In this he follows the precedent of Israelite more than Greco-Roman historiography.

Summaries

The summaries in Acts, like the summaries in the Synoptic Gospels, function as links between narrative segments rather than indicators of literary structure. Luke used summaries to generalize about incidents and also as transitions that introduce and conclude episodes. Luke used a single Markan summary (1:28) in three different places (Luke 4:14, 37; 7:17), just as the Chronicler used the regnal summary of Solomon (1 Kings 10:23–29) in two different places (2 Chron. 1:14–17; 9:22–28). Luke took over five Markan summaries (cf. Mark 1:28 in Luke 4:37; Mark 1:32–34, 39 in Luke 4:40–41, 44; Mark 3:7–12 in Luke 6:17–19; Mark 6:12–13 in Luke 9:6). He also created several of his own (Luke 1:80; 2:40, 52; 7:21). Acts contains three major summaries that deal with the ideal character of the earliest Christian community in Jerusalem (2:43–47; 4: 32–35; 5:11–16). In addition, Acts contains many shorter summary sentences (e.g., 1:14; 8:1b–4; 9:31; 11:19–21; 19:11–12; 28:30–31).

The Content of Luke-Acts

The dramatic structures that characterize the other Gospels have no real counterpart in Luke and/or Acts. The other Evangelists depict the increasing conflict between Jesus and his adversaries, culminating in his death (their apparent victory over him), and his resurrection (his victory over them). In the absence of the kind of causal relationships between episodes necessary for a plot, Luke uses two complex intersecting themes to give *movement* to the story. One theme is the characteristic response to messengers of God or prophets: rejection (primarily by Jews) and acceptance (primarily by Gentiles). This theme shapes the prophetic image of Jesus, structures many individual episodes, and determines the basic structure of both books.

The second theme is divine guidance which arranges human events in accordance with a predetermined plan called "the will of God" (Luke 7:30; Acts 2:23; 4:28; 5:38f.; 13:36; 20:27). Throughout Luke-Acts, events are guided by various types of supernatural revelation appropriate to a Jewish-Christian setting (signs, dreams, visions, prophetic oracles). These elements occur in the other Gospels, but in Luke-Acts they set the stage for Jesus' life and ministry, and punctuate critical stages in the growth and development of early Christianity. The Greco-Roman conception of "fate" has a functional counterpart in Luke-Acts in the necessity of the fulfillment of prophetic predictions in Scripture.

The Prophet as an Endangered Species

After narrating Jesus' baptism (presented as the outpouring of the Spirit on a prophet) and temptation, which frame a genealogy (Luke 3:21–4:13), Luke includes a brief summary of Jesus' activities and successes through the Spirit (4:14–15). Immediately following is a dramatic episode about Jesus in the synagogue at Nazareth (4:16–30), widely regarded as programmatic for Luke-Acts. Jesus reads Isaiah 61:1–2, then delivers a homily in which he claims to be anointed with the Spirit (i.e., a prophet). When the audience takes offense, he retorts, "No prophet is acceptable in his own country," and cites Old Testament stories about how Elijah and Elisha were sent to Gentiles rather than Israelites. Anger transforms the worshipers into a violent mob. They drag Jesus out of town to a precipice with the intention of throwing him to his death. Miraculously, he passes unharmed through their midst and departs, abruptly and mysteriously. This first public act of Jesus couples his rejection with an attempted lynching, prefiguring his ultimate rejection, execution, and resurrection triumph.

In Luke-Acts, the prophetic status of Jesus is given greater emphasis than in any of the other Gospels (cf. Luke 4:24; 7:16, 39; 9:8, 19; 24:19). Traditions depicting Jesus as the eschatological Mosaic prophet of Deuteronomy 18:15–18 are preserved, though not exploited, in Acts 3:22–23; 7:37. Luke's interest in the prophetic status of Jesus is connected with the motif of the violent fate of the prophets, i.e., the widespread Jewish view that suffering and martyrdom were inevitable for a true prophet (Acts 7:52; cf. Neh. 9:26). Luke uses several sayings from Q to promote this view (6:22–23; 11: 47–48, 49–51; 13:34–35). Jesus is rejected and killed, not *primarily* because his words and behavior antagonize Jewish authorities, but because he is a prophet of God.

Divine Guidance

The first two chapters of Luke narrate an extraordinary amount of revelatory activity including miraculous signs, visions, and prophecies. The Holy Spirit (referred to 17 times in Luke and 57 times in Acts) is mentioned seven times in these two chapters. Angels appear and announce the births of John to Zechariah, and of Jesus to Mary and a group of shepherds. Elizabeth, Zechariah, Simeon, and Anna all utter prophecies inspired by the Holy Spirit. Zechariah is temporarily struck dumb as a sign of unbelief. Elizabeth gives birth to John in spite of advanced age, and Jesus is conceived by a virgin through the Holy Spirit. All of this, in a Jewish-Christian idiom, reflects the Greco-Roman view that great events are presaged by supernatural signs and oracles (particularly the births of great men). The angelic and prophetic announcements of the births of John (1:13–18, 68–79) and Jesus (1:32–33; 2:29–35, 38) function as evaluative summaries of their careers and achievements. John's Nazirite life-style and prophetic ministry of preaching repentance are highlighted, as are Jesus' roles as eternal Davidic king, savior of

Jews and Gentiles, and the conflicts he will cause. Polybius observed that most historians used prefaces to evaluate kings and prominent men (10.26.9–10). Luke does this *indirectly*. Luke 1–2 is *introductory* since 3:1–2 contains a chronological synchronism, a historical convention indicating a new narrative phase (Thucydides 2.2.1; Dionysius of Halicarnassus 9.61; Josephus, *Wars* 2.284; *Ant.* 20.257). Luke 3:1–3 also contains the second of two lengthy periodic sentences in Luke-Acts, a feature confirming its structural importance. Luke introduces the careers of *both* John and Jesus with similar devices because his intentions are historical rather than biographical. The rest of the Gospel narrative presupposes that Jesus, filled with the Spirit at his baptism (Luke 3:22), continued to minister in the power of the Spirit (Luke 4:1, 14, 18).

The theme of the power and activity of the Holy Spirit continues in Acts (1:5, 8). The Spirit is poured out upon Jewish believers in a dramatic initial experience (Acts 2), corresponding to Jesus' baptism. As in Luke 1–2, prophetic speeches are uttered by people filled with the Spirit (4:8; 7:55f.; 13:9–11). Gentiles are brought to belief through visions (9:1–9; 10:3–6). Divine guidance is given to Christian leaders through visions (10:10–16; 16:9–10; 18:9–10; 22:17–21; 23:11; 27:23–24). Prophetic oracles are delivered by inspired prophets (11:27–28; 13:1–3; 15:28; 20:23; 21:4, 10–11). Paul, the single most influential individual in the spread of Christianity to the Gentiles, is converted through an epiphany of the exalted Jesus (Acts 9:1–9; 22:3–21; 26:12–23). The three evangelistic tours of Paul and his companions are introduced by a prophetic commission of Barnabas and Paul (13:1–3). Paul and Silas were divinely directed to extend their second evangelistic tour to Europe through a vision (16:9–10). Paul stayed eighteen months in Corinth in obedience to a vision (18:9–10).

Prophetic Fulfillment

The motif of the fulfillment of biblical prophecy pervades Luke-Acts, though absent from Luke 1–2. Unlike Matthew and John, Luke (preferring indirect narration) does not insert editorial comments to indicate the fulfillment of Scripture in and through various events in the life of Jesus. Yet of all the Evangelists he most clearly states the theoretical basis for prophetic fulfillment (Luke 24:26), a program repeated in the appearance of Jesus to his followers in Luke 24:44–47. When Jesus predicts his death and resurrection, the necessity that Scripture be fulfilled is emphasized (Luke 9:22; 18:31; 22:22; cf. 24:7). Apostles and evangelists argue not only that Jesus is the Messiah (Acts 5:42; 9:22; 17:3; 18:5, 28) but also that the suffering of the Messiah occurred in fulfillment of Scripture (Acts 2:23; 3:18; 4:28; 13:36; 17:3; 20:27; 26:23).

During the Hellenistic period Greco-Roman historians narrated events with the conviction that the will of man was controlled by Chance of Luck, personified as *Tychē,* a universal goddess for the Greeks (Pliny, *Natural History* 2.5.22), and as *Fortuna,* a Roman goddess of particular individuals and cities (Tacitus, *Annals* 6.22). Ancient conceptions of Fortune ranged from mechanical determinism to personal deities who could intervene in human affairs. The role of fate in determining human events in Greco-Roman historiography had its beginnings in Greek epic and dramatic poetry. There anthropomorphic deities intervened regularly in human affairs. While the epic conception of gods controlling human events disappears in prose history, all supernatural influence does not vanish. The prophetic oracle, for example, became a stock literary device functioning as an "exciting force" in the plots in such epics as the *Iliad* and the *Odyssey,* the *Argonautica* of Apollonius of Rhodes, Vergil's *Aeneid,* Lucan's *Civil War,* and others. Oracles functioned similarly in tragedy.

Herodotus assumed that human events were shaped by the gods (7.139; 8.13; 9.65). He believed in oracles and their fulfillment, and included more than eighty of them, twenty-seven in verse (e.g., 8.77). He also included twenty revelatory dreams (e.g., 1.34; 2.141; 3.124; 7.19), and forty portents of impending disaster (6.27; e.g., 9.120). These supernatural communications disclosed the divine purpose in human history. For Thucydides and Polybius the supernatural played no role at all. Yet for Polybius, *Tychē* was a way of accounting for factors outside of human control and not subject to rational comprehension (36.17), i.e., what insurance policies now refer to as "acts of God."

Divine Intervention

Miracles permeate Luke-Acts, and the author uses them without apology. Lucian advised would-be historians to tell myths but to season them with skepticism (*History* 60). This reflects the penchant of Hellenistic historians to relate wonders, but advise the readers to judge the truth for themselves (Herodotus 2.123; 5.45; Dionysius, *Roman Antiquities* 1.48.1), a practice followed by Josephus (*Ant.* 1 108; 2.348; 3.81). In the face of Hellenistic skepticism, Luke insists that Jesus established his resurrection from the dead "with many convincing proofs" (Acts 1:3). Even miracles fall under the heading of the "exact information" *(asphaleia)* he promises to provide in Luke 1:4. Luke-Acts contains six exorcisms (four in Luke, two in Acts), eighteen healings (twelve in Luke, six in Acts), six epiphanies (three in Luke, three in Acts), five rescue miracles (one in Luke, four in Acts), one gift miracle (Luke), and four punitive miracles (one in Luke, three in Acts). The importance of miracles in Luke-Acts is also indicated by the frequency with which they are mentioned in summaries (Luke 4:40–41; 6:17–19; 7:21; Acts 2:43–47; 5:12–16; 19:11–12). One epiphany story, the conversion of Paul, is found in three versions (Acts 9:1–22; 22:4–16; 26:9–18), while the Ascension story is found in two versions side by side (Luke 24:44–53; Acts 1:6–11). Greek historians often recorded variant versions of a tradition, either expressing their own preference for the most plausible one or else leaving that decision to the reader (Herodotus 3.3; 4.11, 179; 7.150, 167, 214; Polybius 1.36.4; Dionysius, *Roman Antiquities* 4.2.1). Luke may, like other Hellenistic historians, be transmitting variant versions without making his procedure explicit.

Divine Retribution

Another feature that Luke-Acts has in common with Greco-Roman and Israelite-Jewish historiography is a concern with the theme of *divine retribution*. In ancient legal systems there was a basic concern that the punishment fit the crime. Ancient criminal codes often made use of the principle of *lex talionis* ("the law of retaliation"), i.e., the principle of retaliation by infliction of the same injury (basically a form of limited liability). The biblical phrase "an eye for an eye, and a tooth for a tooth" (Ex. 21:24), is a famous expression of this principle. In the Twelve Tables, the first codified form of Roman law dating to ca. 450 B.C., the same principle is found. In the ancient world there was a widespread belief in a moral order in which fate or the gods dealt out justice for crimes unpunished by civil authorities or outside their jurisdiction. Such divine retribution could take the form of *lex talionis*, or a similarly suitable punishment.

Divine retribution is a frequent theme in Acts. Herod Agrippa is struck down by the angel of the Lord for arrogance, accepting praise for his divine rhetorical abilities (12:20–23). The angel of the Lord as an agent of divine retribution is an Old Testament figure (2 Sam. 24:16; 2 Kings 19:35), but the incident itself is based on historical tradition (Josephus, *Ant.* 19.343–350). Acts also recounts the death of Judas (1:18–19), though the motif of divine retribution is not explicit. Among the other retributive miracles in Acts are the deaths of Ananias and Sapphira (5:1–11), the blinding of Elymas (13:6–12), and a demoniac's attack on the seven sons of Sceva (19:13–16).

Just as the monotonous pattern of disobedience and unfaithfulness to God exhibited by Israel resulted in the division of the kingdom and the capture of both Samaria and Judea according to the Deuteronomic historian (2 Kings 17:7–23; 21:11–15), so Acts emphasizes the continuing Jewish rejection of the gospel and its proclaimers (e.g., 4:1–3; 7:54–8:3; 9:23–25; 13:45; 14:2, 19; 17:5, 13; 18:12–17; 19:8f.; 21:27–36). The speech of Stephen summarizes Israelite history in terms of Jewish rejection of divine revelation; they "always resist the Holy Spirit" (Acts 7:51). For this reason Paul and others turn from Jews and bring the gospel to Gentiles in Asia Minor (13:46–47), Greece (18:6), and Rome (28:25–28). Yet Paul goes right back to other synagogues (14:1; 18:19). Jewish blindness and Gentile receptivity fulfill Isaiah's prophecy quoted by Paul in Acts 28:26–27 (Isa. 6:9–10). Paul's concluding statement in Acts 28:28 indicates that Israel has been rejected and the Gospel will henceforth go out only to the Gentiles.

The Function of Luke-Acts

Scholars have proposed a number of possible purposes for Luke-Acts: (1) to defend Christianity against heresy, possibly Gnosticism, (2) to defend the legitimacy and antiquity of Christianity as the authentic continuation of Judaism for the benefit of Roman authorities, (3) to polish up Paul's tarnished reputation, (4) to edify Christian readers by demonstrating Christianity's truth and superiority over Judaism and Hellenism, (5) to entertain Christian readers, and (6) to continue biblical history.

While there is some validity in many of these proposals, Luke's own explicit statement of purpose to Theophilus in Luke 1:4 should be emphasized: "That you may know the truth [*asphaleia*] concerning the instruction you have received." He wants to provide his patron with "exact information" *(asphaleia)* about the historical and theological basis for the Christian faith. However, even this explicit statement can be understood in various ways. Two complementary ways of understanding it are that Luke intended (1) to awaken or strengthen faith, and (2) to present Jesus and the apostles as paradigms of Christian life and thought. Although the Gospels of Mark, Matthew, and Luke functioned similarly (see chapter 2), the second point requires amplification when applied to Luke-Acts, since the author did not limit himself to a narrative focusing on Jesus but gives equal space to describing important developments in earliest Christianity.

By ca. A.D. 50, Christianity was a religious movment needing definition, identity, and legitimation. (1) Christianity needed *definition* because during the first generation of its existence, it exhibited a broad spectrum of beliefs and practices, sometimes manifested in splinter groups making exclusive claims. The many intra-Christian controversies reflected in the Pauline letters continued into the second century. Hostile critics like the philosopher Celsus (late second century A.D.) naturally lumped all "Christians" together. Origen, attempting to refute him, found it necessary to make "we"/"they" distinctions between different kinds of Christians: the orthodox and the heretics. (2) Christianity needed *identity* because, unlike other ancient Mediterranean religions, it had ceased to remain tied to a particular ethnic group (i.e., it had increasingly looser relations to Judaism). Some Jewish Christians, like Peter and Paul, apparently advocated that Christians (whether Jews or Gentiles) ignore or regard as nonessential the traditional signs of Jewish social and religious identity (circumcision, Sabbath and festival observance, dietary restrictions, and the wearing of religious paraphernalia, such as phylacteries and fringes). The occasional adoption of Jewish customs by Gentile Christians indicates a desire for identification with Judaism. On the other hand, struggles against "Judaizing" by Paul and others reflect a Christian identity crisis (Gal. 5:2–12; Phil. 3:2–3; Col. 2:16; Ignatius, *Magnesians* 8.1; 10.3). Further, Christian congregations were fully comparable neither to religious groups nor to philosophical schools. Most religious groups focused on distinctive ritual practices with little or no concern for ethical or theological issues. Christianity, emphasizing both ethics and theology, superficially resembled a philosophical school (e.g., Cynicism, Stoicism, or Epicureanism). Some Christian teachers, like Justin Martyr (died ca. A.D. 165), regarded Christianity as the true philosophy and themselves as Christian philosophers. (3) Christianity needed *legitimation,* because no religious movement or philosophical sect could be credible unless it was rooted in antiquity. Luke provided legitimation by demonstrating the Jewish origins of Christianity and by emphasizing the divine providence which was reflected in every aspect of the development and expansion of the early church.

Luke-Acts provided historical definition and identity as well as theological legitimation for the author's conception of normative Christianity. Luke defines Christianity not only in terms of a particular conception of Jesus but also in terms of the role of the twelve apostles as an official group guaranteeing the tradition (Judas' replacement reconstitutes the Twelve, Acts 1:15–26). Yet he does not know the kind of apostolic succession first found in *1 Clement* 44 (the martyred James is not replaced, cf. Acts 12:2). While Luke regularly equated "the apostles" with "the twelve," this equation is found elsewhere only in Matt. 10:2 and Rev. 21:14. Originally the apostles and the Twelve apparently constituted different groups (cf. 1 Cor. 15:3–7). Yet apart from the account of Pentecost and the appointment of seven "deacons" (Acts 2:14; 6:2, 6), they play no role in Acts. He emphasizes the rite of laying on of hands as an institutional means for expanding Christianity (Acts 6:6–7; 8:17–19; 9:12, 17; 13:3; 19:6). The bestowal of the Spirit (sometimes linked with the laying on of hands) occurs only when one of the Twelve or their representative is present. This is in addition to the emphasis on divine guidance in the expansion of the faith discussed above. Further, Luke implicitly discredits deviant forms of Christianity, such as those in his day who regarded Simon Magus as a founding figure (Acts 8:9–24; cf. the later evaluations of Simon's key role in spawning heresy in Justin, *1 Apology* 1.26, 56; Irenaeus, *Against Heresies* 1.27.1), or those who still follow John the Baptist (Acts 18:24–26; 19:1–7), or those who use the name of Jesus for magical purposes (Acts 19:13–16).

More than half of Acts centers on Paul, not biographically or personally, but as a representative of the kind of apostolic Gentile Christianity that Luke himself represented. Paul's mission to the Gentiles had provoked conflict with some of his Jewish Christian peers in his own lifetime, as attested by Gal. 2; Phil. 3:2–11; and 2 Cor. 10–13. Late in the second century some Jewish Christian groups, driven to a defensive stance by the growing dominance of Gentiles in the church, expressed their opposition by anti-Pauline writings (e.g., the *Kerygmata Petrou*, or *Preaching of Peter*, and the Pseudo-Clementine *Homilies* and *Recognitions*, core sections of which originated before A.D. 300). They saw Paul as the founder of a deviant form of Christianity, while Peter and James were founders of the true way. Luke (writing ca. A.D. 90) stands midway between the occasional conflicts experienced by Paul and the hardened, "sectarian" oppositions that emerged in the next century.

Luke-Acts as General History

Luke was an eclectic Hellenistic Christian historian who narrated the early history of Christianity from its origins in Judaism with

Jesus of Nazareth through its emergence as a relatively independent religious movement open to all ethnic groups. He did not, it is true, set out to narrate *all* aspects of early Christianity from ca. 4 B.C. to A.D. 60. He focused on the mission and message of Jesus and the twelve apostles, which merged with the activity of Paul. He silently passed over traditions he must have known concerning Christianity's early penetration into Syria, the East, Egypt, Rome, and Spain. From Christianity's beginnings until ca. A.D. 325, when Eusebius of Caesarea supposedly created the "new" genre of church history (*Church History* 1.1.30), no literary work had appeared that attempted to narrate the origins and development of early Christianity, with the exception of Luke-Acts. Eusebius' main achievements, besides rectifying some of Luke's omissions (*Church History* 2), were to emphasize the purity of the church until the time of Trajan (A.D. 98–117), when various heresies began to emerge with the absence of the apostles (*Church History* 3.32.7–8), and to extend Christian history down to his own day. Luke, rather than Eusebius, should be credited with creating the "new" genre of church history. His achievement is remarkable in view of the early date of his work (ca. A.D. 90) and the long period that elapsed before he found an imitator and continuator in Eusebius.

Literary Models Used by Luke

The primary models used by Eusebius were Luke-Acts and Josephus. But what were Luke's models? One very important model and source was the Gospel of Mark, which Luke modified in four significant ways: (1) He framed Mark with large blocks of narrative material. (2) He rewrote Mark in a more elevated literary style. (3) Following the Hellenistic convention of using one source at a time, he intercalated a large section of Jesus' teachings from another source (Q) into the middle of Mark (9:51–18:14). (4) The many literary parallels between Luke and Acts reveal the author's intention to provide the kind of literary unity for his second book that he had achieved in his first. Mark was a direct model for Luke's first book, and an indirect model for his second.

A second important model, one that shaped the entire composition in a more comprehensive way, was *general history,* an eclectic genre of Greco-Roman history. General and antiquarian histories focused on the history of a particular people (typically the Greeks or Romans) from mythical beginnings to a point in the recent past, including contacts (usually conflicts) with other national groups in various geographical theaters. The general history of the Greeks, for example, was not the history of the Greeks in Greece, but the history of the Greeks wherever they lived in the Mediterranean world (chiefly Greece, the islands, central Italy, and western Asia Minor). In the Near East, Israel developed a form of general history earlier than the Greeks, but which had a geographical focus only on *Palestine,* particularly Jerusalem. Diaspora Judaism (Jews living outside Palestine) was never the subject of either late Israelite or early Jewish historiography (though it was emphasized in pious fiction, e.g., Esther, Daniel, Tobit).

Following the conventions of Hellenistic general history, Luke selectively treated the history of early Christianity outside of Palestine, wherever its representatives contacted significant persons in important places throughout the Mediterranean world. Yet he combined this with Israelite historiographical conventions by emphasizing Palestine (particularly Jerusalem) to a greater extent than his sources. Unlike the writers of the other Gospels, Luke both begins and ends his first book in Jerusalem, which becomes the point of departure for world evangelization (Acts 1:8). By stressing the Old Testament and Jewish heritage of early Christianity, he underlines both its antiquity and its legitimacy.

The "National Consciousness" of Luke-Acts

"National consciousness" is the awareness of members of a national group of a unity (usually based on common language, land, and customs) that sets them apart from other peoples. General history reflects the rise of national consciousness, a phenomenon that appeared in the Hellenistic world only after the demise of the city-state as an independent political entity. During the Hellenistic period the genres of general and antiquarian history were adopted by native intellectuals (like Manetho, Berossus, and Josephus) in regions controlled first by the Greeks and later by the Romans. They wrote propagandistic and apologetic narratives emphasizing the key role that their nations played in world civilization. These histories all reflect a national consciousness clarified and defined by the conflicts of their native cultures with Hellenism.

Luke's dependence on the conventions of general history made it natural to conceptualize Christianity on analogy to an ethnic group. He presents Christianity as an independent religious movement in the process of emerging from Judaism to which it is its legitimate successor. His use for the term "Christians" facilitated this conception (Acts 11:26; cf. 26:28). *Christianoi* was formed using the borrowed Latin adjectival ending *-anus* ("belonging to"), on analogy with political groups in the ancient world such as Pompeiani ("adherents of Pompey"), Sullani ("Sulla's veterans"), or Herodiani ("adherents of Herod"). Luke intentionally uses *Christianoi* for the first time when he shifts his narrative focus from Palestine and Jerusalem to the Greco-Roman world. Christians are also labeled, usually by outsiders, as adherents of "the Way" (Acts 9:2; 19:9, 23; 22:4; 24:14, 22), as "the Nazarenes" (Acts 24:5), and as a "sect" (*hairesis*, Acts 24:5, 14; 28:22), analogous to the sects of the Pharisees and Sadducees (Acts 5:17; 15:5; 26:5). These labels all serve to identify Christians as a distinct group, analogous to political or partisan groups, and a fitting subject for historical treatment.

Luke-Acts provides historical justification for the theological conception of Christianity's "national consciousness," for Luke understands Christianity as a separate, identifiable group that emerged from Judaism. He did not invent this conception. Paul was the first to express the view that Christians were a *people* with political and historical self-consciousness. He used the three categories of Jews, Greeks, and the church of God (1 Cor. 10:32). He also regarded Christians as aliens whose true citizenship was in heaven (Phil. 3:20; cf. 1 Peter 1:17; 2:11). He thought of Christianity as transcending racial differences (Gal. 3:28; 5:6; 1 Cor. 12:13; cf. Col. 3:11; Eph. 2:11–12). Ignatius too referred to the church as a single body composed of both Jews and Gentiles (*Smyrneans* 1.2). The distinctiveness and separateness of Christians was recognized by outsiders (cf. Origen, *Against Celsus* 8.2) and insiders (1 Peter 2:9; Justin, *Dialogue with Trypho* 119), culminating in the conception of Christians as a "third race" (*tertium genus;* cf. *Epistle to Diognetus* 5–6; Tertullian, *To the Nations* 1.8).

The Apocryphal Acts

By the end of the first century the twelve apostles had become revered founding figures of the past (Rev. 21:14), who both exemplified (*1 Clement* 5.5–7) and proclaimed the gospel and were guardians of Christian truth. The Greek word *apostolos* means "envoy," and in the apocryphal (i.e., noncanonical) narratives in which they figure prominently, they are uniformly presented as itinerant missionaries. The five earliest apocryphal acts, the Acts of Paul, Thomas, Peter, Andrew, and John, were composed anonymously between A.D. 175 and 225, and are examples of *popular* literature written by and for lower-class Christians. The nine extant papyrus and parchment fragments of apocryphal acts from the third and fourth centuries A.D. are all in codex form, an indication of popularity. This literature has often been labeled heretical (i.e., Gnostic), though it probably arose in "popular" Christianity, where both "orthodoxy" and "heterodoxy" can be misleading labels. Most of the apocryphal acts were produced in Asia Minor, though the *Acts of Thomas* originated in Syria. They are not entirely fictional, but combine oral traditions (in some cases reaching back into the first century) with creative imagination. One major problem in understanding this literary genre is the puzzling relationship between apocryphal acts, the canonical book of Acts, the ancient novel, and late lives of philosophers.

The Content of the Apocryphal Acts

The *Acts of John* was written in Greek ca. A.D. 150, perhaps in Asia Minor, and first mentioned by Eusebius (*Church History* 3.25.6), who labels it heretical. About 70 percent of the original work survives. The reconstructed order of the text in Hennecke-Schneemelcher places the chapters as follows: 18–37a, 87–105, 37b–86, 106–115. The composition falls into three parts: (I) John's first stay in Ephesus (18–37a, 87–105, 37b–55); (II) his trip to Smyrna (55–61); and (III) his second stay at Ephesus (62–115). The first section has seven episodes: (1) the healing of Cleopatra and the resurrection of Lycomedes (19–25); (2) the portrait of John (26–29); (3) the public healing of a group of old women (30–37); (4) a lengthy "sermon" by John used to frame several Jesus traditions (87–105); (5) John's prayer which destroys the temple of Artemis (37–45); (6) the resurrection of a pagan priest (46–47); (7) the resurrection of a man killed by his son (48–54). The Smyrna section contains three episodes: (1) the pronouncement story about John and the partridge (56–57; the only such story in the apocryphal acts); (2) John's departure speech (58–59); and (3) the miracle of the expelled bedbugs, or John as a temporary exterminator (60–61). The third section, John's second stay in Ephesus, consists of three episodes: (1) the death and resurrection of Callimachus, Drusiana, and Fortunatus (63–86); (2) John's last speech and eucharist (106–110); and (3) his martyrdom (111–115).

The *Acts of Andrew* (late second century) survives in several major fragments. Two sections are extant, the account of a journey and the martyrdom of Andrew. Andrew is depicted as traveling through Asia Minor and Greece, preaching, making converts, and performing one miracle. One fragment contains a single episode, the exorcism of the soldier Varianus, brother of a pious Christian virgin (9.7–10.11; 14.24–15.28). The tension in this scene is increased by a speech of Andrew that intercalates the circumstances leading up to the exorcism, including the attempt by a sorcerer to magically seduce the virgin using a *paredros daimōn*, "assisting deity" (10. 11–14.24). The procedure involved in this attempt at love magic has an exact parallel in the *Papyri Graecae Magicae* IV.1850–1859. Another fragment begins with a sermon of Andrew from prison. Maximilla, his convert, lives in continence to the consternation of her husband, the proconsul Aegeates, who imprisons Andrew. In prison, Andrew delivers a long homily to Maximilla and Stratocles (5–10); later Maximilla returns and hears another sermon (15–18; here the text breaks off). In the reconstructed martyrdom of Andrew, the apostle gives several homilies from the cross before dying. After his death, Maximilla remains steadfastly celibate; Aegeates commits suicide by jumping to his death.

The *Acts of Paul*, according to Tertullian, was written by a presbyter from Asia Minor (*On Baptism* 17), ca. A.D. 190. Dennis R. MacDonald proposes that the traditions behind the work were transmitted by women to legitimate their celibate ministry. He proposes that the Pastoral letters opposed this legendary image of Paul (1 Tim. 4:3 opposes celibacy; v. 7 warns against tales told by old women). The fragmentary beginning describes Paul's conversion and early travels. In the section on Paul and Thecla (which circulated separately), Paul preaches a gospel of continence at Iconium, and Thecla is converted (5–6). She adopts a life of continence, breaking off her engagement. An angry fiancé stirs up the population against Paul, who is imprisoned (15–17). At night Thecla bribes the jailers and visits Paul in jail but is discovered (18–19). Paul is then expelled from Iconium and Thecla condemned to be burned (20–21). Rain prevents the execution and Thecla is released and follows Paul (22–24). Together they travel to Antioch, where Alexander (an Antiochian nobleman) falls in love with Thecla but is rebuffed and publicly humiliated by her, and for this she is condemned to death (26–27). She finds a temporary protector in Tryphaena (a historical queen of Pontus in the mid-first century A.D., attested by inscriptions on coins), a rich woman for whose deceased daughter Thecla prays (28–29). When Thecla is thrown to the beasts, they attack each other rather than her (33). Thecla throws herself in a pit of water, thereby baptizing herself (34). More animals and more torture prove ineffective, and finally when Tryphaena faints and is thought dead, Alexander relents and releases Thecla (36–39). After rejoining Paul at Myra, she returns home alone to Iconium to preach the gospel, and then to Seleucia, where she eventually dies (40–43). Subsequent sections of the *Acts of Paul* relate his mission at Myra, Sidon, Tyre, Ephesus, Philippi (at this point letters exchanged between Paul and the Corinthians are quoted, including the apocryphal *3 Corinthians*), Corinth, Italy, and finally Rome, where he undergoes martyrdom.

The *Acts of Peter*, first mentioned in Eusebius, *Church History* 3.3.2, was written in Greek toward the end of the second century and survives only in three fragments and one extended passage. The fragments contain the story of Peter's daughter (she is paralyzed, but Peter refuses to heal her permanently since her physical condition is conducive to virginity); the story of the peasant's daughter (whom Peter raises from the dead); and a few lines from a speech of Peter. The largest section deals with Peter and Simon Magus. When Paul goes to Spain (1–3), Simon arrives in Rome and troubles the church. Peter also arrives (in obedience to a vision) and restores the church. The conflict between Simon and Peter includes a debate (23–24) and a contest of miracles (25–29). Simon flies through the air, but at the prayer of Peter falls and eventually dies (32). Four concubines of Agrippa take an oath of celibacy, as does Xanthippe the wife of Albinus, a friend of Caesar (33–34). The work closes with the martyrdom of Peter (36–40).

The *Acts of Thomas* was written in Syriac in Syria ca. A.D. 225, the only apocryphal acts to survive in complete form. It describes the mission of Thomas to India. The text consists of fourteen episodes (each but the last designated a *praxis*, an "act," in the Greek translation). Many episodes are only loosely connected with the trip to India (e.g., 30–38, 39–41, 42–50, 51–61). In the first "act," the Lord (disguised as Thomas) breaks up a honeymoon (11–13). Thomas then leaves for India with Abban the merchant and arrives at the palace of King Gundaphorus (17–29). Agreeing to build a palace for the king, he distributes the money to the poor instead, thus building him a heavenly palace (fortunately the king's dead brother has seen the palace and returns to life to tell the king before Thomas is punished). The following episodes deal with talking animals (30–41), exorcisms (42–50; 62–81), the resurrection of a murdered maiden (51–61), and spreading the gospel of continence (82–133); the book concludes with the martyrdom of Thomas (159–170, a section that may have circulated separately).

Literary Features of Apocryphal Acts

Literary Form

The apocryphal acts lack conventional plots. The literary focus is the individual episode. These episodes are loosely framed by chronological accounts of the travels and adventures of apostles, usually culminating with martyrdom. The episodic character of these works made it comparatively easy to break off sections for separate circulation (e.g., *Acts of Paul and Thecla, Martyrdom of Paul*). Individual episodes often focus on miraculous healings or resurrections, and there is a tendency to prolong the tension and emphasize the melodramatic potential of narratives dealing with human suffering and grief (e.g., *Acts Jn.* 19–25, 30–37; *Acts Andr.* [Pap. Copt. Utrecht 1], pp. 9–15). Though the authors usually use the third person, occasionally the first-person plural is found (*Acts Jn.* 19, 60–62, 72–73).

Constituent Literary Forms

The proclamation of the gospel is a central feature of the apocryphal acts, and (as in the canonical Acts), *speeches* are the literary vehicles used. Thus *missionary sermons* emphasizing the gospel of continence occur frequently (e.g., *Acts Thom.* 33–36, 39; *Acts Jn.* 33–36, 39). *Homilies* emphasizing virtues and vices addressed to Christians are even more common (*Acts Thom.* 28, 82–86, 94; *Acts Jn.* 29, 67–69, 103–104, 106–107; *Acts Pet.* 2, 7, 20). Other types of speeches include (1) expository speeches (Peter's speech in *Acts Pet.* 17 provides background information on Simon; John relates experiences with the earthly Jesus in *Acts Jn.* 87–102); (2) farewell addresses (*Acts Jn.* 58–59; 106–107; *Acts Thom.* 142–149); and (3) a eulogy (*Acts Jn.* 67–69).

Extant portions of the *Acts of Peter* contain three *summaries* similar to those in canonical Acts; e.g., *Acts Pet.* 29: "From that same hour they venerated him [Peter] as a god, and laid at his feet such sick people as they had at home, so that he might heal them" (Hennecke-Schneemelcher, II, 313; cf. *Acts Pet.* 31; 33; 34; *Acts Thom.* 59). In general this narrative technique is rarely used.

Liturgical forms include (1) prayers (*Acts Jn.* 22, 41, 82, 85, 108, 109, 112–114; *Acts Pet.* 2); (2) hymns (*Acts Thom.* 6–7, the Wedding Hymn; 108–113, the famous Hymn of the Pearl); and (3) liturgies connected with chrismation, i.e., anointing with oil (*Acts Thom.* 27, 121, 132, 157), the eucharist (*Acts Thom.* 50, 133, 158; *Acts Pet.* 5; *Acts Jn.* 109f.), and baptism (*Acts Thom.* 157).

Literary Motifs

Apostles as Holy Men

Each of the five apocryphal acts centers on the activities of a particular apostle engaged in an itinerant mission of spreading the gospel of continence (in the *Acts of Paul* the focus oscillates between Paul and Thecla). The apostles are presented using ancient "holy man" imagery. This stereotyped image includes the following features: (1) The teaching and behavior of the holy man are consistent and regularly expressed in an ascetic and continent life-style (cf. *Acts Jn.* 113; *Acts Thom.* 20, 96, 139—reflecting both internal and external freedom). (2) The itinerant life-style of the holy man is both a correlative of his asceticism (detachment from normal pleasures and possessions) and a necessary means for communicating a divine message to people. (3) The spiritual power inherent in the holy man is expressed by clairvoyance (*Acts Pet.* 2; *Acts of Paul* 11.1; *Acts Jn.* 46, 56f.) and the ability to perform miracles that legitimate both his holiness and the divine character of his mission. (4) Holy men usually have a marginal social status, expressed by their ascetic life-style and indicated by charges that they practice magic (see below). (5) The primary social setting of the holy man is the circle of his disciples and followers.

The Gospel of Continence

All apocryphal acts share the view that sexual continence and asceticism are essential features of Christianity (*Acts Thom.* 84). An essential part of the proclamation of the gospel is the requirement of sexual asceticism as a behavioral expression of commitment to the truth of the gospel (though castration is frowned on; cf. *Acts Jn.* 53f.). In *Acts Thom.* 101, Charisius quotes the message of Thomas (Hennecke-Schneemelcher, II, 495): "It is impossible for you to enter into the eternal life which I proclaim to you, except you rid yourselves of your wives, and likewise the women of their husbands" (cf. *Acts of Paul* 3.12). This gospel of continence is also reflected in a summary of how people responded to Peter's preaching in *Acts Pet.* 34 (Hennecke-Schneemelcher trans.):

> And many other women besides fell in love with the doctrine of purity and separated from their husbands, and men too ceased to sleep with their own wives, since they wished to worship God in sobriety and purity.

A predictable pattern provides a plot with many episodes: a prominent woman, upon conversion, either remains a virgin or withdraws from her marriage, practicing sexual abstinence (Maximilla in *Acts Andr.;* Thecla in *Acts of Paul;* Mygdonia and Tertia in *Acts Thom.;* Xanthippe in *Acts Pet.;* and Drusiana in *Acts Jn.*). The jilted lovers or husbands are understandably angry and seek to have the apostles arrested and executed. Miraculous rescues regularly resolve the conflict except in the final episode, which recounts the apostle's martyrdom. A similar motif is found in legends surrounding philosophers (Diogenes Laertius 6.96, LCL trans.):

> She [Hipparchia] fell in love with the discourses and the life of Crates, and would not pay attention to any of her suitors, their wealth, their high birth or their beauty. But to her Crates was everything.

The difference, of course, is that Hipparchia *married* Crates, and they presumably philosophized together ever after.

Visions, Dreams, and Oracles

As in the canonical book of Acts, divine guidance through dreams and visions is a common literary device in the apocryphal acts. In the *Acts of Peter,* Paul and Peter are commanded in visions to go to Spain and Rome (1, 5). Theon, the pilot of the ship bearing Peter to Rome, receives a vision (5). Ariston is commanded by Paul in a vision to leave Rome. The success that Peter will have over Simon is revealed by Jesus in a night vision (16). The deceased Peter appears in a vision to Marcellus (40). Epiphanies of Jesus are experienced in waking visions (*Acts Pet.* 5, 21, 35). Similarly John is guided by visions and dreams (*Acts Jn.* 18, 48). Thomas is commissioned in a night vision to go to India (*Acts Thom.* 1) and receives guidance along the way (30). Heavenly voices predict Paul's death by Nero (*Acts Pet.* 1) and inform John that he will give glory to the Lord in Ephesus (*Acts Jn.* 18; cf. John 12:28f.).

Miracles and Wonders

Miracles and wonders are so essential to this genre that the apocryphal acts have been described as Christian "aretalogies" (collections of miracle stories told for propagandistic purposes) framed by missionary travels. Miracles of healing, exorcism, and resurrection are often the subject of dramatic episodes accentuating the element of pathos, and crowds are usually present (e.g., *Acts Jn.* 19–25). Such miracles, often accompanied by sermons, result in dramatic conversions (e.g., *Acts Jn.* 37–45, 63–86; *Acts Thom.* 30–38). Resurrections from the dead occur frequently. In the *Acts of John,* John raises four people from the dead (23, 51, 75, 80) and delegates others to do the same (24, 46f., 82f.). He heals Cleopatra and resurrects her husband Lycomedes in a lengthy melodramatic scene filled with pathos and moving speeches (19–24). When Simon kills a boy using sorcery, Agrippa the prefect resurrects him at Peter's command (*Acts Pet.* 25–26); Peter resurrects a widow's son (27) and also the dead senator Nicostratus, whom Simon could not raise (28). A young man who killed his fiancée raises her from the dead with the help of Thomas (*Acts Thom.* 53–55), and she proceeds to describe hell (55–57). Two exorcised women die and are raised from the dead (75–81).

More conventional miracles of healing also occur. Peter heals a blind old woman, and then a group of blind old women (*Acts Pet.* 20–21). John heals several old women in the theater after first preaching to the assembly (*Acts Jn.* 30–37). Exorcisms also occur and are frequently characterized by elaborate and moving dialogue speeches by the apostle and the demon. Thomas (with the obligatory dramatic speeches) frees a woman from a demonic incubus (*Acts Thom.* 42–49). The only miracle in the extant fragments of the *Acts of Andrew* is an exorcism.

Punitive miracles occur with some frequency. In the *Acts of Peter,* the adulteress Rufina is struck with paralysis when she tries to partake of the eucharist (2). A talking infant has Simon struck dumb (15). In *Acts of Thomas* 51, the hands of a murderer who receives the eucharist become withered. An instance of *lex talionis* occurs when the cupbearer who slapped Thomas is killed by a lion and his severed hand is brought into the feast by a dog as Thomas predicted (*Acts Thom.* 5, 8).

Among the wonders reflected in the apocryphal acts are loquacious animals, including a lion (*Acts of Paul* 7), a dog (*Acts Pet.* 9, 12), a serpent (*Acts Thom.* 31–33), a colt (39–40), and an ass who preaches (78–79). A seven-month-old child prodigy lectures Simon (*Acts Pet.* 15). Marcellus, acting at Peter's suggestion, restores a broken statue (*Acts Pet.* 11); Peter causes a smoked fish to live and swim (*Acts Pet.* 13). Thomas persuades a serpent to heal a man whom it killed, and the serpent itself dies when it sucks out the poison (*Acts Thom.* 30–33). Prison doors open miraculously (*Acts Thom.* 151), and bright lights appear at night (*Acts Thom.* 153, 155).

Accusations of Sorcery

Ancients had an ambivalent attitude toward magic (consisting of *sorcery*, a learned skill, and *witchcraft*, an inherent "talent"). Magic was both feared for its malevolent effects, necessary for protection, and a means for achieving antisocial ends (without anyone being the wiser). The accusations of sorcery that occur in all five apocryphal acts constitute a literary motif used in the following connections: (1) Apostles are often labeled sorcerers by opponents without specific reasons being given (*Acts of Paul* 7; *Acts Pet.* 4). (2) Sexual continence is regarded as an effect of sorcery (*Acts Thom.* 96, 98, 101, 134; *Acts of Paul* 15, 20). (3) Apostles and other virtuous Christians find themselves in conflict with pagan magicians (*Acts Andr.* 10.11–40; *Acts Pet.* 16–29). (4) Eucharistic water and bread and oil used for anointing are regarded by pagans as *materia magica* (*Acts Thom.* 152). (5) The Christian use of the name of Jesus is regarded as magical (*Acts Jn.* 31; *Acts Thom.* 96).

Literary Function

The implicit yet conscious intention of the authors of the apocryphal acts was both edification and entertainment. The chief vehicles for edification are the apostolic speeches, which give expression to distinctive Christian beliefs and practices that separate the authors and their audiences from the world of paganism. In this way they legitimate the Christian worldview by appealing to the paradigmatic stories of the founding apostles. The *Acts of Paul* have a special function relating to the figure of Thecla. This work legitimates the preaching, teaching, and perhaps baptismal ministries of women in the late first- and early second-century church.

Episodes in the apocryphal acts frequently have a strong allegorical tinge which fits in with the emphasis on edification. The episode of John's portrait (*Acts Jn.* 26–29) provides the apostle with an opportunity to reveal the true colors that should be used to express the inner person: kindness, goodness, and brotherly love. When John causes a dead priest of Artemis to be resurrected, he tells him that he is not really "living" unless he believes in Jesus (*Acts Jn.* 47; cf. 52), which he promptly does. Peter gives a sermon while hanging upside down on a cross using that position as a metaphor for the first man's headlong fall to earth, which is repeated in human birth (*Acts Pet.* 38–39).

The Ancient Novel

The "novel," i.e., fictional prose narratives emphasizing the themes of love, travel, and violence (usually within the framework of a story of two lovers separated and finally reunited after many trials), first appeared in the late Hellenistic or early Roman imperial periods (first century B.C. to first century A.D.). The *Odyssey*, a kind of proto-novel, has many novelistic features even though it is in verse and exhibits a more complicated structure than any extant Greek novel. Through the influence of Erwin Rohde a century ago, Greek novels were thought *late* (fifth or sixth centuries A.D.), *mediocre*, and *serious*. All of these judgments have since been revised. Papyrus finds suggest that the earlier novels originated no later than 150 A.D., and the earliest of all, Chariton's *Chaereas and Callirhoë*, is now dated between the first century B.C. and the first century A.D. Other important surviving examples of the genre include Xenophon's *Ephesiaka* (second century A.D.), Iamblichus' *Babyloniaka* (second century A.D.), Longus' *Daphnis and Chloe* (second half of the second century A.D.), Achilles Tatius' *Leucippe and Clitophon* (end of the second century A.D.), and Heliodorus' *Ethiopika* (fourth century A.D.). Though Latin novels are not as relevant for present purposes as Greek novels, two important examples are Apuleius' *Metamorphoses* (second century A.D.) and Petronius' *Satyricon* (first century A.D.).

The Greeks had no special generic term for the novel, which they variously designated a "tale" *(ainos, diēgēma)*, "story" or "fiction" *(mythos)*, "narrative" *(logos)*, "history" *(historia)*, or "report" *(akousma)*. In later antiquity novels were commonly referred to as "fictitious tales" *(plasmatika)*, or "dramatic tales" *(dramatika)*. Greek novels, unlike their Roman counterparts, were never really acceptable in literary circles, despite the fact that the first novels were probably written for educated circles in Hellenistic Asia Minor at a time when the classical period (480–330 B.C.) was looked back upon with nostalgia. Most novels used the classical age as a chronological setting (Xenophon's *Ephesiaka* is an exception). Ancient critics thought poetry was the more appropriate literary vehicle for fiction, and regarded imaginative narratives in which the elements of edification and instruction (Latin: *utilitas*) were absent as unsuitable for adult consumption (Macrobius, *Commentary on the Dream of Scipio* 1.2.6–16).

Though the Greek novel was influenced by such earlier genres as history, biography, fabulous travel descriptions, and erotic poetry, Ben Perry regarded it as the most formless of ancient literary forms, reflecting the open society within which it originated. According to B. P. Reardon, the novel functioned as the myth of Greco-Roman society with its central theme of the lonely traveler searching for his beloved as an expression of the individual's sense of isolation in the world. The novel reached the zenith of its popularity in the second and third centuries A.D., and it sometimes circulated in codex (i.e., book) form rather than the more literarily acceptable roll form, a possible indication of popularity. Of the thirty-two surviving novel fragments from the first to the third centuries A.D., three are in codex form: Achilles Tatius (one fragment from the second century, another from the third) and the recently discovered *Phoinikika* of Lollianus (second century). The heroine is really the focal character in many novels, suggesting their popularity among women. Some may even have been written by women. A. Scobie has proposed that itinerant storytellers read novels to households or lower-class groups, though the evidence for this attractive proposal is slim (Quintilian, *Institutes* 5.11.19; Pliny, *Letter* 2.20.1). The heyday of the Greek novel coincided with the popularity of Christian apocryphal acts of apostles (second and third centuries A.D.), and many scholars (including Ernst von Dobschütz, Rosa Söder, and Richard Pervo) have emphasized their generic relationship.

The Genre of the Apocryphal Acts

Apocryphal Acts and the Greek Novel

The generic affinity between the apocryphal acts and the Greek novel has been thoroughly examined by Rosa Söder. She selected five "essential novelistic" features occurring in various combinations in ancient novelistic literature: (1) the demonstrations of supernatural power by the hero (i.e., the aretalogical element), (2) the travel theme, (3) religious or philosophical propaganda, (4) the love theme, and (5) interest in the exotic and unfamiliar (the teratological element). While aretalogical and teratological elements occur frequently in the apocryphal acts, they are absent from Greek novels. Yet the erotic element, which is prominent in the Greek novels, is absent from the apocryphal acts. According to Söder, the connection between the ancient novels and the apocryphal acts is only indirect. The latter have closer ties with a literary genre not otherwise preserved: popular narratives centering on the adventures, wonders, and romances of real or imaginary heroes.

The love theme, which is central to the novels, is treated in an entirely different way in the apocryphal acts. While the Greek novel narrates the involuntary *temporary* separation and final reunion of lovers, the apocryphal acts emphasize the *permanent* separation of lovers (virgins from fiancés, wives from husbands). Yet while the temporary separation of lovers moves the plot in Greek novels (functioning as the exciting force), the motif of permanent separation in the apocryphal acts provides dramatic tension only for individual episodes. In many episodes in the apocryphal acts, tension is generated by the desire for sexual abstinence on the part of converted women and the desire of unconverted lovers or husbands for normal sexual or conjugal relations. The apostles, depicted as holy men, act as agents of the supernatural world in facilitating this religiously motivated "alienation of affection." The apocryphal acts, in contrast to the Greek novel, exhibit a negative view of the world reflecting the outlook of the Christian communities that produced them.

The travel theme functions in different ways in both types of literature. In most Greek novels travel to distant places prolongs the tension of the plot, which is moved by the separation of two lovers (testing and proving their mutual fidelity). Travel accounts also provide entertainment for readers by describing exotic features of faraway places and peoples. Yet the travel theme is not indispensable. It is missing in Longus' *Daphnis and Chloe*, is hardly significant in the *Acts of Peter*, and even in the *Acts of Thomas* is only mentioned three times (3–4, 16–17, 68–71). Even in the apocryphal acts that emphasize travel to a greater extent *(Acts of Paul, Acts Jn., Acts Andr.)*, itineraries loosely connect individual dramatic episodes, while the composition as a whole lacks dramatic unity.

Apocryphal Acts and Canonical Acts

The titles of the apocryphal acts imitated the title *Praxeis*, which was affixed to the canonical Acts before A.D. 150. The generic links between the canonical and apocryphal acts go beyond the imitation of a title, for it is likely that the former inspired the production of the latter. There are important similarities and differences between canonical Acts and the apocryphal acts. (1) The author of canonical Acts presents his work as *history*, while it is clear that the authors of the apocryphal acts were basically writing fiction. (2) While the apostles are depicted as stereotypical holy men in the apocryphal acts, this imagery is only marginal in canonical Acts (e.g., the healing qualities of Peter's shadow, Acts 5:15; Paul's miraculous handkerchiefs, 19:12). (3) While the literary focus of the apocryphal acts is the individual episode, canonical Acts, while lacking a "plot" in the conventional sense, nevertheless has chronological movement toward a goal, the proclamation of the gospel in Rome. Yet despite these superficial differences, it seems clear that the canonical Acts has provided a literary paradigm for the apocryphal acts.

Apocryphal Acts and Lives of Philosophers

Apocryphal acts are not biographies, for they show little direct concern with the lives of the apostles before Jesus' death and resurrection. The figure of the apostle is chiefly of interest as a messenger of God who both exemplifies and proclaims Christian truth. There are therefore many similarities between apostles depicted in the apocryphal acts and contemporary biographies of philosophers (e.g., Philostratus' *Life of Apollonius* and the lives of Pythagoras by Iamblichus and Porphyry). There are, for example, striking similarities between the *Acts of Thomas* and the *Life of Apollonius* of Philostratus (born ca. A.D. 170). Both Thomas and Apollonius travel to the exotic land of India; both have dealings with nobility (Thomas visits the Indian king Gundaphorus); both preach, perform miracles, and experience persecution and suffering. Yet the suppressed eroticism of *Acts of Thomas* has no counterpart in the *Life of Apollonius,* and the structure of *Acts of Thomas* is more complex than that of the novels.

Conclusions

Richard Pervo, in his attempt to link the apocryphal acts with canonical Acts and the ancient novel *generically,* objects to the view that the themes of love and travel are generic hallmarks of the novel (Apuleius' *Metamorphoses* is not a love story, and Longus' *Daphnis and Chloe* lacks travel). Pervo provides a comprehensive definition of ancient novels as lengthy and entertaining fictional prose narratives that project the ideal individual and social aspirations of the readers onto characters who accomplish these ideals by transcending the limits of ordinary life. In this definition, only the term *fiction* distinguishes the novel from the various forms of ancient historiography. That is, Pervo's definition is so broad that a *type* rather than a *genre* of ancient literature has been defined. The apocryphal acts have several features in common with the Greek novel, the canonical Acts, and the second- and third-century lives of philosophers. The distinctive traditions of popular Christianity have been combined with the form and function of traditional fiction to provide a new vehicle for the entertainment and edification of ordinary Christians in late antiquity.

For Further Study

On Luke-Acts: Henry J. Cadbury, *The Making of Luke-Acts* (Macmillan Co., 1927); Leander E. Keck and J. Louis Martyn, eds., *Studies in Luke-Acts* (Abingdon Press, 1966). A dated but still useful survey to about 1960 is C. K. Barrett, *Luke the Historian in Recent Study* (Fortress Press, 1970). See also I. Howard Marshall, *Luke: Historian and Theologian* (Exeter: Paternoster Press, 1970), and Robert Maddox, *The Purpose of Luke-Acts* (Edinburgh: T. & T. Clark, 1982). C. H. Talbert has edited two volumes of helpful studies on Luke-Acts: *Perspectives on Luke-Acts* (Association of Baptist Professors of Religion, 1978), and *Luke-Acts: New Perspectives from the Society of Biblical Literature Seminar* (Crossroad Publishing Co., 1984). Two collections of important essays by Jacob Jervell are *Luke and the People of God* (Augsburg Publishing House, 1972) and *The Unknown Paul: Essays on Luke-Acts and Early Christian History* (Augsburg Publishing House, 1984).

On Luke: For a review of research on Luke, see M. Rese, "Das Lukas-Evangelium: Ein Forschungsbericht," *ANRW* II.25.2, 2258–2328. The most important commentary is Joseph A. Fitzmyer, *The Gospel According to Luke*, 2 vols., Anchor Bible (Doubleday & Co., 1981–85). Another excellent recent commentary is I. Howard Marshall, *The Gospel of Luke: A Commentary on the Greek Text* (Wm. B. Eerdmans Publishing Co., 1978).

On Acts: The history of scholarly research on Acts is reviewed by W. Ward Gasque, *A History of the Criticism of the Acts of the Apostles* (Wm. B. Eerdmans Publishing Co., 1975). For a conservative perspective on Acts research see F. F. Bruce, "The Acts of the Apostles: Historical Record or Theological Reconstruction," *ANRW* II.25.2, 2569–2603. Recent research is summarized and critiqued by Eckhard Plümacher, "Acta-Forschung 1974–1982," *Theologische Rundschau* 48 (1983), 1–56; 49 (1984), 105–169. The best commentaries on Acts include Gerhard Schneider, *Die Apostelgeschichte*, 2 vols. (Freiburg: Herder, 1980–82); Ernst Haenchen, *The Acts of the Apostles, A Commentary* (Westminster Press, 1971); Martin Dibelius, *Studies in the Acts of the Apostles*, ed. by H. Greeven (London: SCM Press, 1956).

On the Genre of Luke-Acts: Richard I. Pervo, *Profit with Delight: The Literary Genre of the Acts of the Apostles* (Fortress Press, 1987); S. P. Schierling and M. J. Schierling, "The Influence of the Ancient Romances on Acts of the Apostles," *Classical Bulletin* 54 (1978), 81–88; Charles H. Talbert, *Literary Patterns, Theological Themes and the Genre of Luke-Acts* (Scholars Press, 1974).

Formal Features of Luke-Acts: *Language and Style:* H. J. Cadbury, *The Style and Literary Method of Luke*, Harvard Theological Studies, 6 (Harvard University Press, 1920); John C. Hawkins, *Horae Synopticae: Contributions to the Study of the Synoptic Problem*, 2nd ed. (Oxford: Clarendon Press, 1909), pp. 174–197. *Literary Patterns:* W. Radl, *Die Parallelen von Lukas-Evangelium und Apostelgeschichte* (Frankfurt: Lang, 1979); Charles H. Talbert, *Literary Patterns, Theological Themes and the Genre of Luke-Acts* (Scholars Press, 1974).

A volume containing a mine of information on Luke-Acts in connection with ancient literary and epigraphical forms is Frederick W. Danker, *Benefactor: Epigraphic Study of a Graeco-Roman and New Testament Semantic Field* (Clayton Publishing House, 1982).

Form Criticism of Acts: Martin Dibelius, "Style Criticism of the Book of Acts," in idem, *Studies in the Acts of the Apostles*, ed. by H. Greeven (London: SCM Press, 1956), pp. 1–25; Eduard Norden, *Agnostos Theos: Untersuchungen zur Formengeschichte religiöser Rede* (Darmstadt, 1956).

On the Prefaces of Luke-Acts: H. J. Cadbury, "Commentary on the Preface of Luke," *Beginnings*, vol. 2, 489–510. An excellent recent discussion with full bibliographical references is Richard J. Dillon, "Previewing Luke's Project from His Prologue (Luke 1:1–4)," *CBQ* 43 (1981), 205–227. See also Vernon K. Robbins, "Prefaces in Greco-Roman Biography and Luke-Acts," *Perspectives in Religious Studies* 6 (1979), 94–108. An important recent article is Loveday Alexander, "Luke's Preface in the Context of Greek Preface-Writing," *NovT* 28 (1986), 48–74.

On Genealogies: The two basic works on biblical genealogy are M. D. Johnson, *The Purpose of the Biblical Genealogies* (Cambridge: University Press, 1969), and Robert R. Wilson, *Genealogy and History in the Biblical World* (Yale University Press, 1977). On Greek genealogy see Molly Broadbent, *Studies in Greek Genealogy* (Leiden: E. J. Brill, 1968). The Greco-Roman background is stressed in W. Speyer, "Genealogie," *RAC*, IX, cols. 1145–1268. See particularly W. S. Kurz, "Luke 3:23–38 and Greco-Roman Biblical Genealogies," in *Luke-Acts: New Perspectives from the Society of Biblical Literature Seminar*, ed. by C. H. Talbert (Crossroad Publishing Co., 1984), pp. 169–187.

On Dramatic Episodes: The most important study is E. Plümacher, *Lukas als hellenistischer Schriftsteller* (Göttingen: Vandenhoeck & Ruprecht, 1972), pp. 80–136. On Acts 27:1–28:16, see M. P. O. Morford, *The Poet Lucan: Studies in Rhetorical Epic* (Oxford: Basil Blackwell, 1967), pp. 20–36, and S. M. Praeder, "Acts 27:1–28:16: Sea Voyages in Ancient Literature and the Theology of Luke-Acts," *CBQ* 46 (1984), 683–706, which refers to the relevant primary and secondary sources. See also G. B. Miles and G. Trompf, "Luke and Antiphon: The Theology of Acts 27–28 in the Light of Pagan Beliefs About Divine Retribution, Pollution, and Shipwreck," *HTR* 69 (1976), 259–267, expanded and critiqued by D. Ladouceur, "Hellenistic Preconceptions of Shipwreck and Pollution as a Context for Acts 27–28," *HTR* 73 (1980), 435–449.

On Speeches: An essential earlier study is H. J. Cadbury, "The Speeches of Acts," *Beginnings*, vol. 5, 402–427. The basic modern study is Martin Dibelius, "The Speeches in Acts and Ancient Historiography," in idem, *Studies in the Acts of the Apostles*, ed. by H. Greeven (London: SCM Press, 1956), pp. 138–185. Particularly excellent is Paul Schubert's "The Final Cycle of Speeches in the Book of Acts," *JBL* 87 (1968), 1–16. Ulrich Wilckens, *Die Missionsreden der Apostelgeschichte* (Neukirchen-Vluyn: Neukirchener

Verlag, 1961), doubts the authenticity of the six speeches to Jewish audiences but finds traditional patterns in those directed toward pagans. Two helpful articles are the analyses of the mission speeches by Eduard Schweizer, "Concerning the Speeches in Acts," in *Studies in Luke-Acts*, ed. by L. E. Keck and J. L. Martyn (Abingdon, 1966), pp. 208–216, and Paul's defense speeches by Jerome Neyrey, "The Forensic Defense Speech and Paul's Trial Speeches in Acts 22–26: Form and Function," in *Luke–Acts*, ed. by C. H. Talbert (Crossroad Publishing Co., 1984), pp. 210–224.

On Symposia: Important secondary literature is cited and the three Lukan passages discussed in E. S. Steele, "Luke 11:37–54—A Modified Hellenistic Symposium?" *JBL* 103 (1984), 379–394. The single most important discussion of the genre is Josef Martin, *Symposion: Die Geschichte einer literarischen Form* (Paderborn: Verlag Ferdinand Schoeningh, 1931). On the symposion and the Jewish Seder, see S. Stein, "The Influence of Symposia Literature on the Literary Form of the Pesah Haggadah," *JJS* 8 (1957), 13–44. For a recent critical review of Stein's proposal see Baruch M. Bokser, *The Origins of the Seder* (University of California, 1984), pp. 10–12, 50–66.

On "We" Passages: An important recent article that discusses the possible interpretations is E. Plümacher, "Wirklichkeitserfahrung und Geschichtsschreibung bei Lukas: Erwägungen zu den Wir-Stücken der Apostelgeschichte," *ZNW* 68 (1977), 2–22. Jacques Dupont, *The Sources of the Acts*, tr. by K. Pond (Herder & Herder, 1964), pp. 75–165, reviews research and supports the itinerary hypothesis. Vernon K. Robbins, "By Land and by Sea: The We-Passages and Ancient Sea Voyages," in *Perspectives on Luke-Acts*, ed. by C. H. Talbert (Association of Baptist Professors of Religion, 1978), pp. 215–242. Robbins' proposals are persuasively qualified by Colin J. Hemer, "First Personal Narrative in Acts 27–28," *TB* 36 (1985), 79–109. E. Haenchen, " 'We' in Acts and the Itinerary," *Journal for Theology and the Church* 1 (1965), 65–99. G. I. Davies, "The Wilderness Itineraries: A Comparative Study," *TB* 25 (1974), 46–81, is a mine of information about Near Eastern and Greco-Roman itinerary literature.

On Ancient Novels: The best general introduction to the Greek novel is Thomas Hägg, *The Novel in Antiquity* (University of California Press, 1983), with an extensive annotated bibliography on pp. 235–250. An exceptionally important treatment is B. P. Reardon, *Courants Littéraires Grecs des IIe et IIIe siècles après J.-C.* (Paris: Les Belles Lettres, 1971), pp. 309–405. Also important are Ben Edwin Perry, *The Ancient Romances: A Literary-Historical Account of Their Origins* (University of California Press, 1967), and A. Scobie, *Aspects of the Ancient Romance and Its Heritage* (Meisenheim/Glan, 1969). The classical study on the subject is Erwin Rohde, *Der griechische Roman und seine Vorläufer*, 2nd ed. (Leipzig: Teubner, 1900). For a guide to recent research see G. N. Sandy, "Recent Scholarship on the Prose Fiction of Classical Antiquity," *Classical World* 67 (1974), 321–359. On individual novels, see Albert Henrichs, *Die Phoinikika des Lollianos: Fragmente eines neuen griechischen Romans* (Bonn: Rudolf Habelt Verlag, 1972), which should be read in conjunction with Jack Winkler, "Lollianos and the Desperadoes," *JHS* 100 (1980), 155–181. See also B. P. Reardon, "Theme, Structure and Narrative in Chariton," in *Later Greek Literature*, ed. by John J. Winkler and Gordon Williams, Yale Classical Studies, 27 (Cambridge: University Press, 1982), pp. 1–27; Gareth L. Schmeling, *Chariton* (Twayne Publishers, 1974); Sophie Trenker, *The Greek Novella in the Classical Period* (Cambridge: University Press, 1958); John J. Winkler, *Auctor & Actor: A Narratological Reading of Apuleius' The Golden Ass* (University of California Press, 1985).

On Apocryphal Acts: Indispensable for extensive introductory articles and translations into English of the major apocryphal acts is Edgar Hennecke, *New Testament Apocrypha*, ed. by Wilhelm Schneemelcher, tr. by R. McL. Wilson et al, vol. 2 (Westminster Press, 1966). François Bovon et al., *Les actes apocryphes des apôtres: christianisme et monde païen* (Geneva: Labor et Fides, 1981), is an indispensable work containing many important articles and a recent bibliography. Idiosyncratic but valuable is Steven L. Davies' *The Revolt of the Widows: The Social World of the Apocryphal Acts* (Southern Illinois University Press, 1980). E. von Dobschütz, "Der Roman in der altchristlichen Literatur," *Deutsche Rundschau* 111 (1902), 87–106, first proposed a generic link between the apocryphal acts and the novel. Important discussions of the "holy man" image are Peter Brown, "The Rise and Function of the Holy Man in Late Antiquity," *JRS* 61 (1971), 80–101, and G. Fowden, "The Pagan Holy Man in Late Antique Society," *JHS* 102 (1982), 33–59. See also A. F. J. Klijn, *The Acts of Thomas* (Leiden: E. J. Brill, 1962). Dennis Ronald MacDonald, *The Legend and the Apostle: The Battle for Paul in Story and Canon* (Westminster Press, 1983), is an excellent study in which oral traditions behind the *Acts of Paul* are seen reflected (and opposed) in the Pastoral letters of Pseudo-Paul. See also Richard I. Pervo, *Profit with Delight: The Literary Genre of the Acts of the Apostles* (Fortress Press, 1987); E. Plümacher, "Apokryphe Apostelakten," *RE*, suppl. vol. XV (Munich, 1978), cols. 11–70; S. M. Praeder, "Luke-Acts and the Ancient Novel," *Society of Biblical Literature: 1981 Seminar Papers*, ed. by K. H. Richards (Scholars Press, 1981), pp. 269–292; William M. Ramsay, "The Acta of Paul and Thekla," in idem, *The Church in the Roman Empire Before A.D. 170* (London: Hodder & Stoughton, 1897), pp. 375–428; S. P. Schierling and M. J. Schierling, "The Influence of the Ancient Romances on Acts of the Apostles," *Classical Bulletin* 54 (1978), 81–88; Rosa Söder, *Die apocryphen Apostelgeschichten und die romanhafte Literatur der Antike* (Stuttgart: W. Kohlhammer, 1932); R. McL. Wilson, "Apokryphen, II. Apokryphen des Neuen Testaments," *Theologische Realenzyklopädie*, III, 341–348.

5

Letters
in the Ancient World

The letter form exhibited great flexibility in the ancient world. Virtually any type of written text could be sent to individuals or groups in an epistolary format. Most letters, whether ancient or modern, are written communications addressed to individuals or groups from whom the sender is separated by distance or social status. The letter is therefore a substitute for oral communication and could function in almost as many ways as speech. In ancient times letters were usually carried by messengers, but not all messengers carried letters. Messengers also transmitted oral messages or oral elaborations of written letters. The Greek word *epistolē* ("epistle") originally referred to an *oral* communication sent by messenger (Herodotus 4.10.1; Thucydides 7.11.1). Whether people met personally or sent messages (oral or written), etiquette prescribed an opening greeting and a concluding farewell.

The overlap between letter and speech suggests two important dimensions for understanding the former. First, oratory was very important in the Greco-Roman world and rhetoric occupied a central role in ancient education. Though primarily connected with oral delivery, rhetoric had a profound effect on all genres of literature including letters. A knowledge of ancient rhetorical theory, therefore, can contribute to understanding letters written by ancients (like Paul and Ignatius) who had more than a basic education. Second, throughout the ancient world there was a high degree of social stratification. Consequently, systems of etiquette prescribed socially appropriate modes of behavior and speech for relating to persons of higher, equal, or lower social status in various situations. In letters, where the sender communicates with a person or group, the social status and relationship of sender and receiver will inevitably influence both *what* is said and *how* it is said.

The relationship between written and oral communication, how-ever, can be exaggerated. While there are many similarities between written letters and oral communications, there are also significant differences in language, style, and structure. We do not write the way we speak. Neither did the ancients. Oral communication, for example, tends to be *linear* or *sequential*. The immediate context for a statement is the preceding statement and the "interpretive" para-linguistic features of gesture, tempo, inflection, rhythm, and voice quality. While written texts can also be linear, the reader has the advantage of being able to reread earlier sections of a document not completely understood or fully appreciated on the first reading. Yet since written texts must do without the paralinguistic features of speech, they must be written in a special way to function without an "interpreter" (Plato, *Phaedrus* 275e).

The "letter" was the most popular literary form in early Christi-anity. It is also the most problematic since it exhibits more variety and flexibility than any other literary form. There are twenty-two "letters" in the New Testament. Twenty are independent writings; two are embedded in the text of Acts. They include (1) written communications between individuals (1–2 Timothy, Titus, 2–3 John); (2) written communications between individuals and specific groups (most of Paul's letters); (3) circular letters sent to several communities (Galatians, Ephesians, James, 1–2 Peter, Jude); (4) the letter form used as a framing device for another genre (Revelation); (5) an anonymous homily with an epistolary conclusion but without an epistolary prescription (Hebrews); and (6) "embedded" letters (Acts 15:23–26; 23:26–30). The seven embedded "letters" in Rev. 2–3 are not really letters but prophetic proclamations patterned after ancient royal and imperial edicts. First John has been called a letter, but lacks the salutation and conclusion typical of ancient letters.

Of the fifteen individual compositions by nine authors of the Apostolic Fathers (written ca. A.D. 90–140), twelve are in letter form. The seven letters of Ignatius include paraenetic letters written to five churches and one individual (Polycarp of Smyrna), and one letter of advice written to the Roman church. Polycarp's letter to the Philippians is primarily paraenetic. *First Clement* is a lengthy letter of advice written from Rome to the Corinthian church. The *Epistle to Diognetus* is a protreptic ("persuasive") letter that tries to convince the reader of the truth of Christianity. *Barnabas* is an extensive homily based on a convoluted exegesis of the Old Testament. The *Martyrdom of Polycarp* is an account of the circumstances leading up to the execution of Polycarp written up as a circular letter. The great variety evident in this brief survey of early Christian letters underscores the ambiguity of the "letter" form.

Greco-Roman Letters

Early Christian letters have many formal similarities to the ancient papyrus letters recovered from Egypt by the thousands from the garbage dumps where they were discarded and from the cardboard coffin liners into which they were recycled. Yet while nearly all the papyrus letters are relatively brief, many early Christian letters are quite lengthy. Their very length suggests a comparison with the longer literary and official letters of antiquity preserved in epistolary collections, embedded in literary narratives or inscribed on stone.

Adolf Deissmann, a pioneer in the comparative analysis of ancient letters, defined them as private personal conversations between people separated by distance. Because he saw similarities between the recovered papyrus Greek common letters and the authentic letters of Paul, he distinguished *true letters* (which are natural, spontaneous, and private) from *literary letters* or *epistles* (mechanical, artistic, and public). Deissmann considered all of the authentic letters of Paul, together with 2–3 John, as *true letters,* but the Pastorals and most of the Catholic letters (Hebrews, James, 1–2 Peter, Jude) as *epistles.* Deissmann's influential distinction between letters and epistles has obscured rather than clarified the spectrum of possibilities that separated the short personal letter from the literary letters of antiquity. There are, for example, no really private letters among Paul's authentic letters. Nor was Deissmann sensitive to stylistic differences between papyrus letters and Pauline letters. The letters of Paul and Seneca, for instance, exhibit a dialogical style quite different from anything found in papyrus letters.

Letters and Rhetoric

The vast majority of ancient letters were relatively short communications written for a specific occasion and discarded soon afterward. By the first century B.C., rhetoric had come to exert a strong influence on the composition of letters, particularly among the educated. Their letters functioned not only as means of communication but also as sophisticated instruments of persuasion and media for displaying literary skill.

Earlier Greco-Roman rhetorical handbooks have little to say about the art of letter writing. The two most important treatments of epistolary theory are *On Style* 4.223–235 (ca. first century B.C.), incorrectly ascribed to Demetrius of Phalerum, and *Epistolary Styles* (fourth to sixth centuries A.D.), erroneously ascribed to Proclus or Libanius. Cicero's familiarity with Greek epistolary theory indicates that handbooks on epistolography were circulating during the first century B.C. Also important is Pseudo-Demetrius' *Epistolary Types* (first century B.C. or later), and an appendix entitled "On Letter Writing" in the *Rhetorical Arts* of Julius Victor (fourth century A.D.).

Types of Letters

Aside from Deissmann's distinction between real letters and literary epistles (which had the advantage of simplicity), few typologies of Greco-Roman or early Christian letters have been proposed and none widely adopted. Distinctions between private and official letters, documentary and nondocumentary letters, have proven only slightly less problematic than Deissmann's distinction between nonliterary and literary letters.

One ancient method of categorizing letters was by *content*. Cicero, for example, distinguished between news letters, domestic letters, letters of recommendation, letters of consolation, and letters promising assistance (*To Friends* 2.4.1; 4.13.1; 5.5.1). A. N. Sherwin-White (1966), synthesizing up to thirteen ancient types, suggests eight types: (1) public affairs (including history, anecdotes, gossip); (2) character sketches; (3) patronage; (4) admonitions; (5) domestic affairs; (6) literary matters (e.g., composition, criticism); (7) scenic; and (8) social courtesy.

Treatises on ancient epistolary theory provided lengthy lists of letter types together with short samples. The *Epistolary Types* of Pseudo-Demetrius, for example, describes twenty-one types (e.g., friendly, commendatory, blaming, reproachful, consoling, censorious). Forty-one epistolary types are discussed by Pseudo-Libanius in *Epistolary Styles*. These epistolary types generally conform to many of the nineteen aspects of epideictic oratory elaborated by Quintilian (3.4.3), and most of them are subtle variations of the Greek letter of advice *(logos protreptikos* or *logos parainetikos)*. These types all focus on the purpose of the body of the letter and ignore formal epistolary features found in the openings and closings (opening and closing formulas are usually omitted from ancient model letters). Pseudo-Libanius recommends that epistolary prescripts be very plain: "X to Y, greetings" (*Epistolary Styles* 51). Recently Stanley Stowers (1986) has proposed a typology of six epistolary types of Greco-Roman letters largely based on ancient epistolary theory: (1) letters of friendship; (2) family letters; (3) letters of praise and blame (functions of epideictic rhetoric); (4) hortatory letters (with seven subtypes: paraenetic letters, protreptic letters, letters of advice, admonition, rebuke, reproach, and consolation); (5) letters of recommendation (or mediation); and (6) accusing, apologetic, and accounting letters (functions of juridical rhetoric), found in letters of petition. Stowers recognizes that while some epistolary types conform to one of the three species of rhetoric (judicial, deliberative, epideictic), others resist such categories (e.g., letters of exhortation). Following the epistolary theorists, Stowers views letters *functionally,* i.e., in terms of the actions that people intended to perform through them. Consequently one must understand the typical social occasions that provided the context for letter writing, i.e., the Greco-Roman social conventions for communicating with equals or with people of higher or lower status. Stowers' typology is significant because it applies to the full spectrum of Greco-Roman letters, from the bottom to the top of ancient society. Letters of exhortation and advice is a complex category and many letters of this type exhibit mixtures of various types of exhortation.

The epistolary typology proposed by Stowers has disadvantages as well as advantages. Ancient official letters, an important and influential type of correspondence, play little or no part in his typology. Further, many types of literary letters, embedded letters, or the use of epistolary conventions to frame literary works are not considered. For these reasons we shall survey Greco-Roman letters in terms of three additional categories—private or documentary letters, official letters, and literary letters—though rigid boundaries cannot be placed between these categories.

Private or Documentary Letters

Documentary (i.e., nonliterary) private letters constitute the common letter tradition of antiquity, a tradition that remained stable from the Ptolemaic period (third century B.C., the date of the earliest papyrus letters) to the Roman period (third century A.D. and later). The thousands of ancient papyrus letters preserved by the dry Egyptian climate provide the bulk of our knowledge of the ancient Greek common letter tradition. Such letters functioned in three basic ways: to maintain contact with family and friends, to communicate information, to request information or favors. Private letters therefore include several types determined by function: (1) letters of request or petition; (2) letters of information; (3) letters of introduction; (4) letters of order and instruction; (5) family letters; and (6) business letters (contracts, leases, receipts, etc.). While some letters exhibit only one function, others function in several ways.

The conventions of modern American personal and business letters are relatively fixed. Private letters in the Greco-Roman world were even more stereotyped. The ancient Greek letter regularly consisted of three parts: opening formulas, main part or body, and closing formulas. This basic structure with its constituent stereotyped features and formulas changed only slightly through the centuries.

The *prescript* of the ancient letter typically contained three elements, the superscription (sender), the adscription (addressee), and the salutation: "X [nominative] to Y [dative], greetings [*chairein*]." A more formal variant (used in petitions, complaints, and applications) is "To Y [dative] from X," usually omitting the salutation. These two patterns are found from the third century B.C. to the third century A.D. Many variations are also found. The basic pattern of Greek epistolary prescripts was subject to various forms of amplification and elaboration. The superscription and adscription could be expanded through the addition of epithets, titles, terms of relationship ("X to his sister Y") and endearment ("X to my dearest friend Y"), and geographical location. The salutation was also capable of expansion by using adjectives or adverbs emphasizing degree ("warmest greetings") or by adding a health wish ("greetings and health"). This capacity for amplification allowed the Christian letter to develop its own distinctive features.

The *formula valetudinis* or health (*hygiainein*) wish (also found at the close) often followed the prescript: "If you are well, it would be excellent. I too am well." Since there are several health formulas that exhibit some variation, the health wish might better be described as a *topos* or theme. The *errōsthai* wish (from the third century B.C. on) could occupy a separate position at the beginning of the main part of the letter separate from the prescript, or it could be joined syntactically to the salutation of the prescript: "greetings and best wishes" [*chairein kai errōsthai*].

The *proskynēma formula*, a prayer (often of thanksgiving; *proskynēma* means "act of worship"), frequently either follows or is blended with the formula of health. Compare Hunt-Edgar, no. 97: "Isias to her brother Hephaestion, greeting. If you are well and other things are going right, it would accord with the prayer which I make continually to the gods." Another example from Hunt-Edgar is no. 120: "Antonius Longus to Nilous his mother, very many greetings. I pray always for your health; every day I make supplication for you before the Lord Serapis." This prayer report formula appears in the first century A.D. and remains popular until the fourth century.

The *closing greeting,* or *aspazesthai* wish, sometimes occurs in place of the *hygiainein* wish at the beginning of the main part of the letter, but by the first century B.C. it is placed most often at the end of the letter.

The *closing formulas* most commonly used were *errōso* or *errōsthe* ("farewell"), and also the verb *(di)eutychei* ("farewell" or "best wishes"), frequently with the date. The closing formula could also be omitted.

Formulas at the conclusion of the main part include "take care of yourself that you might be well" (from the third century B.C.). This was gradually replaced by the *aspazesthai* ("greeting") formula, from the first century B.C. on, in which the writer asks the recipient to greet acquaintances not directly addressed and/or conveys the greetings of others. There is also the illiteracy formula ("X writes on behalf of Y"), usually in business letters and official letters. Oath formulas occur at the end of certain types of business letters such as sworn declarations and various official statements.

Official Letters

Official letters are those which are written from a government head or representative to others in an official capacity. The form and style of official letters is similar to private letters. The ancients were very familiar with such letters since they were often published by posting or by inscription on stones placed in prominent places for public viewing. Publication meant that they were tools for influencing public opinion.

By the second century B.C. the Hellenistic monarchies in the Greek east had developed bureaucracies with royal chanceries whose staff drew up and preserved official governmental correspondence and kept archival copies of all royal edicts. Typically, a city's request was presented to the king by ambassadors. The request could be the acceptance of honors voted to the monarch, for which various favors might be asked in return (e.g., arbitration of a dispute, settlement of a legal point). The king would then draft a reply which the chancery staff would put in finished form. The king added a concluding "farewell" himself. The heads of these royal chanceries gave such letters a distinctive form and style. The prescripts reflect the conventions of the private letter: "X [nominative] to Y [dative], greetings [*chairein*]," and concludes with *errōsthe* ("farewell"), written on the original document by the king himself. Rhetoric influenced chancery correspondence only very slowly. C. Bradford Welles, editor of the standard collection of these royal letters, distinguished between two basic forms of official letters, one containing a statement or announcement alone (e.g., praise, royal decision, or a favor), and another containing a statement that is the basis for an order.

During the Republic, official Roman correspondence took the form of letters sent by the Roman Senate or magistrates to officials of foreign cities outlining official policy in particular matters. During the Empire, diplomatic correspondence was very common. *Epistulae principum* ("imperial epistles") and *rescripta* (written responses by the emperor to the queries of officials) were the primary means for the emperor to create law and convey his will to provincial cities. *Epistulae principum* were issued only by the *Ab epistulis,* the imperial bureau (with both Greek and Latin departments) concerned with the emperor's private and official correspondence.

Official Roman letters of the late Republic and early Empire addressed to Greek cities followed Hellenistic models. Senatorial decrees and other official communications were translated into Greek (a measure taken for no other language group under Roman authority) and published as inscriptions. They usually begin with a typical epistolary prescript: "X [nominative] to Y [dative], greetings [*chairein*]." The adscript includes the name of the city in the genitive and the name or names of city officials or governing bodies in the dative. After 150 B.C. official letters sometimes include the health formula after the greeting. Motives for writing, such as information or requests from Greek envoys, are then mentioned. Also included are the names of the Greek envoys, where they met the magistrate, and the information they brought. The body of such letters then included such matters as (1) the bestowal of various benefits, (2) the restoration of land, (3) decisions and edicts, (4) arbitration, (5) the communication of *senatus consulta* ("resolutions of the senate"). Diplomatic letters conclude with a wish for the well-being of the addressee, usually *errōsthe* ("farewell") in imitation of Hellenistic letters.

Literary Letters

Literary letters are those which were preserved and transmitted through literary channels and were valued either as epistolary models, as examples of literary artistry, or as vignettes into earlier lives and manners. They exhibit wide variety, including (1) real letters written by an educated person with no thought of publication (e.g., many of the *epistulae commendaticidae* or letters of recommendation by

Cicero, Pliny, and Fronto); (2) real letters written with a broader public in view (Cicero, Pliny, Libanius); (3) ideal letters using a "high" style and written with publication in view (Horace, Ovid, Seneca, Statius); (4) fictional letters using epistolary conventions to frame human interest stories or interesting anecdotes (Alciphron, Aelian, Philostratus); (5) fictional letters composed for insertion in historical and fictional narratives and/or those written as rhetorical exercises as if by some famous person (Achilles Tatius, Chariton); (6) letter-essays (*syggrammata;* Pseudo-Demetrius, *On Style* 4.228), in which essays or treatises on various subjects are prefaced by an epistolary prescript (Plutarch, Fronto).

Letters of Recommendation

Commendationes or letters of recommendation played an increasingly important role in upper-class society from the end of the Roman republic to late antiquity. They are the Roman counterpart of the Greek letter of introduction mentioned in the epistolary theorists (Pseudo-Demetrius, *Epistolary Types* 2; Pseudo-Libanius, *Epistolary Styles* 8). Many letters of this type are preserved in the epistolary collections of Cicero (106–43 B.C.), Pliny (ca. A.D. 61–112), Fronto (A.D. 100–166), and Libanius (A.D. 314–393). The collection of Cicero's letters, made during the principate of Nero (ca. A.D. 60), contains numerous letters of recommendation that served as models for later writers (cf. the ten *commendationes* to Acilius in *To His Friends* 13.30–39). The Roman empire was fundamentally a patronage system in which *vertical* bonds between people of different classes or orders took precedence over *horizontal* relationships between equals (thus effectively preventing an ancient "class consciousness"). The reciprocity ethic (favors bestowed incurred obligation) permeated all aspects of life, between people and the gods, within families, and among friends. Influential patrons could recommend their clients for administrative positions under the control of those (like the emperor) who could exercise personal discretion in such appointments. The patronage system meant that officials characteristically used their position to secure benefits for family and friends. Influential men like Cicero, Pliny, and Fronto recommended their protégés on the basis of moral qualities (e.g., uprightness, soberness, intelligence, diligence; cf. Fronto, *To Marcus* 5.37; cf. *To Friends* 1.1–5, 8; *To Pius* 9) rather than professional skills. The Roman conception of friendship had an important utilitarian aspect —i.e., the mutually beneficial exchange of various kinds of goods and services—since there were no impersonal institutional means for distribution. A letter of recommendation was in effect an act of friendship, addressed to one friend on behalf of another friend.

Letter-Essays

Letter-essays are treatises that make only a limited use of some epistolary conventions, particularly in opening formulas. Epistolary prefaces, for instance, appear for the first time in the scientific treatises of Archimedes (287–212 B.C.), both addressed and dedicated to friends. Seneca was the first rhetorical writer to use epistolary prefaces (all of his *Moral Epistles* have them). Quintilian introduces his *Institutes* with a double preface, one epistolary and the other rhetorical (revealing the close relationship between the two types). Pliny the Elder's *Natural History* also has a prose epistolary preface. The *Lives of the Sophists* (written after A.D. 202) of Philostratus has a prefatory letter. The *Rhetoric to Alexander,* a late third-century rhetorical handbook, is prefaced by a bogus letter with the prescript "Aristotle to Alexander, best wishes [*eu prattein*]," and concluded by a simple "farewell" *(errōso).*

Plutarch wrote several letter-essays. *On Tranquility* is a deliberative essay written in response to the addressee's request. Two other deliberative letter-essays are *Consolation to His Wife* (written when he learned, while abroad, of the death of their child) and *Conjugal Precepts* (advice to newlyweds). A fourth letter-essay is *On the Generation of the Soul* (a treatise on Plato's doctrine of the soul requested by his two sons). Plutarch always uses *eu prattein* ("best wishes") as a salutation, a formula used frequently in literary letters.

Philosophical Letters

The first century A.D. was a period when moral philosophers increasingly made use of the letter form as a vehicle for instruction. The letters of Plato and Aristotle were important models in this development (Plato's *Letter* 7, for example, was influential on later writers). The letters of Epicurus were among the most important models for this development. Several of his letters survive (actually philosophical treatises in epistolary form), though the one to Pythocles is of doubtful authenticity. Three letters are preserved in Diogenes Laertius 10.34–83, to Herodotus (epitomizing Epicurus' philosophy of nature), to Pythocles (summarizing his meteorology at the request of Pythocles), and to Menoeceus (summarizing Epicurean morality). The Letter to Menoeceus is a symbouleutic (protreptic) letter urging the study of philosophy.

Many pseudepigraphical letters and letter collections made their debut, including the lengthy collection attributed to Hippocrates (some of which exhibit the diatribe style), and the collections of Cynic letters attributed to such philosophers as Socrates, Anacharsis, Crates, Diogenes, and Heraclitus. The diatribe is transformed into epistolary form in the first century A.D. through Seneca, on the one hand, and the many collections of pseudepigraphical Cynic letters on the other (e.g., Diogenes, Heraclitus, Crates).

Novelistic Letters

Novelistic letters are fictional, often pseudepigraphical attempts to present stories and anecdotes about great past personalities. Some of these letters probably orginated as rhetorical exercises in *prosōpopoiia*, i.e., writing a speech in character for a famous historical or mythical person. During the early imperial period (first century A.D.) an unknown author proficient in Asianic rhetoric wrote several letters in imitation of Hippocrates. The author appears to be both a physician and a rhetorician (*Letter* 23.1); he is proficient at *prosōpopoiia*. The letters of Pseudo-Hippocrates are written with a basically apologetic motive, reflecting the rivalry between the medical schools at Cos and Cnidos represented by Hippocrates and Ctesias, respectively. The novelistic features of the Hippocratic letters are evident in *Letters* 3–5 (which circulated in excerpt form apart from the main corpus). They were popular because of the image of the ideal physician represented by Hippocrates: Artaxerxes writes to Hystanes offering a reward to Hippocrates if he will come to the Persian court (*Letter* 3), and Hystanes relays the message to Hippocrates (*Letter* 4). Hippocrates responds to Hystanes, refusing the offer and adding that he will not help enemies of the Greeks (*Letter* 5). Hippocrates' moral code, which leads him to treat the destitute sick rather than the wealthy Persian king, made this exchange popular.

Imaginative Letters

The main purpose of this type of letter is to entertain and delight the reader. The earliest collections of such letters go back to the second and third centuries A.D. Authors writing in this genre included Alciphron, Aelian, Aristaenetus, and Theophylactus (second through seventh centuries A.D.). The letters of Philostratus, while similar, purport to be his own. Fictional epistolography had many implicit rules, such as the exploitation of earlier writers, and the use of certain types of names for the correspondents (real names from the historical past, names from the characters in Greek comedy, and suitably metaphorical names). A collection of 122 fictional letters in four books was written by Alciphron (ca. third century A.D.). Following the nostalgic archaism of his day, he attributed them to Athenian fishermen, farmers, prostitutes, and freeloaders of the fourth century B.C., attempting to capture imaginatively the lives and outlooks of people many centuries earlier. Philostratus wrote a collection of 73 racy love letters to both boys and women.

Embedded Letters

Authors of historical, biographical, and fictional narratives of the Hellenistic period often inserted letters for documentary or dramatic reasons. While epistolary prescripts and postscripts tend to be abbreviated or eliminated in edited collections of letters, they are often left intact in embedded letters. It is therefore difficult to determine whether they are genuine, genuine but abbreviated, or simply inventions. Embedded letters in histories and biographies can be as fictional as those in novels. Diogenes Laertius, in his fanciful lives of the sages who preceded the philosophers, regularly inserts bogus letters where a list of writings is found for later philosophers (Thales, 1.42–44; Solon, 1.64–67; Chilon, 1.73; Pittacus, 1.81). One of the earliest Greek historians to use embedded letters (which function like speeches) was Thucydides. The letter of Nicias (7. 10–15), for example, reads like an oration and contains neither opening nor closing epistolary formulas. Nicias reportedly wrote a letter rather than trust the messenger's memory, and thus sent written and oral messages together (7.8.2). Similarly Thucydides quotes the substance of a letter of Pausanias to Xerxes (1.128.7), again without opening or closing formulas, but the response from Xerxes (1.29.3) has the characteristic Persian epistolary prescript: "Thus says King Xerxes to Pausanias." A letter of Themistocles found in Thucydides 1.137.4 is later transformed into a speech by Plutarch (*Themistocles* 28.1–2) and Diodorus Siculus (11.56.8).

Letters are regularly used as dramatic devices by the Greek novelists (Achilles Tatius 1.3.6; 5.18.2–6; 5.20.4–5; Chariton 4.5.8; 8. 4.2–3, 5–6). Philostratus' *Life of Apollonius*, which combines biographical with novelistic elements, contains 20 letters (e.g., 2.46; 4.27; 4.46 [four letters]; 6.29; 8.7.3), including excerpts from three letters (1.7, 24; 4.22). Most of these letters have the conventional form: "X [nominative] to Y [dative], greetings [*chairein*]," and the letters conclude with *errōso* or *errōsthe* ("farewell"). Some of these may be authentic.

Letters as Framing Devices

Epistolary prescripts and postscripts could be used to frame almost any kind of composition. The epistolary conventions of many letter-essays, philosophical letters, and novelistic and fictional letters functioned frequently in this way. In fictional and pseudepigraphical letters the epistolary conventions often function as a legitimating device setting the composition back to an earlier period or attributing it obviously to a famous person of the past. The letter form was frequently used for various types of legal documents. According to Roman law, a letter containing a legal document is enacted only when the addressee (or the latter's secretary or messenger) receives it. Sales, for example, could be concluded by letter, or a person could express some desires to an heir in a letter which then has the status of a codicil. Letters could also serve to acknowledge debts. In these cases the letter form is a convenient way of indicating the sender and recipient and of formalizing the transaction. Many legal documents, such as marriage contracts, divorce decrees, leases and wills, were written with formal opening and closing epistolary conventions.

Letter Collections

The Romans were more avid writers and collectors of letters than the Greeks. While Cicero, Horace, Seneca, and Pliny all had intentions of publishing some or all of their letters, the first Greek author to publish a collection of his own letters was Gregory Nazianzus (ca. A.D. 329–389). The seventeenth-century English classicist Richard Bentley persuasively demonstrated that ancient collections of Greek letters attributed to Phalaris, Themistocles, Socrates, and Euripides were forgeries. In consequence, the shadow of doubt has fallen on many other such collections, though some contain at least some authentic letters.

Some important representative collections of ancient Greek letters include those by Isocrates, Demosthenes, Epicurus, Apollonius of Tyana, and Libanius. The letters of Aristotle, surviving only in fragments, were collected and published after his death (384–322 B.C.). A collection of nine letters of Isocrates (436–338 B.C.) is still extant, though the authenticity of several is debated. A collection of six letters of Demosthenes (384–322 B.C.) has been preserved, four of which are authentic and two doubtful. Similarly a collection was made of the letters of Epicurus (341–270 B.C.), which became influential as models for philosophical letters.

A collection of 97 letters and letter fragments make up the correspondence of Apollonius of Tyana (died ca. A.D. 97); some may be authentic (e.g., *Letter* 71). In addition, 20 letters (*Letters* 98–117, following Hercher's numbering) are quoted in the *Life of Apollonius.* Philostratus claims to have used letters of Apollonius as sources (1.2, 23–24, 32). That suggests the existence of a collection. Philostratus also knows a collection of letters that Apollonius exchanged with Euphrates (5.39; *Letters* 1–8, 14–18, 60). While all of the letters of Apollonius have abbreviated openings (i.e., the name of the recipient in the dative, or "to the same person"), closing salutations (*errōso* or *errōsthe*) occur just four times (*Letters* 14, 43, 47, 53).

One of the great pagan letter writers of late antiquity was the Antiochean rhetorician Libanius, who wrote more than 1,600 letters. Libanius had an extensive network of personal connections, largely maintained by correspondence. Many letters recommended former students for employment to provincial governors (*Letters* 154, 161, 807). Others were letters of introduction requesting private hospitality for traveling students and friends (*Letters* 268, 704). He also reported on students' progress by writing reassuring letters to parents (*Letters* 141, 190, 324). For Libanius, letter writing was an art. Rigidly adhering to epistolary convention, he limited letters to a single topic. News and information extraneous to the letter were left to the bearer (*Letters* 753, 1429). Most of his letters have three sections: (1) expressions of friendship to recipient, (2) praise to the bearer, and (3) the main business of the letter. It was conventional to omit everything extraneous to the main purpose of the letter. Personal feelings (personal experiences, private ideas and opinions, etc.) were not expressed in letters except through such conventional *topoi* as longing, friendship, jealousy at the preference for another friend, consolation for a bereavement. Not to write when someone was going to see a person's friend was an injury (*Letters* 212, 326, 410). It was also bad manners to write to a stranger, and the beginning of a friendship demanded special justification (*Letters* 95, 448, 645, 836), since such a relationship might lead to a demand for favors. Libanius and his educated friends wrote with a wider public in view, for they publicly read letters received (*Letter* 1264; *Oration* 1.175), and expected recipients of theirs to do the same. Libanius consciously tried to give his letters a timeless quality so that they might have a permanent value transcending the original circumstances of their composition.

Important collections of Latin letters are attributed to Cicero and Pliny the Younger. The 931 letters of Cicero's extant correspondence between 68 and 43 B.C. were published posthumously (ca.

A.D. 60) in four collections (*To Friends, To Atticus, To Quintus,* 27 letters; *To Brutus,* 25 letters). Cicero intended to publish a small selection of his letters (*To Atticus* 16.5) that would illustrate his literary abilities (*To His Friends* 16.17.1), but he died without accomplishing this intention. Cicero kept copies of some of his letters (*To Friends* 7.25.1), and recipients such as Atticus retained them, perhaps pasting them together into rolls. Cornelius Nepos (*Atticus* 16. 2–4) refers to eleven rolls of Cicero's letters owned by Atticus. These perhaps constituted eleven of the sixteen books of letters to Atticus published later.

Pliny (A.D. 61–112) published nine books of 358 letters arranged chronologically. He usually limited letters to one theme, avoided excessive length, and used a style appropriate to the subject. The distinctive character of his letters suggests an origin in the oratorical digression, which characteristically treated the praise of persons or places, descriptions of places, and narratives of historical or legendary events (Quintilian 4.3.12). The literary character of Pliny's letters is also evident in his use of standardized opening phrases indicating the subject of letters.

Epistolary Topoi

The *topoi* ("themes" or "commonplaces") of ancient friendly letters have been investigated principally by Heikki Koskenniemi (1956) and Klaus Thraede (1970). The *topoi* they discuss all revolve about the theme of friendship, perhaps the most important type of ancient letter. Koskenniemi examined the views of Greco-Roman epistolary theorists and concluded that the ideal letter should exhibit three basic features, all connected with the tradition of Greek friendship: (1) *philophronēsis,* the "friendship" between the writer and the recipient, (2) *parousia,* the anticipated "presence" or "reunion" of the writer and the recipient after a period of separation, and (3) *homilia,* a conversation between the writer and the recipient leading to fellowship and communion. Thraede's study of literary letters (Cicero, Ovid, Seneca, Pliny, and Christian letters of late antiquity) focuses on the *topoi* of the letter as (1) a conversation between friends, (2) a surrogate for the presence of a friend, (3) a consolation for separation, including (4) resultant expressions of longing, and (5) expressions of joy on receiving a letter. As important as these themes are, there are many others that require investigation.

The Greek term *topos* (Latin *locus*) literally means "place" and was used by ancients to refer to either a "theme" or an "argument." The phrase *koinos topos* (Latin: *communis locus*) means "commonplace" and refers to a recurring *theme* (e.g., friendship), consisting of a cluster of constituent stereotypical *motifs* which develop various thematic components (friendship motifs include equality, reciprocity, mutual trust, unlimited help in times of need, willingness to make the highest sacrifice, frankness, and loyalty). A *topos*, therefore, is not a literary form, nor is it exclusively a line of argumentation (see below), but rather a common theme taken up in a variety of literary forms (maxims, exempla, stories, domestic codes, stock epithets, themes for amplification, etc.). While *topoi* themselves are not necessarily hackneyed and trite, their constituent motifs can be. *Topoi* are recognizable because they are found in many different authors. The view that *topoi* are stereotyped and have universal applicability is sometimes understood to mean that they do not fit the specific situation to which they are applied. However, the arsenal of motifs that the rhetoricians propose under each *topos* suggests the opposite. A large stock of motifs equips the orator to adjust his remarks to the rhetorical situation (Cicero, *Divisions of Oratory* 3.8).

This understanding of *topos* originated with Aristotle, who used the phrase *idioi topoi* ("particular topics") to describe the main themes appropriate for certain types of oratory (Aristotle, *Rhetoric* 1.4–15). In symbouleutic or deliberative oratory, he maintained, there are five principal topics about which an orator must have a detailed knowledge: ways and means, war and peace, national defense, imports and exports, and legislation. Later rhetorical handbooks outlined the structure and *topoi* appropriate for various kinds of speeches. Menander (third century A.D.) wrote a handbook on types of epideictic speeches in which he suggests four *topoi* for an *epithalium* ("wedding speech"): (1) the groom's family, (2) the bride's family, (3) the bridal couple, and (4) description of the bridal room (2.6). Under each of these *topoi* he suggests various kinds of subjects (i.e., motifs) that the orator can use to enlarge on the main theme.

Aristotle also used the term *topos* to mean "argument" (*topos* literally means the "place" where appropriate arguments are found). For Aristotle *enthymemes* (i.e., statements with supporting reasons usually introduced by "for" or "because"), the rhetorical counterparts of logical syllogisms, are constructed out of *topoi*. He used the phrase *koinoi topoi* ("general topics") of arguments that could be used in any kind of speech (Aristotle, *Rhetoric* 2). They consist of four *topoi:* (1) the possible and the impossible, (2) past fact, (3) future fact, and (4) degree. Another kind of *topos* had nothing to do with subject matter, but comprises *strategies of argumentation* appropriate for all types of oratory (twenty-eight *topoi* are discussed in Aristotle, *Rhetoric* 2.22–23; cf. his *Topics;* Cicero, *Topics; On Oratory* 2.30–36). Following Aristotle, ancient rhetoricians distinguished between *topoi* as "themes" or "arguments" (Quintilian 5.10.20; 10. 5.12).

Aramaic and Jewish Epistolography

Many caches of ancient Near Eastern letters on clay tablets have been discovered by archaeologists. Three of the most important finds include thousands of Mari letters discovered at Tell Hariri in Syria (from the reign of Zimrilim, ca. 1730–1700 B.C.), the Ras Shamra letters from north Syria (ca. 1400 B.C.), and the letters from Tell el-Amarna in Egypt (ca. 1400–1360 B.C.). The diction of these letters has close ties to the oral message, since messengers read them aloud to the addressees. However, the epistolary traditions of the ancient Near East most relevant for understanding early Christian letters are those preserved in Aramaic, Hebrew, and Greek.

Aramaic Letters

Aramaic letters are important because Aramaic was widely used in diplomacy and commerce from the eighth century B.C. through the Hellenistic period (336–331 B.C.), when it was gradually replaced by Greek. More than 120 Aramaic letters have been preserved on papyrus, parchment, and ostraca (pieces of broken pottery), nearly all from the fifth or fourth centuries B.C. These include several letters embedded in Aramaic portions of the Old Testament (four in Ezra 4:8–6:18; 7:12–26; two in Dan. 2:4b–7:28), and in rabbinical literature. Nearly all of the Aramaic letters are private or official letters. Very few are literary letters like Dan. 4:1–37 and 6:25–27, written for publication.

Joseph Fitzmyer has proposed a five-part schema of the Aramaic letter: (1) prescript, (2) initial greeting, (3) secondary greetings, (4) main part, (5) concluding statement. The prescript of Aramaic letters exhibits five different patterns: (a) "To Y, your servant/brother/son X, [greetings]" (e.g., Ezra 4:11–16); (b) "To Y from X, [greetings]"; (c) "From X to Y, [greetings]"; (d) "X to Y, [greetings]" (e.g., Ezra 7:12–26); and (e) "To Y, [greetings]" (e.g., Ezra 4:17–22; 5:7–17). In some papyrus letters the prescript begins with "Greetings to Temple Y," an apparent invocation of the deity of the place addressed. The initial greeting was sometimes omitted in official correspondence. The greeting takes two forms: a *shalom* ("peace," "greetings") formula and a *berakah* ("bless") formula. Secondary greetings (conveyed by the writer for others) are occasionally found. An example of an Aramaic letter is this one from Bar Kosiba (Bar Kochba), written ca. A.D. 132–135 (Yadin, p. 126):

> Letter of Shimeon bar Kosiba, peace!
> To Yehonathan son of Be'aya [my order is] that
> whatever Elisha
> Tells you do to him and help
> him and those with him.
> Be well.

Hebrew Letters

Hebrew letters include 48 documentary letters, nearly all written on ostraca (and consequently very short), from 630–586 B.C. The only extant letters in Hebrew from the Roman period are five of the fifteen Bar Kosiba letters (A.D. 132–135; of the others, eight are in Aramaic and two in Greek). All are papyrus except one Aramaic letter written on a wooden slat. In addition there are many embedded letters in the Old Testament. The *Greek* letters of relevance here are those written by Jews in Greek (as the two Greek Bar Kosiba letters) and those embedded in Greek narrative literature which are either translations of Hebrew or Aramaic letters or pretend to be. Some of these letters reflect the epistolary conventions of Hellenistic Judaism, of great importance because of the potential influence on early Christian letter writing.

According to the analysis of Dennis Pardee (1982), the forty-eight extant documentary Hebrew letters exhibit the following conventional features: (1) the address (which may double as a greeting with name and epithet of sender but only rarely the name and epithet of the recipient); (2) greetings (which may be part of address, occur without an address, or be omitted); (3) formula for transition to main part; (4) a final greeting: *shalom* (only Bar Kosiba letters); and (5) the signature (only Bar Kosiba letters). There are no final greetings, dates, or signatures before the Bar Kosiba period (A.D. 132–135). Some of these elements require comment. (1) The *prescript* in letters contains an address (sender and receiver) and a formula of initial greeting. The address in Hebrew letters from 630 to 586 B.C. usually exhibits one of two forms: (a) "To Y [+ epithet or title], greetings," or (b) "From X to Y, [greetings]." Only four Hebrew letters before A.D. 135 contain the sender's name (the messenger bringing the ostracon would transmit that information). The Bar Kosiba letters exhibit a different opening formula: "From X to Y

[+ epithet or title], greetings [*shalom*]." Both the name of the sender and the name of the recipient are part of prepositional phrases using the *mn-* . . . *l-* formula ("from . . . to"). (2) The single word of initial greeting in all the Bar Kosiba letters is the term *shalom* ("peace," "greetings"). (3) The transition from the prescript to the main part of the letter is usually marked by a special word which can be translated "and now," or "now," or in the Bar Kosiba letters, "that."

A late example of a Hebrew letter is this Bar Kosiba letter (Yadin, p. 133):

> From Shimeon bar Kosiba to the men of En-Gedi To Massabala and to Yehonathan bar Be'ayan, peace. In comfort you sit, eat and drink from the prosperity of the House of Israel, and care nothing for the brothers.

There are also thirteen letters or portions of letters in Mishnaic Hebrew embedded in Tannaitic literature (set in the first century A.D.). Here is one of several Gamaliel letters (Pardee, 1982, p. 187):

> From Simeon b. Gamaliel and from Yohanan b. Zakkai to our brothers in the Upper and Lower Galilee and to Simonia and to Obed Bet Hillel: Well-being [*shalom*]! Be it known to you that the fourth year [of the septennial cycle] has arrived. But as yet the sacred items have not been removed. Now then, quickly bring olive-heaps for these impede the Confession. Nor is it we who have begun to write to you. Rather, our ancestors used to write to your ancestors.

The "From X to Y, well-being [*shalom*]" pattern is found also in the Hebrew Bar Kosiba letters. This letter and the other two Aramaic Gamaliel letters are encyclicals written to ensure proper tithing.

In the Hebrew Old Testament, eleven letters are embedded in narrative literature. All opening formulas have been removed (closing formulas were not used until the Roman period), leaving just the main part or a summary of the original letter. The earliest letter fragment in the Old Testament is the single sentence quoted from a letter of David to Joab about Uriah (2 Sam. 11:15). (For the other instances see 1 Kings 21:8–10; 2 Kings 5:5–6; 10:1–3, 6; 19:10–13 [=Isa. 37:10–13]; Jer. 29:4–23, 26–28; Neh. 6:6–7; 2 Chron. 2: 10–15; 21:12–15.) Similarly the apocryphal Letter of Baruch (located at the end of *2 Baruch*) has an epistolary opening and closing. This is a fabricated festal letter, similar to those in Esther 9:20–32 (Purim) and 2 Maccabees 1:1–2:18 (Hanukkah).

Hellenistic Jewish Letters

The Septuagint (the Greek translation of the Hebrew Bible) includes a number of Jewish religious writings collectively designated "Apocrypha" (some of which are included in the Old Testament of Eastern Orthodoxy and Roman Catholicism). The Apocrypha and the "Pseudepigrapha" (documents written under a pseudonym) contain many embedded letters that exhibit great variety. Some were simply translated from Hebrew or Aramaic into Greek. Others (some authentic, some spurious) were originally written in Greek and reflect a variety of epistolary conventions and functions.

First Maccabees, originally composed in Hebrew, contains twelve official letters, of which two are attributed to Jews. One is from a group of besieged Jews to Judas and his brothers (1 Macc. 5:10–13), and one from Jonathan to the Spartans (12:6–18). The prescript of this last letter reads: "Jonathan the high priest, the senate of the nation, the priests, and the rest of the Jewish people to their brethren the Spartans, greetings." This is a typically Greek prescript. None of these letters closes with an epistolary formula.

Second Maccabees, an anonymous abridgment and embellishment of a Greek work by Jason of Cyrene, contains seven embedded letters, two of which are Jewish (2 Macc. 1:1–9; 1:10–2:18). The first is an authentic Jewish festal letter, originally in Hebrew or Aramaic, with a prescript in an appropriate Hebrew epistolary style: "To their Jewish brethren in Egypt, greetings (from) the Jewish brethren in Jerusalem and those in the land of Judea, good peace" (1:1). The prescript is followed by a prayer that has particular relevance for understanding the Pauline epistolary thanksgivings:

> May God do good to you, and may he remember his covenant with Abraham and Isaac and Jacob, his faithful servants. May he give you all a heart to worship him and to do his will with a strong heart and a willing spirit. May he open your heart to his law and his commandments, and may he bring peace. May he hear your prayers and be reconciled to you, and may he not forsake you in time of evil. We are now praying for you here.

The second letter, found in 1:10–2:18, is spurious. It has a typical Greek prescript: "X [nominative] to Y [dative], greetings [+ health formula]." This letter is also pertinent to the study of Pauline letters since it contains a thanksgiving prayer immediately following the prescript that is a close parallel to the Pauline thanksgivings (1:11): "Having been saved by God out of grave dangers we thank [*eucharistoumen*] him greatly for taking our side against the king."

The so-called *Letter of Aristeas,* written ca. 100 B.C. (which despite its traditional title is not a letter), contains three letters (29–32, 35–40, 41–46). Only the third is Jewish, though in form it is thoroughly Hellenistic: "Eleazar the High Priest to his true friend King Ptolemy, greetings. Yourself fare well and Queen Arsinoe your sister, and the children: so will it be well as we wish; we too are in good health." The concluding greeting is "farewell" (*errōso*).

First Esdras contains versions of four letters (none of which are Jewish) quoted in slightly different form in Ezra: (1) 1 Esdras 2: 17–24 (LXX 2:13–18), which exhibits greater conformity to typical Aramaic epistolary form than its parallel in Ezra 4:11–16; (2) 1 Esdras 2:26–29 (LXX 2:20–24), parallel to Ezra 4:17–22; (3) 1 Esdras 6:7–22, interesting because it shows that *chairein* can translate *šlm:* "To king Darius, greetings [*chairein*]," parallel to Ezra 5:7–17: "To Darius the king, peace [*shelama'*]"; (4) 1 Esdras 8:9–24 (=Ezra 7:12–26; here Ezra is more Semitic since the beginning of the body is introduced with "and now"; the "greetings" [*chairein*] in 1 Esdras 8:9 has no counterpart in the Hebrew Ezra).

In the Septuagint the expanded form of Esther contains two letters: 3:13a–g; 8:12a–x. Both are official letters from the Persian king Artaxerxes. The *Paraleipomena of Jeremiah* (ca. A.D. 125) contains a prophetic letter of Baruch to Jeremiah (6.19–25). The prescript and opening prayer are striking (my trans.):

> Baruch, the servant of God, writes to Jeremiah in the captivity of Babylon: Rejoice [*chaire*] and be overjoyed, for God has not permitted us to leave this body sorrowing for the city which was laid waste and outraged.

While not an exact parallel to the Pauline thanksgivings, it is very close. The letter has no closing formulas. Closely related is the apocryphal Letter of Jeremiah (ca. second century B.C.), supposedly a copy of a letter that Jeremiah sent to the Babylonian exiles "to give them the message which God had commanded him" (preface). Neither an epistolary prescript nor closing formulas are part of the text. The Letter of Jeremiah has the distinction of being one of the few literary letters preserved independently of narrative embedment. Finally, *1 Enoch* 91–108 has been labeled "The Letter of Enoch" because of the subscription found in the Greek version (confirmed by an internal reference to "this letter" in 100.6). The entire section is in the form of a final testament (and thus comparable to 2 Peter). More recently it has been proposed on the basis of the Aramaic fragments that the letter is limited to *1 Enoch* 92.1–93.2. However, no epistolary forms characterize either textual unit.

Here is a translation of one of the two Greek Bar Kosiba letters (Yadin, p. 132):

> Ailianos to Yonanthes the brother, greetings [*chairein*]. Simon Khosiba has written to me that you must send the . . . for the needs of the brothers. . . . [Ailia]nos. Be well, my brother [*errōso adelphe*].

Fifty-three Greek papyrus letters written by or about Jews in Greco-Roman Egypt (from the third century B.C. through the Byzantine period) are collected in the *Corpus Papyrorum Judaicarum* (including thirteen petitions). For the most part these letters reflect the forms and themes typical of pagan papyrus letters. The prescript usually contains the pattern "X to Y, greetings" (*CPJ*, nos. 4–6, 135, 424, 436, 439–444). Some of the letters contain interesting features (*CPJ*, no. 4; 257 B.C.):

> Toubias to Apollonios greeting. If you and all your affairs are flourishing, and everything else is as you wish it, many thanks to the gods! I too have been well, and have thought of you at all times, as was right.

The phrase "many thanks to the gods" is surprising in a Jewish letter. This stock formula is also found in the opening line of a bogus letter attributed to Periander: "Many thanks to Pythian Apollo" (Diogenes Laertius 1.99).

Josephus also includes many letters in his historical works. The messages exchanged by Solomon and Hiram (1 Kings 5:1–9) are transformed into letters in *Ant.* 8.50–54, the first with a thanksgiving period (8.52). Eupolemus reworks these letters (adding some) into even more typical Hellenistic letters, though the blessing (Eusebius, *Preparation for the Gospel* 9.34) is derived from 1 Kings 5:7 (=2 Chron. 2:12). *Antiquities* 16.166–173 contains five letters. Two are from the Jewish king Agrippa, and three from Roman officials. All have the typical Greek prescript "X to Y, greetings"; none have closing formulas. In *Antiquities* 17.134–139, Josephus quotes three Jewish letters, one without a prescript, two in with the "X to Y" pattern (without a salutation), none with closing formulas.

Summary

In contrast to the enormous number and variety of Greek and Latin letters from antiquity, very few distinctively Jewish documentary letters (whether in Aramaic, Hebrew, or Greek) have survived. A relatively large number of letters were embedded in narratives written in Greek (or translated into Greek) by Hellenistic Jews. Yet nearly all of these letters exhibit Hellenistic epistolary conventions.

In the following chapter it will become evident that early Christian letters, too, owed far more to Hellenistic than to oriental epistolary conventions.

Yet one important type of Jewish letter, the *encyclical,* had an important influence on early Christian epistolography. Such letters were carried by envoys *(šaliaḥim)* and were a major means whereby Jewish authorities in Palestine communicated with Diaspora communities (cf. Acts 9:1; 28:21). Encyclicals were used for many administrative purposes, including the regulation of holy day observance. Messengers were sent from Palestine with letters announcing the appearance of the New Moon in six important festival months so that the festival days might be accurately fixed (M. *Rosh Ha-Shanah* 1.3–4; 2.2). The texts of some of these letters are preserved in T. *Sanhedrin* 2:6. The more general *festal letter* encouraging observance of various holy days was also common (2 Macc. 1:1–10; 1:11–2:18; Esth. 9:20–32).

For Further Study

On Ancient Letters Generally: J. Schneider, "Brief," *RAC,* II (1954), cols. 563–585; I. Sukutris, "Epistolographie," *RE,* suppl. vol. V (1931), pp. 210f. The single best introduction to Greco-Roman letters, with many ancient letters in translation and numerous observations on early Christian letters, is Stanley K. Stowers, *Letter Writing in Greco-Roman Antiquity* (Westminster Press, 1986). Several important essays are found in John L. White, ed., *Studies in Ancient Letter Writing, Semeia* 22 (1981).

On Greco-Egyptian Papyrus Letters: The best recent introduction to documentary papyrus letters, including many translations, is John L. White, *Light from Ancient Letters* (Fortress Press, 1986). Also important is idem, *The Body of the Greek Letter,* SBL Dissertation Series, 2, 2nd ed. (Scholars Press, 1972). Indispensable for identifying collections of published papyri is J. F. Oates, R. S. Bagnall, W. H. Willis, and K. A. Worp, *Checklist of Editions of Greek Papyri and Ostraca,* 3rd ed., *Bulletin of the American Society of Papyrologists,* Suppl. 4 (Scholars Press, 1985). Still indispensable is F. J. Exler, *The Form of the Ancient Greek Letter: A Study in Greek Epistolography* (Catholic University of America, 1923). The classic studies on the subject are those by Adolf Deissmann: *Bible Studies,* tr. by A. Grieve (Edinburgh: T. & T. Clark, 1901), esp. pp. 3–59, and *Light from the Ancient East,* tr. by L. R. M. Strachan (London: Hodder & Stoughton, 1927), pp. 143–246. For many Greek letters, with translations, see A. S. Hunt and C. C. Edgar, *Select Papyri,* 2 vols. (Harvard University Press, 1932–34). See also Clinton W. Keyes, "The Greek Letter of Introduction," *AJP* 56 (1935), 28–44, and Chan-Hie Kim, *The Familiar Letter of Recommendation* (Scholars Press, 1972).

On Official Letters: Robert K. Sherk, *Roman Documents from the Greek East: Senatus Consulta and Epistulae to the Age of Augustus* (Johns Hopkins Press, 1969); C. Bradford Welles, *Royal Correspondence in the Hellenistic Period* (Yale University Press, 1934).

On Greco-Roman Literary Letters: The most extensive collection of texts is still Rudolph Hercher, *Epistolographi Graeci* (Paris: Didot, 1873). Two important formal analyses are by Heikki Koskenniemi, *Studien zur Idee und Phraseologie des griechischen Briefes bis 400 n. Chr.* (Helsinki: Akateeminen Kirjakauppa, 1956), and Klaus Thraede, *Grundzüge griechisch-römischer Brieftopik* (Munich: C. H. Beck, 1970). The standard discussion of Roman literary letters, though Seneca is omitted, is Hermann Peter, *Der Brief in der römischen Literatur* (Leipzig: Teubner, 1901). On ancient epistolary theory, with translated texts prefaced by a discussion, see Abraham J. Malherbe, "Ancient Epistolary Theorists," *Ohio Journal of Religious Studies* 5 (1977), 3–77. *Letters of Recommendation:* For the social setting see Richard P. Saller, *Personal Patronage Under the Early Empire* (Cambridge: University Press, 1982); Hannah Cotton, *Documentary Letters of Recommendation in Latin from the Roman Empire* (Königstein: Hain, 1981); Clinton W. Keyes, "The Greek Letter of Introduction," *AJP* 56 (1935), 28–44; Chan-Hie Kim, *The Familiar Letter of Recommendation* (Scholars Press, 1972). *Cynic Letters:* Harold W. Attridge, *First-Century Cynicism in the Epistles of Heraclitus* (Scholars Press, 1976); Abraham J. Malherbe, ed., *The Cynic Epistles* (Scholars Press, 1977). *Demosthenes:* Jonathan A. Goldstein, *The Letters of Demosthenes* (Columbia University Press, 1968). *Hippocrates:* A. E. Hanson, "Papyri of Medical Content," in *Papyrology*, ed. by Naphtali Lewis, Yale Classical Studies, (Cambridge: University Press, 1985), pp. 25–47; O. Philippson, "Verfasser und Abfassungszeit der sogennannten Hippokratesbriefe," *Rheinisches Museum* 77 (1928), 293; Dimitrios T. Sakalis, "Beiträge zu den Pseudo-Hippokratischen Briefen," *Formes de pensée dans la collection Hippocratique*, ed. by F. Lasserre and P. Mudry (Geneva: Librairie Droz, 1983), pp. 499–514. *Horace:* W. Allen et al., "Horace's First Book of *Epistles* as Letters," *Classical Journal* 68 (1972–73), 119–133. *Libanius:* J. H. W. G. Liebeschuetz, *Antioch: City and Imperial Administration in the Later Roman Empire* (Oxford: Clarendon Press, 1972), pp. 17–23; O. Seeck, *Die Briefe des Libanius zeitlich geordnet.* Texte und Untersuchungen, 15 (1906). *Pliny:* A. N. Sherwin-White, *The Letters of Pliny: A Historical and Social Commentary* (Oxford: Clarendon Press, 1966); H. W. Traub, "Pliny's Treatment of History in Epistolary Form," *TAPA* 86 (1955), 213–232. *Pythagoras and Pythagoreans:* Alfons Staedele, *Die Briefe des Pythagoras und der Pythagoreer* (Meisenheim: Verlag Anton Hain, 1980). *Seneca:* Hildegard Cancik, *Untersuchungen zu Seneca Epistulae Morales* (Hildesheim: Georg Olms Verlag, 1967).

On Letters and Rhetoric: Abraham J. Malherbe, "Ancient Epistolary Theorists," *Ohio Journal of Religious Studies* 5 (1977), 3–77. *Ancient Education:* S. F. Bonner, *Education in Ancient Rome* (University of California Press, 1977); A. D. Booth, "Elementary and Secondary Education in the Roman

Empire," *Florilegium* 1 (1979), 1–14; idem, "The Schooling of Slaves in First-Century Rome," *TAPA* 109 (1979), 11–19; M. L. Clarke, *Higher Education in the Ancient World* (London: Routledge & Kegan Paul, 1971); R. A. Kaster, "Notes on 'Primary' and 'Secondary' Schools in Late Antiquity," *TAPA* 113 (1983), 323–346.

On Aramaic and Israelite-Jewish Letters: A. Cowley, *Aramaic Papyri of the Fifth Century B.C.* (Oxford: Clarendon Press, 1923), contains the texts and translations of 25 Aramaic letters. See also Joseph A. Fitzmyer, "Some Notes on Aramaic Epistolography," *JBL* 93 (1974), 201–225. For extensive bibliography and texts and translations of the extant letters together with commentary, see Dennis Pardee, *Handbook of Ancient Hebrew Letters* (Scholars Press, 1982), and his earlier article "An Overview of Ancient Hebrew Epistolography," *JBL* 97 (1978), 321–346. See also Yigael Yadin, *Bar Kokhba* (Random House, 1971). *Hellenistic Jewish Letters:* V. A. Tcherikover, A. Fuks, and M. Stern, *Corpus Papyrorum Judaicarum*, 3 vols. (Harvard University Press, 1957–64).

6

Early Christian Letters
and Homilies

Since Adolf Deissmann, research on Greco-Roman letters has taken three different routes: *formal literary analysis, thematic analysis,* and *rhetorical analysis,* each discussed in detail in chapter 5. In addition, New Testament scholars have used another method, *form criticism,* first applied to the Synoptic Gospels, to identify and analyze various types of fixed traditional forms, both oral and written, that have been preserved in early Christian letters and homilies. In this chapter each of these approaches will be applied to the epistolary and homiletic literature of the New Testament and the Apostolic Fathers.

Formal Literary Analysis

The formulaic features of ancient letters (particularly documentary papyrus letters) have been extensively analyzed in comparison with New Testament letters. Considerable progress has been made, not only with regard to opening and closing formulas, but also in the matter of epistolary forms, which tend to be found at the beginning and end of the body or central section of ancient letters. Yet there are limitations in this approach, since the analysis of the central section of early Christian letters remains problematical.

Framing Formulas

Since the Pauline letters are the earliest and most complex early Christian letters, epistolary conventions found in them can provide a framework for discussing early Christian epistolary formulas. These letters, like most ancient letters, consist of three basic elements: the opening and closing formulas and the central section of the letter which they bracket. In most Pauline letters the basic elements of the epistolary prescript have each been expanded in a distinctive way. The body consists of the central section, which often closes with travel plans and exhortation. The closing consists of doxology, greetings, and benediction. Many of these features are derived from Greco-Roman or Jewish epistolary conventions.

Opening Formulas

The formulaic opening of the Pauline letters consists of two basic elements: the prescript (superscription or sender, adscription or addressee, and salutation) and the thanksgiving.

In superscriptions, Paul usually identifies himself with epithets such as "apostle" and "servant" (lacking only in 1 and 2 Thess.). Most of Paul's letters list co-senders; Romans, Ephesians, and the Pastorals are exceptions. He is identified as an apostle in all but four letters (Philippians, 1–2 Thessalonians, Philemon). The term "servant" is used either in combination with "apostle" (Titus 1:1; cf. 2 Peter 1:1) or alone (Phil. 1:1; cf. James 1:1; Jude 1), and the term "prisoner" is used once (Philemon 1). Three times Paul is identified with the phrase "an apostle of Christ Jesus by the will of God" (2 Cor. 1:1; Eph. 1:1; Col. 1:1). This is expanded in 2 Timothy 1:1: "according to the promise of life which is in Christ Jesus." Among the authentic letters, Galatians and particularly Romans stand out as distinctive, with exceptionally long phrases qualifying Paul's status (Gal. 1:1–2a; Rom. 1:1–6), because his status was questioned by the Galatians and unfamiliar to the Romans. In Roman diplomatic *epistulae,* the sender usually identified himself with appropriate titles, underlining their official character. Official letters sent by Roman emperors contained impressive strings of imperial titles. Similarly, the use of epithets in early Christian letters suggests their function as "official" correspondence.

All Pauline letters except the Pastorals have similar salutations, found in simplest form in Paul's earliest letters: "Grace to you and peace" (1 Thess. 1:1). Paul may have used the term "grace" *(charis)* as a word play on the usual epistolary "greetings" *(chairein).* The closest parallel is found in a pseudepigraphic letter attributed to Baruch, originally written in Hebrew ca. A.D. 100 (*2 Baruch* 78.2): "Mercy and peace to you." Paul's use of "peace" probably reflects the Hebrew and Aramaic salutation *šlm.* In New Testament letters, the simple *chairein* salutation occurs only in James 1:1 and in two embedded letters (Acts 15:23; 23:26). The salutation "grace to you and peace" was expanded by making the source explicit (cf. Col. 1:2: "Grace to you and peace *from God our Father"*) and was further amplified in the other eight letters to: "Grace to you and peace from God our/the Father and the/our Lord Jesus Christ." Galatians 1: 3–5 is singular, for the salutation is expanded into a doxology.

The presence of an optative verb in the salutation in 1–2 Peter, Jude, *1 Clement*, Polycarp's *Philippians*, and the *Martyrdom of Polycarp* reflects another distinctive pattern: "May grace and peace be multiplied to you" (1 Peter 1:2; cf. *1 Clement*, preface). This pattern is amplified in 2 Peter 1:2 by the addition "in the knowledge of God and of Jesus our Lord." Jude 2 (cf. Polycarp, *Philippians*, preface) varies 1 Peter: "May mercy, peace and love be multiplied to you." This pattern is combined with the Pauline pattern in *Martyrdom of Polycarp*, preface: "Mercy, peace and love from God the Father and our Lord Jesus Christ be multiplied." A similar salutation occurs in three letters attributed to a Rabbi Gamaliel (I or II?), written in Aramaic, possibly the preferred language of written communication in the eastern Diaspora: "May your well-being [*selam*] increase!" (J. *Sanh.* 18d; B. *Sanh.* 18d; Tos. *Sanh.* 2.6). Two letters from the Aramaic section of Daniel have the same salutation (Dan. 3:31; 6:26). The Theodotianic Greek text of Daniel 4:1 and 6:26 ("may peace be multiplied to you") is verbally identical with 1 Peter 1:2 (though the Christian term "grace" is missing). Further, the three letters of Gamaliel were *encyclicals* directed to three regional groups of Diaspora Jews, the brothers of Upper and Lower Galilee, of the Upper and Lower South, and of Babylonia. James, 1–2 Peter, and Jude have some of the characteristics of these and other Jewish encyclical letters. First Peter is explicitly directed "to the exiles of the dispersion in Pontus, Galatia, Cappadocia, Asia, and Bithynia," while Jude and Second Peter are directed to all Christians in general. Another letter presented as an encyclical (two copies were sent to different groups) is the pseudepigraphal letter of Baruch to the brothers in Babylon and the nine-and-a-half tribes beyond the Euphrates (*2 Baruch* 77.17–19; 78.1–86.3).

All of the authentic Pauline letters except Galatians and 2 Corinthians insert a prayer of thanksgiving immediately after the salutation (e.g., Rom. 1:8–17; 1 Cor. 1:4–9; Phil. 1:3–11). Second Corinthians 1:3–7 has a benediction where a thanksgiving is expected. These prayers all begin with the phrase "I give thanks to God always for you" (or the equivalent), using the Greek verb *eucharistein* ("to give thanks"), which quickly became a technical term for the Lord's Supper (Ignatius, *Ephesians* 13.1; Justin, *1 Apology* 65–66). The thanksgivings in two of the Pastoral letters (1 Tim. 1:12–17; 2 Tim. 1:3–5) use an entirely different idiom, and the prayer in 1 Peter 1:3–12 is really a "eulogy" or benediction, since it begins, like 2

Cor. 1:3–7, with the term *eulogētos* ("blessed [be]"). Ephesians 1: 3–14 is a "eulogy" followed by a thanksgiving (1:15–23).

The inclusion of a prayer or a religious or nonreligious expression of gratitude after the salutation has parallels in ancient letters. The *proskynēma* formula follows the salutation in Greek papyri beginning with the first century A.D. Similar prayers are found in the same position in some Hellenistic Jewish letters (2 Macc. 1:1–9; 1:10–2:18, the closest parallel to the Pauline thanksgiving; *Paraleipomena of Jeremiah* 6.19–25). Speeches occasionally begin with an expression of gratefulness (Dio Chrysostom, *Oration* 48.1, thanks the city magistrate who permitted the assembly). Seneca begins a letter by expressing gratitude for receiving letters frequently from a friend (*Moral Epistles* 40.1).

The thanksgiving period is not just ornamental. It often praises the recipients, functioning as an exordium aimed at securing their goodwill. As such it is a functional equivalent to introductory sections of official letters that praise the recipients. Pauline thanksgivings usually encapsulate the main themes of letters, like the thanksgiving periods in papyrus letters and introductions of speeches. The length of the thanksgiving reflects the degree of intimacy between writer and recipients. The longer thanksgivings of Philemon and 1 Thessalonians reflect cordial relations. They are missing from Galatians and 2 Corinthians, reflecting strained relations.

Closing Formulas

Paul's letters always conclude with a *charis* benediction. Before that several optional epistolary formulas are often found, in this order: (1) peace wish, (2) request for prayer, (3) secondary greetings, (4) holy kiss, (5) autographed greeting (various positions).

Paul replaced the usual formulas of final greetings *(errōso* or *errōsthe)* with a *charis* ("grace") benediction: "grace [*charis*] . . . be with you," which characterizes all Pauline letters but Ephesians (and just six other Christian letters through the sixth century A.D.). This benediction always comes last (except in 1 Cor. 16:23). The benediction contains three basic elements: (a) "grace," (b) the divine source of that grace, and (c) those who benefit from that grace. The benediction of Paul's earliest letter exhibits the basic pattern: "The grace/ of our Lord Jesus Christ/ be with you" (1 Thess. 5:28; cf. Rom. 6:20; 1 Cor. 16:23; 2 Cor. 13:14; Gal. 6:18; Phil. 4:23; 2 Thess. 3:18; Philemon 25). This Pauline pattern is also followed in Revelation 22:21 and *1 Clement* 65.2. The latter joins the benediction to an epistolary doxology. Just two elements are found in Colossians and in several non-Pauline letters: "Grace/ be with you" (followed with slight variations in 1 Tim. 6:21; 2 Tim. 4:22; Titus 3:15; cf. Heb. 13:25). A different form of blessing concludes *Barnabas* 21.9: "May you be saved, children of love and peace. The Lord of glory and all grace [be] with your spirit."

A typical Pauline peace wish is found in Phil. 4:9: "and the God of peace will be with you." This formula is found near the end of all the Pauline letters except 1 Corinthians and Philemon.

A request for prayer occasionally is made at the end of Pauline and Deutero-Pauline letters (Rom. 15:30–33; 1 Thess. 5:25; 2 Thess. 3:1; Col. 4:3; Eph. 6:18–20; cf. Heb. 13:18).

Secondary greetings (greetings conveyed to the recipients by the author from others) are frequently found at the conclusion of Hellenistic letters after the first century B.C., using the *aspazesthai* ("send greetings to") formula. Early Christian letters often use this form, e.g., Philemon 23–24: "Epaphras, my fellow prisoner in Christ Jesus, sends greetings [*aspazetai*] to you, and so do Mark, Aristarchus, Demas, and Luke, my fellow workers." Secondary greetings occur in every authentic Pauline letter but Galatians; they are absent from the doubtful 2 Thessalonians and from the Deutero-Pauline Ephesians and 1 Timothy. The longest section of secondary greetings is found in Rom. 16:3–16 (twenty-six people are greeted); the shortest is 2 Cor. 13:13: "All the saints greet you." Among the non-Pauline New Testament letters, concluding secondary greetings occur in Heb. 13:23–24; 1 Peter 5:13–14; 2 John 13; 3 John 15.

Several times the recipients of Paul's letters are told to greet each other with a "holy kiss" (Rom. 16:16; 1 Cor. 16:20; 2 Cor. 3:12; 1 Thess. 5:26). This uniquely Christian greeting, which elsewhere occurs only in 1 Peter 5:14, is perhaps simply an enactment of Paul's greetings to each of them. The practice is later attested as part of the early Christian liturgy (Justin, *1 Apology* 65; Tertullian, *On Prayer* 14). When Ignatius says "the love of X greets you" (*Trallians* 13.1; *Romans* 9.3; *Philadelphians* 11.2), he may be alluding to this custom.

A personal "autographed greeting" is found at the end of five of Paul's letters (1 Cor. 16:21; 2 Thess. 3:17; Col. 4:18; Gal. 6:11; Philemon 19), e.g., 1 Cor. 16:21: "I, Paul, write this greeting with my own hand." In many papyrus letters the final greeting is written in handwriting different from that of the rest of the letter, suggesting that it was added by the author (as distinguished from the scribe). Even literary letters reflect this practice (Cicero, *To Atticus* 12:32; 13.28; 14:21). Paul's statement in 2 Thess. 3:17 suggests that he regularly made use of a secretary (cf. Rom. 16:22).

The Central Section

The central section (or body) of the letter is the section containing the information constituting the purpose for which the letter
was written. It is also the section that has proven most resistant to
formal analysis. The central section of ancient letters also contains
formulaic phrases and sentiments, some of which occur toward the
beginning (transitions from the opening to the central section) and
others toward the end (transitions from the main part to the closing). Here we will survey five different types of material found in the
central sections of early Christian letters: (1) internal transitional
formulas, (2) epistolary *topoi*, (3) autobiographical statements, (4)
travel plans, and (5) concluding paraenesis.

Internal Transitional Formulas

The bodies of two of Paul's letters begin with a *disclosure formula*,
"I want you to know, brethren" (Gal. 1:11; Phil. 1:12); two others
begin with the related phrase "I/we do not want you to be ignorant"
(Rom. 1:13; 2 Cor. 1:8). Both phrases can occur *within* letters as a
way of moving into the discussion of an important issue (1 Cor.
12:3; 15:1; 1 Cor. 10:1; 12:1; 1 Thess. 4:13).

Carl Bjerkelund has shown that sentences beginning with "I appeal [*parakalō*] to you (brethren)," or "I beseech [*erōtō*] you (brethren)," constitute a fixed epistolary formula of Greek origin found
in both private and official letters of antiquity. It occurs nineteen
times in Paul (e.g., Rom. 15:30; 16:17; 1 Cor. 4:16; 16:15); the most
revealing instance is Philemon 8–10, in which Paul emphasizes the
fact that he appeals to Philemon rather than commands him, i.e., he
writes in a friendly rather than an authoritative manner. These
sentences have a transitional function indicating a change in subject
and often disclose the main purpose of the letter (2 Thess. 2:1; 1
Cor. 1:10; 1 Thess. 4:1–2, 10b–12). The closest parallels are found
in the diplomatic correspondence of Hellenistic kings, in which the
parakalō sentences emphasize the friendly, personal dimension of
the relationship between the king and his subjects. Though the
formula can introduce paraenesis (Rom. 12:1; 1 Thess. 5:12, 14), it
remains transitional, unrelated to the paraenesis itself.

The *confidence formula*, containing expressions of confidence, occurs several times in Paul (Rom. 15:14; 2 Cor. 7:4, 16; 9:1–2; Gal.
5:10; 2 Thess. 3:4; Philemon 21). Second Corinthians 7:16 is typical:
"I rejoice because I have perfect confidence in you." Stanley Olson

finds four variations in these expressions of confidence, all of which have parallels in ancient papyrus letters: (1) confidence in the recipient's compliance (Gal. 5:10; 2 Thess. 3:4; Philemon 21); (2) request based on confidence (2 Cor. 9:2); (3) pretended confidence as an excuse for making a request (Rom. 15:14; 2 Cor. 9:1–2); and (4) expression of confidence as a polite request (Rom. 15:24).

Epistolary Topoi

An important but neglected subject is the identification and comparative study of epistolary *topoi,* i.e., the themes and constituent motifs used in ancient letters. A comparison between the nonliterary papyrus letters and early Christian letters reveals that they share a number of common epistolary themes and constituent motifs. The most common *topoi* include (1) *letter writing* (Rom. 15:14; 1 Cor. 4:14; 5:9; 7:1; Philemon 21); (2) *health* (2 Cor. 1:8–11; Phil. 2:25–30; 3 John 2); (3) *business* (1 Cor. 16:1–4; 2 Cor. 9:1–5; Phil. 4:14–18); (4) *domestic events* (1 Cor. 5:1–6:11; Phil. 2:25–30; 4:2–4, 14–18); (5) *reunion with addressee(s)* (Rom. 15:14–33; Phil. 3:19–24; 1 Thess. 2:17–3:13; 2 John 12; 3 John 13–14); and (6) *government matters* (Rom. 13:1–7; Titus 3:1–2; 1 Peter 2:13–17). Various combinations of these themes occur frequently in both papyrus letters and early Christian letters.

In several of the hortatory sections of Paul's letters (Rom. 12:1–15:13; Gal. 5:13–6:10; Col. 3:5–4:6; 1 Thess. 4:1–5:22), the exhortations emphasize departing from evil and seeking good. These sections contain a number of *topoi* on various stock themes. Romans 13, for example, contains a series of four *topoi* on authority (vs. 1–5), on paying tribute (vs. 6–7), on love (vs. 8–10), and on the eschatological hour (vs. 11–14). Similarly in 1 Thessalonians 4:9–5:11 there are three separate *topoi* discussed and developed, on love of the brethren (4:9–12), on the fate of the Christian dead (4:13–18), and on times and seasons (5:1–11).

Autobiographical Statements

Throughout his letters, Paul often makes autobiographical statements. Two lengthy ones are found in 1 Thess. 1:2–3:13 and Gal. 1:10–2:21. Many of these statements are located toward the beginning of his letters, often following the thanksgiving (Rom. 1:14–16a; 2 Cor. 1:12–2:17, continued in 7:5–16; 10:7–12:13; Gal. 1:10–2:21; Phil. 1:12–26; 3:2–14; 1 Thess. 2:1–12). Such statements (missing only from 1 Corinthians and Philemon) are often understood as attempts by Paul to defend himself and his gospel from the accusations of opponents.

Yet in Greco-Roman oratory, one of the most important arguments was provided by the establishment of the moral character and conduct of the speaker (*ēthos;* cf. Aristotle, *Rhetoric* 1415a; Cicero, *Divisions of Oratory* 6.22; 8.28; and the *Rhetoric to Herennius* 1.4.8–5.1). Character (*ēthos*) was important for several reasons: (1) the speaker wished to project a likable and trustworthy image of himself; (2) he wished to foster the right impression (and therefore had to know the concerns and situation of his audience); and (3) he wished to present the character of his opponents plausibly but so that his own version would be more persuasive.

According to Gregory Lyons, the autobiographical section in Gal. 1:10–2:21 is structured in accordance with conventional autobiographical *topoi:* (1) *prooimion*—Paul's divine gospel (1:10–12); (2) *anastrophē* ("behavior")—Paul's character (a) as a persecutor (1:13–14); (b) as a preacher of the gospel (1:15–17); (3) *praxeis* ("deeds")—Paul's conduct (1:18–2:10); (4) *synkrisis* ("comparison") —Cephas and Paul (2:11–20); (5) *epilogos* ("epilogue")—Paul does not reject God's grace (2:21). The rhetorical antitheses in this passage and in 1 Thess. 1:2–3:13 do not *necessarily* reflect a point-by-point rebuttal of hypothetical charges.

Travel Plans

Since letters are a primary means of communication between those who are separated, the *topos* of reunion occurs frequently. Robert Funk has described an epistolary form that centers on such visitation talk, which he designated the "Apostolic Parousia" ("arrival"). It usually concludes the main part of Paul's letters. The three modes of Paul's apostolic presence are the letter, envoys, and personal presence. However, the absence of a consistent structure suggests that we are dealing with a *topos* or theme with a number of subordinate motifs. Funk defines the Apostolic Parousia in terms of five elements, some with several subordinate features: (1) mention of Paul's letter-writing activity; (2) mention of his relationship to the addressees; (3) statement of plans for paying a visit (desire to visit, delays in coming, sending of an emissary, announcement of a visit); (4) invocation of divine approval and support for visit; and (5) benefits of the impending visit. There are about twelve examples of the Apostolic Parousia in Paul's letters, though few of the above elements are found in all of them (e.g., Rom. 1:8–15; 15:14–33; 1

Cor. 4:14–21; 16:1–11; Gal. 4:12–20; Phil. 2:19–30; 1 Thess. 2: 17–3:13; Philemon 21–22). Travelogues are found in several Deutero-Pauline letters (Eph. 6:21–22; 2 Tim. 4:6–18; Titus 3:12–14), as well as in other Christian letters (Heb. 13:18–19, 22–23; 2 John 12; 3 John 13–14).

Concluding Paraenesis

One of the distinctive features of Pauline letters and letters written under the influence of the Pauline tradition is the presence of a concluding section of paraenesis (cf. Rom. 12:1–15:13; Gal. 5: 1–6:10; 1 Thess. 4:1–5:22; cf. Col. 3:1–4:6). Yet there are other letters in which paraenesis is not concentrated in the concluding section but is woven throughout the composition (1–2 Corinthians, Philippians; cf. James, Hebrews). Paraenesis is a complex subject that has just recently become the focus of New Testament scholarship. At this point, however, it is helpful to distinguish between *epistolary* paraenesis, which is found in defined concluding sections of some Christian letters, and *paraenetic styles,* which permeate letters (e.g., 1 Thessalonians, Galatians, Colossians).

Paraenesis means "advice" or "exhortation" and refers to general moral and religious instruction that falls between symbouleutic and epideictic rhetoric. Since Judaism, with its rich tradition of ethical monotheism, and the major Hellenistic schools of philosophy (Stoics, Cynics, Epicureans) all emphasized *ethics,* moral exhortation was a common phenomenon throughout the ancient world. Advice *(monitio)* includes, according to Seneca, consolation, warning, exhortation, scolding, and praising (*Letter* 94.39). Paraenesis is really an indirect way of addressing a behavioral problem. Since the content of paraenesis is generally approved by society, it provides a basis of agreement in situations that are potentially divisive.

Paraenesis has several important characteristics: (1) Paraenesis is traditional, reflecting conventional wisdom generally approved by society (Isocrates, *Nicocles* 40–41; Pseudo-Libanius, *Epistolary Styles* 5; cf. Phil. 4:8). (2) Paraenesis is applicable to many situations (Seneca, *Letter* 94.32–35). (3) Paraenesis is so familiar that it is often presented as a "reminder" (Seneca, *Letters* 13.15; 94.21–25; Dio Chrysostom, *Oration* 17.2, 5; 1 Thess. 4:1–2; 2 Thess. 3:6; Phil. 3:1). (4) Paraenesis can be exemplified in exceptional people who are models of virtue (Seneca, *Letters* 6.5–6; 11.9–10; 95.72; 2 Thess. 3:7; Phil. 3:17; 4:9). (5) Paraenesis is usually transmitted by persons who are socially and morally superior to those they address.

Form-Critical Analysis

The central sections of early Christian letters contain a variety of other literary forms that are not typical of ancient letters but received their shape from use, mostly oral, in other settings. The fact that letters functioned in part as surrogates for oral communication encouraged the preservation of these traditions. Another contributing factor is the elastic and inclusive qualities of the letter format. Though form criticism has principally been applied to the Synoptic Gospels, it has also facilitated the identification of oral forms embedded in early Christian letters. The constituent literary forms of Greek and Roman letters, in contrast, remain an unexplored area. The major categories of literary forms surveyed below include liturgical and paraenetic forms.

Liturgical Forms

Paul and other early Christian epistolographers intended their letters to be read aloud to the congregations to whom they were addressed (1 Thess. 5:27; Col. 4:16; Rev. 1:3; 22:18; for an analogous practice in Judaism, cf. *2 Baruch* 86.1). This intended setting accounts for the inclusion of liturgical formulas in Christian letters. Since these formulas were derived from Christian worship, they enabled letters to fit comfortably into liturgical settings. A liturgical setting is indicated by the early tendency to insert a concluding "amen." Although the closing "amen" in Gal. 6:18 (cf. Rom. 15:33) is undisputed in the manuscript tradition, it was probably added at a very early date. Only relatively late letters exhibit an original closing "amen" (Jude 25; cf. 2 Peter 3:18; *1 Clement* 65.2; Polycarp, *Philippians* 14; and variant readings in Ignatius, *Magnesians* 15; *Philadelphians* 11). Several scholars have proposed that the endings of several early Christian letters reflect a liturgical sequence leading up to the celebration of the eucharist after the reading. First Corinthians 16:20–24 (with parallels in Rev. 22:14–21 and *Didache* 9.1–10.7), for example, is often understood as reflecting a fixed liturgical sequence: (1) holy kiss, (2) invitation for believers to come, (3) exclusion of the unworthy, (4) Maranatha (Aramaic for "Our Lord, come!"), (5) promise of grace. One weakness in this proposal is that too little is known of early Christian liturgy. The liturgical forms found in Paul's letters, in addition to the thanksgiving periods discussed above, include (1) *charis* ("grace") benedictions, (2) blessings, (3) doxologies, (4) hymns, (5) confessions and acclamations, and (6) liturgical sequences.

1. The distinctively Christian epistolary salutations and final greetings discussed above are *charis*-benedictions. The formula "the grace of God" which stands behind these benedictions is a theological abbreviation for salvation. *Charis*-benedictions usually lack verbs, which must be supplied. When a verb is used (as in 1–2 Peter and Jude) it is an optative of wish, indicating that these salutations and final greetings are not declarative statements but prayers. As such they have a liturgical character, though we cannot reconstruct their specific role in the liturgy.

2. Early Christian blessings were inherited from Judaism, which used the Hebrew term *baruk* ("blessed") to begin both blessings and doxologies (cf. Gen. 24:27; Ex. 18:10). In Old Testament blessings God is normally referred to in the third person, i.e., "Blessed is the Lord, who . . ." (1 Kings 1:48; Ps. 66:20; 2 Chron. 2:12). The use of the second person, "Blessed are you, Lord . . ." (the most characteristic prayer form of rabbinic Judaism), is found just twice in the Old Testament (Ps. 119:12; 1 Chron. 29:10). The Greek adjective *eulogētos* ("blessed") was used by early Christians in ways similar to the Jewish *berakah* formulas. Paul closely follows the Jewish pattern in three passages: "[God] who is blessed forever! Amen" (Rom. 1:25; 9:5; 2 Cor. 11:31). This basic form could also be expanded, as in 2 Cor. 1:3–4: "Blessed be the God and Father of our Lord Jesus Christ . . ." (cf. Eph. 1:3f.; 1 Peter 1:3ff.; *Barnabas* 6.10; Ignatius, *Ephesians* 1.3).

3. A doxology is a formula or short hymn that ascribes glory or reputation *(doxa)* to God. The basic form of the doxology has three elements: "to whom/ be the glory [*doxa*]/ forever. Amen" (Rom. 11:36; cf. Gal. 1:5; Phil. 4:20; 1 Tim. 6:16; 2 Tim. 4:18; Heb. 13:21; *1 Clement* 32.4; 58.2). Each element can be expanded in a variety of ways (Eph. 3:21; 1 Tim. 1:17; 1 Peter 4:11; Jude 24–25; *1 Clement* 20.12; 65.2). Such doxologies usually conclude a section of text, a practice apparently derived from Hellenistic Judaism (4 Macc. 18:24; 1 Esdras 4:40, 59), since there are no exact parallels in Palestinian Judaism. Doxologies often conclude the central section of letters (Phil. 4:20; 2 Tim. 2:18; Heb. 13:21; 1 Peter 5:11). In three instances a doxology actually concludes a letter (Rom. 16:25–27; 2 Peter 3:18; Jude 24–25; *1 Clement* 65.2). The original setting of the benediction may have been at the close of a sermon.

4. Singing or, more accurately, chanting was an important element in the worship services of early Christians (1 Cor. 14:26; Col. 3:16; Pliny, *Letter* 10.96). A number of hymns or hymnic fragments are preserved in early Christian letters. While they are not metrical like Greek hymns, they do exhibit Semitic poetic parallelism. Chris-

tian letters may include some hymns directed to God (Rom. 11: 33–36; Eph. 1:3–14; 1 Peter 1:3–5; Col. 1:12–14). Several hymns narrate the mission of Christ, often mentioning preincarnation and postresurrection themes (Phil. 2:6–11; Col. 1:15–20; 1 Tim. 3:16; possibly Eph. 2:14–16). Two Christ hymns are quoted by Ignatius of Antioch (*Ephesians* 7.2; 19.1–3).

5. Many confessions (or "homologies," from a Greek word meaning "confession") and acclamations that presuppose a cultic setting are quoted in letters. One very important creedal formula is "Jesus is Lord" (Rom. 10:9; 1 Cor. 12:3; 2 Cor. 4:5; Phil. 2:11; Col. 2:6; cf. Acts 2:39; 19:5). Another is "Jesus is the Son of God" (Rom. 1:4; Heb. 4:14; cf. 6:6; 7:3; 10:29; 1 John 4:15; 5:5). A confessional formula from Hellenistic Judaism, "God is one," also occurs (Rom. 3:30; Gal. 3:20; 1 Cor. 8:4; Eph. 4:6; 1 Tim. 2:5; Ignatius, *Magnesians* 8.2). A related formula is "The Lord is one" (1 Cor. 8:6; Eph. 4:5). A longer creedal statement, variously phrased, juxtaposes the death and resurrection of Jesus as saving facts (1 Cor. 15:3–5; 2 Cor. 5:15; Rom. 4:24–25; 8:34; 10:8–9; 14:9; 1 Peter 3:18; 2 Tim. 2:8). First Corinthians 15:5–8 also appears to contain a conflation of two original separate creedal lists focusing on witnesses to resurrection appearances, one headed by the name of Peter, the second by James. Another formula, developed in the Deutero-Pauline letters, has a twofold structure based on the idea that what was formerly hidden is now revealed (Col. 1:26–27; Eph. 3:4–5; 2 Tim. 1:9–10; Titus 1:2–3).

6. Liturgical sequences are very rare, though Paul does preserve a liturgy of the Lord's Supper in 1 Cor. 11:23–26 that is also preserved in variant versions in the Synoptic Gospels (Mark 14:22–25; Matt. 26:26–29; Luke 22:15–20). Some have argued that 1 Peter 1:3–4:11 preserves a baptismal liturgy, but this is probably incorrect.

Paraenetic Forms

In addition to the various hortatory styles that characterize paraenesis, there are three stereotyped paraenetic forms: vice and virtue lists, codes of household ethics, and the two-ways tradition.

Vice and Virtue Lists

The list is a common literary form used to inventory nearly anything. Virtue and vice catalogs are a relatively common type of list in early Christian literature and exhibit three primary forms: (1)

Polysyndetic lists use connective particles such as "and," "nor," and "or" (e.g., 1 Peter 2:1: "Put away all malice and all guilt and insincerity and envy and all slander"; cf. 1 Cor. 6:9–10). (2) *Asyndetic lists* lack connective particles (e.g., 2 Cor. 12:21: "[They] have not repented of the impurity, immorality, licentiousness which they have practiced"; cf. Rom. 1:29–30; Gal. 5:19–23). (3) *Amplified lists* expand on some or all items. Four of the five vices listed in Col. 3:5, for example, are found in 1 Thess. 4:3–7 in a more discursive form. The traditional content of such lists probably reflects a desire on the part of early Christians to foster greater conformity to contemporary social mores, i.e., culturally determined rules of behavior accepted by Jews, Christians, and pagans. Despite the traditional character of such lists, several of them were specifically aimed at problems experienced by local communities (1 Cor. 5:9–10; 6:9–10; 2 Cor. 12:20–21). Christian vice lists tend to emphasize *social* vices (e.g., covetousness, envy, strife, malice), in contrast to typical Hellenistic moral exhortation, which emphasized personal vices. This is a heritage from Judaism. The greater use of traditional paraenetic forms in post-Pauline letters suggests an increasing emphasis on conformity to Greco-Roman moral values. Double catalogs may reflect a baptismal liturgy (e.g., Gal. 5:17–24; Col. 3:1–17; Eph. 5:3–14), just as the *Rule of the Community* of Qumran (1QS 3.13–4.26) reflects the setting of initiation and *Didache* 7.1 places the extensive virtue and vice lists of the two-ways tradition in a recital preliminary to baptism.

In the New Testament letters there are twenty-three vice lists (a "list" includes three or more items). All but two occur in letters (cf. Matt. and Mark 7:21). Letters contain eight vice lists (e.g., Rom. 13:13; Eph. 5:3–5; 1 Tim. 6:4–5; 1 Peter 4:3), six offender lists (e.g., 1 Cor. 5:10–11; 1 Tim. 1:9–10; 1 Peter 4:5), one mixed vice/offender list (Rom. 1:29–31), and three vice and virtue lists (Gal. 5:19–23; Eph. 4:31–32; Titus 1:7–10).

Vice lists are also common in the Hellenistic moralists. About fifty vice lists occur in the orations of the Stoic orator Dio Chrysostom (A.D. 40 to after 112), many of which have close parallels with those in the New Testament (e.g., 1.13; 2.75; 8.8; 62.2). Lucian of Samosata (born ca. A.D. 120) also has more than fifty vice lists in his surviving writings. Perhaps the longest vice list of all is Philo's list of 147 characteristics of the lover of pleasure (*Sacrifices of Cain and Abel* 32).

The New Testament contains twenty virtue lists (containing a total of sixty-one virtues), all but two of which (Matt. 5:3–11; Heb. 7:26) are in letters (e.g., 2 Cor. 6:6–7; Gal. 5:22–23; Eph. 4:2–3). Dio

Chrysostom also includes more than thirty virtue lists in his orations (e.g., 1.4, 6; 3.5; 23.7; 44.10).

Codes of Household Ethics

Household codes focus on three levels of submission and reciprocal obligations within the extended family: wives to husbands, slaves to masters, children to parents. Several of these codes are found in New Testament letters (Col. 3:18–4:1; Eph. 5:21–6:9; 1 Peter 3:1–7, omitting the child–parent relationship). Submission to governmental authority is emphasized in Rom. 13:1–7 (cf. 1 Peter 2:13–15). In the Pastorals, household codes are found in Titus 2:1–10 and (interspersed with church order codes) in 1 Tim. 2:1–6:1 (cf. Polycarp, *Philippians* 4.1–6.1, which closely corresponds to this passage). If 1 Tim. 3:14f. is used to interpret the surrounding section, it appears that the church (the household of God) is modeled on the domestic household. Christianity applied the household model to relationships within the church itself, producing ecclesiastical station codes (1 Tim. 2:8–15; 6:1–2; Titus 2:1–10; *1 Clement* 1.3; 21.6–9; Ignatius, *Polycarp* 4.1–6.1; Polycarp, *Philippians* 4.2–6.3).

The origin and function of the Christian household codes has provoked a good deal of debate. They are usually thought to have originated in Stoicism. Stoics, however, emphasized the duties of the *individual* rather than the individual in *society*. Recently David Balch has provided a convincing discussion of the origin and history of this kind of moral teaching. Balch traces the origins of the household code back to Plato and Aristotle and discussions of three related *topoi*, "On household management," "On marriage," and "On the constitution" (cf. Aristotle, *Politics* 1.2.1–2; 1.5.1; Dionysius of Halicarnassus, *Roman Antiquities* 2.24.2–2.27.6). The order and strength of the state was thought dependent on the order and strength of the household (disorder in the household produces disorder in the state). The household code is used as an apologetic defense in the face of potential persecution, demonstrating that Christianity is not subversive. Household codes have no missionary purpose, but are directed primarily to Christians. They encourage the submission of pagan members of households (especially wives) to the Christian householder, and also encourage Christian members of pagan households to avoid behavior subversive to the interests and authority of the householder.

The Two-Ways Tradition

The figure of the two ways or paths was widely used in the ancient world as a metaphor for a life of vice or virtue. In early Christianity the two-ways tradition is found in just two letters, Ignatius, *Magnesians* 5.1–2, and *Barnabas* 18–21 (ca. A.D. 125). A very popular metaphor, it occurs in the Egyptian *Book of Two Ways*, in Greek and Roman literature (Hesiod, *Works and Days* 286–292; Xenophon, *Memorabilia* 2.1.21–33; Cebes, *Tabula*), and in Israelite-Jewish literature (Jer. 21:8; Ps. 1:1; Prov. 2:12–15; Sirach 21:10; *Testament of Asher* 1–6; *Rule of the Community* of Qumran, 1QS 3.13–4.26). The tradition is reflected in the two gates of Matt. 7:13–14, but more clearly in *Didache* 1–6 and *Barnabas* 18–21, both drawn from a common source. Both begin similarly: "There are two ways, one of life and one of death, and there is a vast difference between the two ways" (*Didache* 1.1; cf. *Barnabas* 18.1). Ignatius emphasizes life and death as the two ultimate alternatives, but (surprisingly) does not include any moral exhortation.

Epistolary Styles of Discourse

In the ancient world written letters and oral discourse (conversations, speeches) were closely related (Pseudo-Demetrius *Epistolary Types* 223; Cicero, *To Friends* 2.4.1; Seneca, *Letter* 75.1). Ignatius described one of his letters as a "conversation" (*Ephesians* 9.2), and another as an "address" (*Magnesians* 1.1). Paul too used letters to communicate what he might have preferred to say, preach, or teach in person. Preaching, the proclamation of the gospel to pagans and the moral and spiritual exhortation of believers, was an institution of central importance in early Christianity. Christian preaching and teaching was initially shaped by Hellenistic Jewish homiletic traditions, which were gradually displaced by more typically Hellenistic modes of discourse.

Modern scholars have labeled many early Christian compositions as "sermons" or "homilies." Yet these interchangeable terms are not really labels for a literary genre, since New Testament scholarship has not yet been able to define what a sermon is. One major obstacle is the fact that there are no early Christian texts that can be confidently identified as reasonably accurate versions of early Christian sermons. Some sermons (i.e., compositions with a generally didactic character) are framed as letters (Hebrews, James, 1 Peter, *1 Clement*, *Barnabas*), while others lack formal epistolary features (1 John, *2 Clement*). Some were written responses to a particular situation (Hebrews, 1 Peter, *1 Clement*), while others were written for Christians generally (James, *Barnabas, 2 Clement*).

Three types of discourse contributed to preaching and teaching styles in early Christianity: (1) types of Greco-Roman rhetoric (forensic, deliberative, and epideictic oratory), (2) the Greco-Roman diatribe or classroom style, and (3) the Jewish synagogue homily.

Types of Greco-Roman Rhetoric

An important component of literary analysis is rhetorical criticism, the subject of a recent book by George Kennedy (1984). Rhetorical criticism attempts to understand the effect that conventional forms of argumentation and structure used in the Greco-Roman world had on early Christian literary composition. In analyzing early Christian letters, important sources of information include the handbooks of the rhetorical and epistolary theorists, and actual letters. Actual letters include private documentary letters that were never published but reveal ancient epistolary conventions, and published letters, whether in inscriptions, embedment in ancient authors, or in collections that provided models for ancient letter writers.

The subject matter of rhetoric is the *probable,* whereas in philosophy it is the *demonstrable* and in religion the *revealed.* Unlike its pagan counterpart, Christian rhetoric used arguments based on revealed truth. The pragmatic sophists, the traditional practitioners of rhetoric, abandoned the quest for truth for the quest for the most persuasive arguments, and were rivals of the philosophers.

Following Aristotle, ancient rhetorical theorists divided oratory into three types according to the intended effect on the hearer: *judicial* (the most popular type for the simple reason that many were eventually involved, one way or another, in lawsuits), *deliberative,* and *epideictic* oratory. Judicial *(dicanic)* oratory, the oratory of the law courts, attempted to convince judges about *past* events. It had two basic types, accusation and defense. Deliberative *(symbouleutic)* oratory was the oratory of politics and focused on persuading the assembly about a *future* course of action. It also had two basic types, persuasion *(protreptic)* and dissuasion *(apotreptic).* Demonstrative *(epideictic)* oratory is ceremonial oratory and does not ask the audience to make judgments but try to provide pleasure in the *present* by celebrating common values. It also consists of two basic types, praise and blame.

The problem with this rhetorical classification is that it is a little too neat. Aristotle and the rhetorical theorists who succeeded him did not inductively analyze *actual* speeches, but rather prescribed how ideal speeches *ought* to be constructed. While that does not mean that there was no overlap between theory and practice, it does suggest that actual speeches could be more complex and eclectic than the rhetorical handbooks might suggest. Some rhetorical theorists had problems with the rigidity of the system and wanted to expand it (Cicero, *On Oratory* 1.32.145–147; 2.10.40–16.70; 2.23. 98). Most retained the system as important pedagogically but treated the categories with flexibility (Quintilian 3.4.1–16). Speeches whose object was rebuke, encouragement, consolation, teaching, and warning, for example, had no logical place in the threefold rhetorical system (Cicero, *On Oratory* 2.12.50; 2.15.64).

Each type of speech can consist of four elements: (1) *exordium* (introduction), (2) *narratio* (statement of facts), (3) *probatio* (argument), and (4) *peroratio* (conclusion). The introduction and conclusion seek to influence or even manipulate the audience by initially securing their interest and goodwill and end by recapitulating the arguments and making an emotional appeal. The body of the speech *(narratio* and *probatio)* seeks to establish the case. Deliberative speeches often shorten or omit the introduction and omit the *narratio,* since it is future action which is the purpose, not a decision about the past (Cicero, *Divisions of Oratory* 4.13). In order to motivate the audience to accept and act on a recommended course of action in deliberative rhetoric it was important to appeal to their honor and advantage, or self-interest (Quintilian 3.8.1; Cicero, *On Oratory* 2.81.333–337). These motivations were supported by three kinds of arguments: *ēthos:* an appeal to the good character of the audience; *pathos:* an appeal to their emotions; *logos:* an appeal to their reason (Aristotle, *Rhetoric* 1.2.3; 2.4–7; Quintilian 6.2. 9–12).

With few exceptions, early Christian letters were either written with a basically deliberative purpose, or included major deliberative elements. The two basic forms of deliberative rhetoric, persuasion and dissuasion, included not only advice but also most of the features associated with moral and religious exhortation: encouragement, admonition, comfort, warning, and rebuke. Most of Paul's letters, apart from the opening and closing epistolary formulas, consist of three elements. The first is conciliatory; he compliments the addressees for their past performance. The middle section contains advice. The final section contains paraenesis.

The Greco-Roman Diatribe

The diatribe has long been regarded as a literary genre reflecting the oral public preaching style of wandering Cynic and Stoic philosophers. During the Hellenistic period philosophers and rhetoricians were rivals, one reason why ancient rhetorical handbooks never discuss the diatribe. Since the diatribe style permeates Romans 1–11 and appears in patches in other New Testament letters (1 Cor. 15:29–41; Gal. 3:1–9, 19–22; James 2:1–3:12; 4:13–5:6), scholars have supposed that this style was adapted and Christianized from the public preaching style of popular philosophers, perhaps mediated through the Hellenistic synagogue. Recently, Stanley Stowers (upon whom the following discussion is largely dependent) has shown that diatribes did not originate as public lectures, but rather as records of oral classroom discussions and discourses of philosophical schools where the teacher used the Socratic methods of "censure" *(elenktikos)* and "persuasion" *(protreptikos)*. The distinguishing feature of the diatribe is its dialogical or conversational character, a pedagogical method based on the model of Socrates (Dio Chrysostom, *Oration* 13.14–29; Epictetus 2.12). The literary style of the diatribe (basically paratactic) is the result of transforming a rhetorical genre to a written genre, which ranges stylistically from lecture notes in rough draft, *hypomnēmata* (Epictetus' *Discourses* are really Arrian's lecture notes), or in rewritten and polished form, *apomnēmoneumata* (Musonius Rufus, Plutarch). Ancient authors who used this style include Bion and Teles (both third century B.C.), Musonius Rufus, Dio Chrysostom, Horace, Philo, Seneca, Plutarch, Epictetus, and the writer of the pseudepigraphical letters of Heraclitus.

The dialogical style of diatribes makes frequent use of imaginary opponents, hypothetical objections, and false conclusions. The questions and objections of the imaginary opponent and the teacher's responses oscillate between censure and persuasion. Censure exposes contradiction, error, and ignorance. Persuasion overcomes these with a call to the "philosophic" life by describing and illustrating virtue. The imaginary opponent is not a real opponent against whom the author polemicizes, but represents a synthesis of possible objections voiced by students whom he is trying to teach.

The *imaginary opponent* plays a central role in the diatribe: (1) He is abruptly addressed (Epictetus 2.6.16; Plutarch, *Moralia* 525c; Rom. 2:1, 17; 9:19). (2) He is frequently addressed in the vocative as an anonymous "man," or "fool" (Rom. 2:1, 3; 9:20), less commonly as a figure from history or myth representing a negative example, or a personification (Seneca, *Letter* 24.14; Rom. 11:19). (3) The opponent is frequently addressed with a singular "you" (Rom. 2:4, 17; 11:19). (4) An imaginary representative of a group is singled out and indicted for inconsistency (Epictetus 2.9.17; 2.21.11–12; 3.2.8–10; Rom. 3:1). (5) The author responds to an opponent's objection (Epictetus 4.9.5–6; Seneca *Letter* 7.5). (6) The address to the opponent begins with indicting statements or rhetorical questions emphasizing his ignorance (Epictetus 1.12.24–26; Rom. 2:4), error (i.e., wrong behavior or wrong thinking; Epictetus 3.22.81f.; Rom. 2:3; 9:20–24), or inconsistency (Epictetus 2.1.28; Seneca, *Letter* 77.18; Rom. 2:21–22). (7) Vice lists are used (Epictetus 4.9.5–6; Rom. 2:8, 21–23).

Dialogical objections and false conclusions also characterize the diatribe, where they are used primarily for the purpose of indictment: (1) Objections are frequently introduced by expressions like "What then?" (Rom. 3:1) or "Come now, you who say" (James 4:13), or the objector is referred to in the third-person singular or plural: "But someone will ask" (1 Cor. 15:35) or "They say." (2) The adversative particle *alla* ("but") frequently introduces the opponent's objection (1 Cor. 15:35; James 2:18). (3) False conclusions are framed as questions (Seneca, *Letter* 14.15; Plutarch, *Moralia* 527a; Epictetus 1.29.9; Rom. 3:9; 6:1, 15; 7:7; 9:14). (4) Hypothetical objections are posed by the author (Dio Chrysostom, *Oration* 74.8, 23; Rom. 3:1), or attributed to an imaginary interlocutor ("You will say," Rom. 9:19; 11:19). (5) Objections and false conclusions are rejected with such expressions as "not at all!" or "by no means!" (Epictetus 4.8.26–28; Rom. 3:4; 6:2; 9:14; 11:1), and by citing examples (Abraham in Rom. 4:1). (6) Objections or false conclusions are placed at major turns in the argument (Rom. 3:1; 6:1; 7:7; 9:14), and are often restated in subsections (3:9; 6:15; 7:13; 9:19). (7) Ironic imperatives and hortatory subjunctives used ironically are frequent (e.g., "If the dead are not raised, 'Let us eat and drink, for tomorrow we die' "; 1 Cor. 15:32).

Paul was a Christian teacher of both Jews and Gentiles. The diatribe style is a teaching style that he used in dealing with various typical constituencies orally and through letters. He uses the diatribe style extensively in Romans since he knows less about the recipients' situation than he does about communities he himself had founded. His teaching in Romans is therefore not called forth specifically by the epistolary situation but by his past experience as a teacher of Jews and Gentiles. Diatribe style occurs only occasionally in 1 Corinthians and Galatians because he is more familiar with the local situation and tailors his advice more directly to the epistolary situation. The presence of diatribe style in James coheres with the author's extensive use of general paraenetic material not specifically formulated to fit a specific epistolary situation.

The Jewish Synagogue Homily

The homiletic exegesis of Scripture was, of course, a characteristic feature of Judaism, but prior to the formation of the Mishnah (ca. A.D. 200) fixed sermonic patterns did not exist. The origin of the Jewish synagogue sermon is shrouded in obscurity, but by A.D. 70 exegetical preaching was an established custom in Palestine and the Diaspora (Philo, *Moses* 2.215f.; *Special Laws* 2.62; Luke 4:20–27; Acts 13:15). The sermons preached in synagogues or houses of study on Sabbaths and festivals were based on the Torah reading of the day. The great collections of Midrashim (i.e., biblical commentaries such as Genesis Rabbah and Exodus Rabbah) were probably distilled from thousands of sermons preached during the Amoraic period (A.D. 200–500), though nearly all were radically abbreviated and combined with others to form *literary* homilies.

Sermons open in several ways. One type (found in the Tanchuma Midrashim) begins with the formula *Yelammedenu rabbenu* ("May our master teach us"), followed by a halakhic (i.e., "legal") question. Another type that probably reflects actual oral sermons is the "proem" homily, of which about 2,000 are preserved. Proem homilies began with a quotation from a "remote" text from the Writings (the third division of Hebrew Scripture). The object was to link the first text with the first verse of the Torah reading for the day, i.e., to resolve the tension between two seemingly unrelated passages by showing how they were complementary. The proem pattern appeared in the Tannaitic period (first two centuries A.D.) and became popular in the Amoraic period (A.D. 200–500). Only about ten Tannaitic proem sermons are extant, and all deviate from later patterns. By the end of the Tannaitic period (A.D. 200), the proem was still not widely used and had not yet attained a fixed format. The Yelammedenu homilies are much later. The "discovery" of proem homilies in the New Testament (e.g., John 6:31–58; Acts 13:16–41; Rom. 1:17–4:25; 1 Cor. 1:18–3:20) is anachronistic (i.e., these passages may contain homiletic exegesis of Scripture, but they conform neither to the proem or to the yelammedenu types).

Types of Early Christian Letters

Early Christian letters tend to resist rigid classification, either in terms of the three main types of oratory or in terms of the many categories listed by the epistolary theorists. Most early Christian letters are multifunctional and have a "mixed" character, combining elements from two or more epistolary types. In short, each early Christian letter must be analyzed on its own terms. Pseudo-Libanius concludes his list of forty-one styles of letters with the *mixed* style, composed of several styles (*Epistolary Styles* 45, 92, with a sample letter combining praise and blame). Attempts to classify one or another of Paul's letters as *either* judicial *or* deliberative *or* epideictic (or one of their subtypes) run the risk of imposing external categories on Paul and thereby obscuring the real purpose and structure of his letters. Paul in particular was both a creative and eclectic letter writer. The epistolary situations he faced were often more complex than the ordinary rhetorical situations faced by most rhetoricians. Many letters therefore exhibit combinations of styles. Threat and admonition are combined in 2 Cor. 4:14–21. Consolation is found in 1 Thess. 4:13–18. Recommendations are mixed with other epistolary styles in a number of passages (Rom. 16:1–2; 1 Cor. 16:15–18; 2 Cor. 8:16–23; Phil. 2:29–30; 4:2–3; 1 Thess. 5:12–13; Heb. 13:17; Polycarp, *Philippians* 14.1). First Corinthians is a complex combination of paraenesis (3:5–4:21) and advice (5:1–6:11; 7:1–8:13; 10:1–14:39).

Some letters have a single dominant function or purpose reflected in one prevailing style. Philemon and 3 John, for example, are letters of recommendation (*epistolē systatikē*, Pseudo-Demetrius, *Epistolary Types* 2; Pseudo-Libanius, *Epistolary Styles* 55; cf. 2 Cor. 3:1). Such letters played an important role for Christians who visited communities where they were personally unknown (Acts 9:12; 22:5; 1 Cor. 16:3). Romans incorporates protreptic discourse into an epideictic letter; 1 Thessalonians is a paraenetic letter. *First Clement* is a deliberative letter (in 58.2 the author uses the technical term *symboulē*, "advice") in which the author advises the divisive and discordant Corinthian congregation to attain peace and concord (cf. 57.1–2; 63.2; an analogous deliberative speech urging the Nicomedians to seek concord with the Nicaeans is found in Dio Chrysostom, *Oration* 38). Ignatius' letter to the Romans is primarily a deliberative letter of advice (a request), largely lacking the hortatory emphasis found in his other letters.

While it is important to be able to place early Christian letters within the broader setting of a typology of Greco-Roman epistolography (as Stanley Stowers has done), and Jewish epistolography (for which evidence is scanty), the distinctive social features of early Christianity suggest a broader typology in which early Christian letters can be understood. The discussion of individual letters that follows, therefore, is arranged in terms of a typology of two ideal epistolary types. These types are at opposite ends of a spectrum; they consist of (1) *circumstantial,* or dialogical, letters, which are closely linked to specific historical situations, and (2) *general,* or monological, letters, which are unconnected to specific historical settings.

Occasional Letters and Homilies

The *circumstantial* or occasional letter is a written communication between two parties directly acquainted with each other reflecting a particular historical situation. The "epistolary situation" can usually be inferred with relative ease from the text. The message has a dialogical character, i.e., the character of the communication is determined by the relationship between sender and receiver. Such letters tend to be restricted to characteristically epistolary forms and styles. In this section we will discuss the Pauline and Ignatian letters generally, and in more detail 1 Thessalonians, Galatians, 2 Corinthians, Philippians, Philemon, and Hebrews.

The Pauline Letters

Paul is the first Christian writer whose works have survived. Thirteen letters in the New Testament are ascribed to him. Not all are authentic. Those that are (at least Romans, 1–2 Corinthians, Galatians, Philippians, 1 Thessalonians, and Philemon) were written over a fifteen-year period (ca. A.D. 49–64). Four are widely held to be pseudonymous (i.e., written by an unknown person in Paul's name): Ephesians, 1–2 Timothy, and Titus. The authenticity of Colossians and 2 Thessalonians is in doubt. By A.D. 100 a group of ten Pauline letters (all but the Pastorals, 1–2 Timothy and Titus) formed a collection. The Pastorals, written ca. A.D. 100–125, eventually became part of the Pauline corpus, but probably not until late in the second century (they were not included in Marcion's collection of Pauline letters, ca. A.D. 150, and are missing from the earliest papyrus codex of the Pauline letters, P46). A collection of Pauline letters, then, formed an early nucleus for the developing New Testament canon. Not all Paul's letters were preserved (1 Cor. 5:9 refers to a "former letter"; 2 Cor. 2:4 mentions a "sorrowful letter"; Col. 4:16 refers to a letter to the Laodiceans), at least not in their original form. Several Pauline letters show signs of having been edited, i.e., of having major interpolations or consisting of two or more letters shorn of introductory and concluding epistolary features (examples include Romans, 2 Corinthians, and Philippians).

The present canonical order of Paul's letters may reveal the contours of the original collection. Romans is the first and longest (7,094 words or 920 stichoi—a stichos is a line of about sixteen syllables), while Philemon is last and shortest (328 words; 38 stichoi). Aside from Ephesians and the Pastorals, the letters between Romans and Philemon are arranged in order of decreasing length: 1 Corinthians (6,807 words; 870 stichoi), 2 Corinthians (4,448 words; 590 stichoi), Galatians (2,220 words; 293 stichoi), Philippians (1,624 words; 208 stichoi), Colossians (1,577 words; 208 stichoi), 1 Thessalonians (1,472 words; 193 stichoi), 2 Thessalonians (824 words; 106 stichoi). This mechanical arrangement suggests that these nine letters may have existed as a coherent collection antedating the canonical collection which includes Ephesians and the Pastorals. The oldest papyrus codex of the Pauline letters (ca. A.D. 200) lacks the Pastorals and generally follows an order of decreasing lengths, reversing Galatians and Ephesians, though Hebrews (4,942 words) is inserted after Romans. This principle of arrangement is not unknown in the ancient world. The Latter Prophets of the Hebrew Bible (Isaiah, Jeremiah, Ezekiel, the Twelve) are arranged in order of descending length, as are the tractates within each of the six divisions of the Mishnah. Similarly, the 114 surahs of the Qur'an are arranged with the longest surah at the beginning (Al-Baqarah, "The Cow"), and the shortest at the end (Al-Nas, "Mankind").

The Pastorals constitute a short collection arranged in decreasing size: 1 Timothy (1,586 words; 230 stichoi), 2 Timothy (1,235 words; 172 stichoi), Titus (663 words; 97 stichoi). The relatively late date of these works (ca. A.D. 125), their homogeneity, and the evidence of 2 Tim. 4:13 combine to suggest that they were originally written on a codex, probably with the express intention of supplementing the older Pauline corpus. The addition of pseudonymous letters to an existing corpus has analogies in both pagan and Christian epistolary collections (e.g., collections of letters attributed to Plato, Isocrates, Demosthenes, and Ignatius of Antioch).

1 Thessalonians: A Paraenetic Letter

1 Thessalonians, the first letter Paul wrote (ca. A.D. 50), exhibits some distinctive features. The superscript and the salutation are shorter and simpler than usual and it has the longest thanksgiving period of all his letters (1:2–3:13). Further, it is the only Pauline letter in which the "concluding" hortatory section (4:1–5:22) constitutes the main part. The point of the letter is succinctly expressed in 4:1–2, 10b–12: Do what you have done, but even more. The sections "Concerning those who have fallen asleep" (4:13–18) and "Concerning times and seasons" (5:1–11) appear to be responses to questions relayed to Paul from the congregation. Abraham Malherbe has argued that the letter exhibits two paraenetic styles similar to popular moral philosophy. One is paraenetic moral exhortation (clearly evident in chs. 4–5), and the other is the antithetical style which also serves a paraenetic function (evident in chs. 1–3). Paul's use of rhetorical antithesis is evident in 1 Thess. 2:3–4:

> For our appeal does *not* spring from error or uncleanness, *nor* is it made with guile; but just as we have been approved by God to be entrusted with the gospel, so we speak, *not* to please men, but to please God who tests our hearts.

This antithetical style should not be interpreted as Paul's defense of hypothetical accusations. Rather it is a technique that *amplifies* thought by contrasting ideas using negation, antonyms, and other devices (Aristotle, *Rhetoric* 1409b-1410a; Pseudo-Aristotle, *Rhetoric to Alexander* 1435b; Hermogenes, *On Invention* 4.2). This fits the tendency of paraenesis, which also combines the positive "do this" with the negative "stop doing that." Especially in 2:1–12, Paul uses traditional language in response to standard criticisms of wandering philosophers, though not in response to specific attacks. First Thessalonians 1–3 contains many autobiographical features in which Paul rehearses his previous relationship to the community and emphasizes his own role as an example to follow (1:6; 2:14). The exhortation 4:1–5:22 is based on 1:2–3:13. In this style of paraenetic discourse, Paul emphasizes the fact that he is not telling them anything new, but reminding them of what they already know (1:5; 2:1–10).

Galatians: A Deliberative Letter

The epistolary situation reflected in Galatians is that after Paul's departure outsiders ("Judaizers") arrived in Galatia and convinced some that to be a Christian one must first become a convert to Judaism. Some were therefore circumcised. When Paul learned of these developments he was disturbed. He wrote to the Galatians to convince them that the real underlying issue was grace vs. law, and that faith was both prior to and superior to the law as a principle of salvation.

Galatians is often regarded, in whole or in part, as an *apologetic* letter. In his 1979 commentary on Galatians, Hans Dieter Betz has forcefully presented the view that Galatians is an apologetic letter exhibiting the structure of ancient forensic oratory. The apologetic approach to Galatians is based on the assumption that the outside Judaizers were also opponents of Paul who slandered him to discredit his message.

The problem of identifying the charges against Paul is complicated by his use of rhetorical antithesis (e.g., Gal. 1:1): "Paul an apostle —*not* from men *nor* through man, *but* through Jesus Christ and God the Father." Paul uses antithesis again in the important passage in Gal. 1:11–12: "The gospel preached by me is *not* man's gospel, for I did *not* receive it from man, *nor* was I taught it, *but* it came through a revelation of Jesus Christ." It is often thought that a reverse reading of these and other negative statements (e.g., 1: 16–17; 4:14; 5:1, 6, 13; 6:15) reveals the positive accusations of Paul's opponents. Unlike the situation in 1 Thessalonians, in this case Paul *does* have opponents whom he distinguishes from the Galatians themselves (1:7, 9; 5:10, 12; 6:12). Yet since Paul is probably refuting both real and possible charges, we cannot profile either Paul's opponents or their accusations. Normally in forensic speeches of defense the charges are stated clearly; in Galatians they must be inferred.

On the other hand, Galatians can be read as a deliberative letter with some apologetic features. Paul tried to convince the Galatians to change their thinking and their behavior. He tried to help them understand the real relationship between faith and law and to convince them to stop practicing Judaism as if it were a necessary matrix for Christian faith. The thanksgiving period that Paul normally inserts after the prescript has been replaced with a statement of rebuke, which has parallels in papyrus letters. Galatians 1:6–12 is the introduction, in which Paul criticizes the Galatians for switching to another gospel and presents the *stasis* or basic issue of the letter: Paul's gospel is from God not man. The narrative of Gal. 1:13–2:21 has a defensive tone and is intended to establish Paul's credibility, for in deliberative rhetoric the *ēthos* or moral character and conduct of the speaker, if unknown or in doubt, must be established. Galatians 3:1–4:31 uses a range of stock arguments in diatribe (class-room) style which Paul developed in his teaching ministry to argue that the Galatians must understand that faith was both prior to the law and superior to it. The law was intended by God only as an interim measure to point to the necessity of faith in Christ. Thereafter it has no valid role. Finally, Gal. 5:1–6:10 is a paraenetic section in which Paul exhorts the Galatians to change their behavior (i.e., abandon circumcision and all that goes with it) on the basis of the proper understanding true of faith vs. law. While paraenesis can function in both deliberative and epideictic rhetoric depending on whether a change of behavior is envisaged (deliberative) or a set of common values is being reiterated (epideictic), the paraenesis of Gal. 5:1–6:10 functions primarily in a deliberative manner.

2 Corinthians: A Composite Letter

Paul's relationship with the Corinthian Christians was very complex and involved many exchanges of written and oral messages from ca. A.D. 54–56. Paul refers to a "former letter" in 1 Cor. 5:9, and to a "tearful letter" in 2 Cor. 2:4 and 7:8. These have either not survived or have been included, in modified form, in 2 Corinthians. For while 1 Corinthians is not widely regarded as a composite letter, 2 Corinthians may be a conflation of from two to six separate compositions assembled by an unknown editor before inclusion in the Pauline collection. These include (1) 2 Cor. 1:1–2:13; 7:5–16; 13:11–14; (2) 2 Cor. 2:14–6:13; 7:2–4; (3) 2 Cor. 6:14–7:1 (the only possibly non-Pauline segment); (4) 2 Cor. 8; (5) 2 Cor. 9; and (6) 2 Cor. 10:1–13:10 (often identified as the "tearful letter" mentioned in 2:4). The more complicated such partition theories become, of course, the more speculative and less credible they appear. For this reason many scholars argue for the unity of the letter or for a simpler division into two originally separate letters represented by 2 Cor. 1–9 and 10–13.

What some have called a "letter of reconciliation" is preserved in 2 Cor. 1:1–2:13; 7:5–16; 13:11–13. The epistolary prescript (1:1–7) and postscript (13:11–13) have provided the redactional framework for the entire composite letter. The "thanksgiving" (1:3–7) is not typical of Paul's letters since it begins not with "I give thanks" *(eucharistein)* but with a blessing formula *(eulogētos)*. Yet it functions like Paul's thanksgivings by signaling the main theme: the same divine comfort Paul receives by sharing Christ's sufferings can be experienced by the Corinthians in their afflictions. The central section of this letter consists of an extensive autobiographical narrative that both establishes and defends Paul's character and behavior (1:8–2:13 and 7:5–16).

The letter fragments which have the least epistolary integrity are preserved in 2 Cor. 2:14–6:13; 7:2–4. One possible explanation for this is that these fragments do not really constitute an originally independent letter, but rather a lengthy apologetic digression in which Paul defends his apostleship. It begins with a prayer of thanksgiving (2:14–17), but not in the usual form of Paul's introductory thanksgivings. The main section which follows consists of a defense of his apostleship (3:1–6:13 and 7:2–4). Into this apologetic section Paul inserts a digression on Jewish and Christian understanding of the Old Testament (3:12–18). Into this truncated letter, 2 Cor. 6:14–7:1 has been inserted. In its present literary setting it also functions as a digression, as a comparison of the framing verses 2 Cor. 6:13 and 7:2 reveal.

Recently, Hans Dieter Betz (1985) has attempted to place the view that 2 Corinthians 8 and 9 were originally separate letters on a firmer and more objective footing. He proposes that each letter exhibits coherent epistolary structure (lacking only a prescript and postscript) revealing their original independence. Second Corinthians 8 (addressed to Corinth) is a letter mixing advice (8:1–15) with administrative matters (8:16–23), as the following analysis suggests: (1) Introduction (vs. 1–5): The Macedonians, in spite of affliction and poverty, have contributed beyond their means. (2) Statement of facts (v. 6): Titus has been appointed to pick up their contribution. (3) Proposition (vs. 7–8): As they excel in many spiritual virtues, may they excel also in generosity. (4) Proofs (vs. 9–15): It is both honorable and expedient for them to follow their promise with a gift. (5) Commendation of delegates (vs. 16–22). (6) Authorization of delegates (v. 23). (7) Peroration: appeal for acceptance of delegates (v. 24). Betz compares 2 Cor. 8 with letters of appointment given to envoys (cf. Acts 9:12; 22:5). Basically 2 Cor. 8 is an advisory letter (i.e., symbouleutic), and comparable to ancient "official" letters of recommendation, reflecting the legal and administrative conventions of that era (cf. 1 Cor. 16:3).

Second Corinthians 9 (addressed to Christians in Achaia; cf. 2 Cor. 1:1) is a deliberative letter exhibiting the following structure: (1) Introduction (vs. 1–2): Paul has boasted of their willingness to give. (2) Statement of facts (vs. 3–5b): Paul is sending envoys to pick up their contribution lest they should be unprepared when Paul himself arrives and all are embarrassed. (3) Proposition (vs. 5b–c):

The promised contribution has yet to be collected. (4) Proofs (vs. 6–14): Reasons for giving and resultant spiritual and material benefits. (5) Peroration (v. 15): Prayer of thanksgiving.

Second Corinthians 10:1–13:10 (possibly the "tearful letter" mentioned in 2 Cor. 2:4 and 7:8) is a distinctive type of apologetic letter written to refute the charges of opponents who had swayed Corinthian opinion against Paul. When Paul denies (in a rhetorical question) that he is defending himself, he is actually claiming only to forgo argumentation characteristic of forensic rhetoric. Instead he models his defense on philosophical apologies in the Socratic tradition. The accusation against which he mounts a defense is quoted in 2 Cor. 10:10: "For they [i.e., the opponents] say, 'His letters are weighty and strong, but his bodily presence is weak, and his speech of no account.' " In the Socratic tradition, Paul uses sarcasm, parody, and irony as weapons of defense, "boasting" in a fool's speech (11:1–12:18) of his refusal to accept financial support (11:7–12), and of ecstatic visions (12:2–4), failure to be healed (12:7–10), and apostolic signs (12:12).

Philippians: A Letter of Gratitude and Paraenesis

Philippians was written from prison (1:12–14) and mixes gratitude (*apeucharistikos typos;* Pseudo-Demetrius, *Epistolary Types* 21) with paraenesis. Paul expresses gratitude both to God for the exemplary faith of the Philippian Christians and to the community for their financial support and for sending aides like Epaphroditus (1:3–11; 4:10–18). Various styles of paraenesis also pervade the letter: positive exhortation (1:27–2:4, 12–18; 3:1; 4:1, 4–8), warning (3:2), the positive examples set by Paul (1:12–26; 3:4–17) and Christ (2:5–11), and the negative examples set by others whom Paul does not name (3:18–19; 4:9).

One of the main problems in interpreting Philippians is that of the unity of the letter. Philippians is often thought to consist of not one but *three* separate Pauline letters joined together by an unknown editor: (1) 1:1–3:1; (2) 3:2–4:1; (3) 4:10–20 (often labeled a letter of thanks). Philippians 3:2 does depart from the tone of what has preceded, but such changes can be explained as epistolary *digressions.* The travelogue in 2:19–30, though it would normally be placed at the conclusion of the main part of one of Paul's letters, can also occur elsewhere (cf. 1 Cor. 4:14–21; Gal. 4:12–20; 1 Thess. 2:17–3:13). Further, in editing letters the ancient practice usually involved removing just the epistolary prescripts and subscripts. Yet if Philippians is made up of three Pauline letters, the editor has also removed the Pauline thanksgiving periods, which seems unlikely. Further, the pervasive character of paraenesis suggests the unity of the letter.

Philemon: A Letter of Recommendation

The epistolary situation reflected in Philemon, Paul's shortest letter (written from a Rome prison), concerns Onesimus, a runaway slave. Arriving in Rome, he met Paul and was converted. Paul sent him back to his master bearing a letter of recommendation to facilitate reconciliation. A pagan letter of recommendation often compared with Philemon is Pliny's *Letter* 9.21, in which Pliny appeals to Sabinianus to put away his anger and accept back a penitent freedman (*Letter* 9.24 is a follow-up letter of gratitude to Sabinianus for taking his advice). Philemon is not really a *private* letter, for it is addressed to Philemon, Apphia, and Archippus and "the church in your [singular] house," though it is not clear whether the letter is primarily addressed to Philemon or Archippus (i.e., it is uncertain to whom the singular "your" refers). While the request section of Philemon (vs. 8–16) has some similarities to papyrus letters of petition, its structure and argument follow the conventions of deliberative rhetoric. Philemon consists of five parts: (1) prescript (vs. 1–3), (2) exordium, or introduction (vs. 4–7), (3) main part with proofs (vs. 8–16), (4) peroration or concluding summary (vs. 17–22), and (5) postscript (vs. 23–25). Paul's thanksgivings (here vs. 4–7) usually indicate the main themes of his letters, and this one also functions as a *captatio benevolentiae* (an exordium securing the goodwill of the recipient). By praising Philemon, he establishes mutual goodwill and stresses qualities to which he can subsequently appeal (e.g., love, which refreshes the hearts of the saints). In vs. 8–16, Paul is advancing an argument as well as making a request. Using an emotional appeal in vs. 8–10, Paul claims the status to command Philemon, but chooses instead to appeal to his Christian love. He proposes that it is advantageous for Philemon to be reconciled to Onesimus using a pun: he who was "useless" will now be "useful" (Onesimus means "useful"). In vs. 12–14 he appeals to Philemon's honor. Finally in the peroration he restates his request (v. 17), amplifies it (vs. 18–19), appeals to Philemon's emotions (v. 20), and secures his favor (vs. 21–22). Several crucial themes are repeated in the exordium, the main part, and the peroration: love (vs. 5, 7, 9), good (vs. 6, 14), fellowship (vs. 6,17), "heart" (vs. 7, 12, 20). These three parts form a syllogism: if Philemon refreshes the heart of Christians (v. 7), and if Onesimus refreshes Paul's heart (v. 12), then to refresh Paul's heart Philemon must refresh the heart of Onesimus (v. 20).

Hebrews: A Hortatory Sermon

The rhetorical situation of Hebrews, according to many scholars, was the possibility that a particular but unknown group of Jewish Christians might lapse back into Judaism. Accordingly, the author appeals to them to remain firmly within the Christian faith, which is superior to Judaism. The antiquity of this view is reflected in the title "To the Hebrews," inferred from the contents and secondarily added by ca. A.D. 150. Occasional commentators from James Moffatt (1924) to Herbert Braun (1984), however, have correctly argued that this view is based on assumptions not explicitly found in the text. Rather, the original recipients of Hebrews were probably Gentile Christians in danger of lapsing back into paganism. On either view, rhetorically, Hebrews is *epideictic.* The author urges the audience to continue to maintain values and opinions currently held. Hebrews was written ca. A.D. 70–85 (it was used by the author of *1 Clement*) and was addressed to an unknown local community with particular problems and specific experiences (5:11–12; 6:1–12; 10: 25, 32–34; 12:4; 13:7).

Written in excellent Atticizing Greek (apart from the final paraenetic chapter), Hebrews is the only New Testament composition fully deserving the label *Kunstprosa,* "euphonic prose" (cf. Eusebius, *Church History* 6.25.11). Like Luke, Hebrews begins with an elaborate periodic sentence (1:1–4); many others are distributed throughout the composition, giving the prose a flowing quality (e.g., 2:2–4; 3:12–15; 5:1–3, 7–10). The author carefully avoids hiatus (the slight break caused when two vowels come together in successive words or syllables, as in "see easily"), and anacolouthon (breaks in grammatical sequence). He pays conscious attention to patterns of prose rhythm at the conclusion of sentences. An elaborate use of anaphora (a series of lines beginning with the same word) is found in Hebrews 11, in which eighteen sentences, an encomium recounting a series of past Israelite and Jewish models of faith suitable for imitation, each begin with the word *pistei* ("by faith"), building to a moving and eloquent conclusion (11:32–39). The repetition of *pistei* calls to mind the author's use of alliteration. He uses six words beginning with "p" in Hebrews 1:1 (five in 11:28; four in 12:11). The author obviously enjoyed the benefits of a Hellenistic rhetorical education through the tertiary level.

The author labels his work a "word of exhortation [*paraklēsis*]"

(13:22), a phrase elsewhere used of a synagogue sermon (Acts 13: 15), a pep talk by Judas Maccabeus (2 Macc. 15:11), and the substance of an apostolic decree sent by letter (Acts 15:31). The author expects his readers to exhort one another (3:13; a paraenetic *topos* found in Rom. 15:14; 1 Thess. 4:18; 5:11; cf. Rom. 14:19; Jude 20). This mutual exhortation takes place within the setting of congregational worship (10:25), confirming the homiletic character of Hebrews. Several features point toward the rhetorical rather than the literary origin of Hebrews: the use of rhetorical questions (1:5, 13; 3:16–18; 9:14; 10:29; 11:32), the recipients are addressed as "brothers" (3:1, 12; 10:19; 13:22), the presence of rhetorical expressions like "And what more shall I say?" and "Time will fail me if I tell . . ." (11:32).

But is Hebrews a letter? If so, it is atypical for it has an epistolary postscript but no prescript. The anonymity of Hebrews makes it tempting to suppose either that the original epistolary prescript was removed (anonymity was atypical of ancient epistolography), or that a secondary epistolary postscript (13:18–25) was appended. Neither proposal is probable. In spite of the original epistolary conclusion, Hebrews probably originated as an orally delivered sermon (or series of sermons) given literary form and distributed through the inclusion of an epistolary postscript. Further, the concluding paraenetic section in 13:1–17 is epistolary in character, following the pattern of several (though not all) Pauline letters.

The structure of Hebrews remains an unsolved problem. Despite the author's rhetorical training and his epideictic intention, Hebrews is not structured in accordance with the typical patterns of epideictic or (the closely related) deliberative rhetoric. The entire work is *hortatory,* based on the central theme expressed in Hebrews 2:2–4: we must take our revelation more seriously than we have. The rhetorical strategy of the author is based on a comparison (*synkrisis*) between the old and the new. If Israel was punished by God for neglecting the revelation at Sinai, how much more shall we be punished for neglecting our revelation, given its superiority? This superiority is primarily evident in Jesus Christ the Son of God, who is God's final revelation. Jesus (and the new covenant) is superior to angels (1:1–2:18), the old covenant represented by Moses (3: 1–4:13), and the priesthood (4:14–10:31). Hebrews 10:32–12:29 centers on past models of faith and endurance for future imitation: the addressed community's past behavior (10:32–39), a roster of Jewish heroes of faith (11:1–12:1), and Jesus himself (12:2–6). A loosely structured paraenetic section is included (13:1–17). Here the author relaxes the literary character of his Greek. The entire chapter therefore (and not just 13:18–25) exhibits an epistolary character. The doxology of Hebrews (13:20–21) is an *epistolary* doxology since it does not directly conclude the body of Hebrews (otherwise it should be placed after 12:29), but is framed by the conventions of the epistolary postscript (13:18–25; cf. *1 Clement* 65:2) and is located after the epistolary paraenesis in 13:1–17.

The main part of Hebrews (1:1–12:29), therefore, is a complex blend of theological arguments based on the exegesis of the Old Testament punctuated by hortatory appeals. The major hortatory sections (though there is disagreement about their extent) include 2:1–4; 3:7–4:13; 4:14–16; 5:11–6:12; 12:1–17; 13:1–17. The hortatory portions of 1:1–12:29, which reflect the central concern of the author, are primarily *religious* in character and center on the themes of endurance and faith, e.g., 4:14: "Let us hold fast our confession" (cf. 2:1; 4:1, 11; 10:23). Positive exhortations are laced with numerous warnings (2:1–4; 3:7–4:13; 6:4–8; 10:26–39; 12:25–29). The warnings are tempered by the author's assurance that they are scarcely needed (6:9; cf. Rom. 15:14–15). The fact that much of the exhortation is a reminder (2:1) is a typical hortatory *topos*.

The Letters of Ignatius

Ignatius, Bishop of Antioch, was arrested ca. A.D. 115 and taken by land and sea to Rome for execution. His letters, written in expectation of imminent death, read like a testament to the churches of Asia Minor. Unlike the Pauline letters, which were written over a fifteen-year span, Ignatius wrote seven letters within just a few weeks. Ignatius and his military escort arrived in southern Asia Minor, and headed northwest to Troas (probably gathering other prisoners on the way), stopping at Smyrna. There he was permitted visits by delegations from Ephesus (*Eph.* 1.32), Smyrna (*Magn.* 15:1), Magnesia (*Magn.* 2.1), and Tralles (*Trall.* 1.1). He wrote letters to each congregation represented (except Smyrna), and one to Rome (*Rom.* 10.1). Traveling northwest, Ignatius visited Philadelphia (*Philad.* 7.1). From Troas, before crossing over to Europe, he wrote to Philadelphia (*Philad.* 11.2), Smyrna (*Smyr.* 12.1), and Polycarp the bishop of Smyrna (*Polyc.* 8.1). With the exception of the letters to Rome and Polycarp, each was written to communities who had sent representatives to meet Ignatius along the way. They are, implicitly, letters of gratitude.

The popularity of the seven genuine letters of Ignatius encouraged the addition of six spurious letters by a single unknown person by the fifth century A.D. Yet the present collection, arranged not in the order found in the manuscripts but in that mentioned by Eusebius (*Church History* 3.36.1–10), suggests that they originally formed two groups, those written from Smyrna (*Ephesians, Magnesians, Trallians, Romans*), and those written from Troas (*Philadelphians, Smyrnaeans, Polycarp*). Eusebius may be responsible for the fact that they are generally arranged in order of decreasing length. The collection begins with *Ephesians* (the longest 1,778 words) and concludes with *Polycarp* (the shortest, 785 words). Between them are *Magnesians* (1,063), *Trallians* (950), *Romans* (1,032), *Philadelphians* (1,019) and *Smyrnaeans* (1,147). These letters were collected by Polycarp at the request of the Christian congregation in Philippi (Polycarp, *Phil.* 13.1–2).

Opening and Closing Formulas

The opening and closing epistolary formulas used by Ignatius differ from the epistolary style of earlier Christian letters. The superscript in each letter is short and unpretentious: "Ignatius, also called Theophoros." The basic adscript "to the church" is amplified by three structural elements: (1) passive participles describing the benefits each church has received from God (e.g., blessed, foreordained, united, elect); (2) adjectives describing the spiritual greatness of each church (e.g., worthy of blessing); (3) mention of the location of each church. This translation of the *Ephesians* preface exhibits this structure by italicizing the participles and the adjectives mentioned above:

> Ignatius, also called Theophoros, to her who is *blessed* with greatness by the fullness of God the Father, *foreordained* before the ages to be forever destined for enduring and unchangeable glory, *united* and *elected* in true suffering by the will of the Father and Jesus Christ our God, to the church *worthy of blessing* which is in Ephesus in Asia, warmest greetings in Jesus Christ and with blameless joy.

The longest and most ornate adscript is in *Romans*, where (among other flowery features) Ignatius has an asyndetic list of six compound adjectives, each beginning with *axio-* ("worthy"): "worthy of God, worthy of respect, worthy of blessing, worthy of praise, worthy of success, worthy of holiness." Since *Romans* is basically a letter of *request*, Ignatius is obviously working on the assumption that flattery will get him somewhere.

The basic salutation Ignatius favors is "warmest greetings" (*pleista chairein*), a formula first appearing in papyrus letters in the late first century B.C. He usually amplifies it with theologically laden prepositional phrases. The salutation is missing from *Philadelphians*, apparently through oversight. Three times Ignatius includes the *aspazesthai* ("to greet") formula (normally placed in the closing sections of Pauline letters) in prescripts, an epistolary formula attested in papyrus letters for the second through fourth centuries A.D. *(Magnesians, Trallians, Romans)*. While thanksgivings are not placed after the prescripts, Ignatius does include an epistolary thanksgiving toward the end of several letters, perhaps consciously modifying Pauline practice (*Eph.* 21.1; *Philad.* 11.1; *Smyrn.* 10.1).

The postscripts of Ignatian letters exhibit several formal features: (1) There is a typically Hellenistic epistolary closing, "farewell" *(errōsthe,* expanded by various prepositional phrases, such as "in the Lord" *(Polyc.* 8.3), or (the longest), "in the concord of God possessing an unhesitating spirit which is Jesus Christ" *(Magn.* 15.2; cf. *Eph.* 21.2; *Rom.* 10.3; *Philad.* 11.2; *Smyrn.* 13.2). (2) Both personal and secondary greetings occur frequently (e.g., *Magn.* 15.1; *Trall.* 13.1; *Rom.* 9.3; *Philad.* 11.2; *Smyrn.* 11.1; 12.1; 13.1–2). Ignatius occasionally uses the first-person singular verb *aspazomai* ("I sent greetings"), a form attested only for the second century A.D. and later *(Trall.* 12.1; *Smyrn.* 11.1; 12.2; 13.1, 2; *Polyc.* 8.2, 3). (3) Requests for prayer occur often (*Eph.* 20.1; 21.1–2; *Magn.* 14.1; *Rom.* 8.3; *Smyrn.* 11.1). (4) Ignatius regularly uses the verb *graphein* ("to write") in his postscripts, and mentions the place of writing (an unusual feature in Hellenistic letters), e.g., *Eph.* 21.1; *Trall.* 12.1–3; *Rom.* 10.1; *Philad.* 11.2. (5) One postscript includes the date of writing *(Rom.* 10.3), unusual in Hellenistic letters but probably intended to enable the Roman Christians to calculate the approximate time of Ignatius' arrival.

The Main Part

The opening sections of Ignatius' letters exhibit structural parallels with Hellenistic royal diplomatic correspondence, which typically begin with a section praising the recipients (i.e., a *captatio benevolentiae*). Most letters of Ignatius begin this way. Apart from the exordium, the central sections of Ignatius' letters are primarily hortatory and consist of various types of paraenesis, including positive exhortation (*Eph.* 4, 10; *Magn.* 3–9); negative warnings (*Eph.* 5.2–3; *Magn.* 11; *Trall.* 7; *Philad.* 2–3; *Smyrn.* 6–7), positive examples (*Eph.* 12); negative examples (*Eph.* 7). Ignatius' hortatory style is gentle, never authoritarian (*Trall.* 3.3). A characteristic way of summarizing his exhortations, for example, is the impersonal phrase "therefore it is proper for you to do (such and such)" (*Eph.* 2.2; *Magn.* 3.2;

Rom. 12.2; *Smyrn.* 7.2; *Polyc.* 5.2). Following another gentle hortatory technique, Ignatius often urges readers to continue in what
they are already doing (*Eph.* 4.1; *Trall.* 8.1; 12.1; *Smyrn.* 4.1). Ignatius is fond of rhetorical antithesis and, like Paul, makes extensive
use of it in paraenesis (*Eph.* 12.1–2; *Magn.* 3.1; 7.1; 11.1; *Rom.*
4.1–3; *Philad.* 1.1). Ignatius characterizes several of his own letters
as "appeals" or "exhortations" (*parakalein, Eph.* 3.2; *Magn.* 14.1;
Polyc. 7.3), a term synonymous with paraenesis (*Magn.* 6.1; *Smyrn.*
4.1). Ignatius knows that an appeal (appropriate for those of
roughly equivalent status) is a gentler approach than a command
such as an apostle might give (*Eph.* 3.1; *Trall.* 3.3; *Rom.* 4.3). In
Philemon 8–9, which Ignatius probably used as a model, Paul also
appeals to Philemon rather than *commands* him. One of the modes of
exhortation by which he complements his soft style is the frequent
use of first-person plural hortatory subjunctives, e.g., "Let *us* fear
the long suffering of God" (*Eph.* 11.1); "Let *us* love him" (*Eph.*
15.3).

The substance of Ignatius' exhortations and advice varies little
from letter to letter, a fact which suggests that the epistolary situation was primarily determined by Ignatius' own circumstances. In an
ecclesiastical application of the subjection principle characteristic of
the household codes, Ignatius advises Christians to respect and
obey the bishop and the council of elders, earthly representatives
of God or Jesus Christ and the apostles (*Eph.* 4.1–6.2; *Magn.* 6.
1–7.2; *Trall.* 2.1–3.3; *Smyrn.* 8.1–9.2). "Concord," "unity," and
"peace" are code words for subjection to the bishop (*Eph.* 13.1–2;
Philad. 8.1–2), while "strife," "pride," and "division" are caused by
those resisting subjection (*Eph.* 8.1; *Magn.* 6.2). Ignatius also advises Christians to avoid deviant teachers peddling heresy (*Eph.* 9.1;
17.1; *Trall.* 6.1–2; *Smyrn.* 4.1), and to be examples, following the
Lord, of gentleness, faith, love, humility, and endurance (*Eph.* 10.
1–2; *Magn.* 1.2; *Trall.* 4.1–2). He has an overriding theological concern that true Christians fully accept the actual birth, suffering, and
resurrection of Christ. He therefore frequently inserts creedal for
mulas summarizing correct belief (*Eph.* 7.2; 18.2; *Magn.* 11.1; *Trall.*
9.1–2; *Smyrn.* 1.1–2). The closest he comes to a list of virtues is a
list of those for whom heretics show no love (*Smyrn.* 6.2).

General Letters and Homilies

The general letter or homily is a written communication between
two parties only indirectly and loosely connected. Their "relationship" is distant and formal (e.g., the friendship *topos* is usually miss-

ing); the letter deals with matters that tend to transcend specific historical situations; and it emphasizes values widely shared by Christians. The situation of the author determines the content of the communication; the situation of the recipients is usually unknown and the message has the character of a monologue. Such letters tend to avoid or even suppress typically *epistolary* forms and styles for other types of discourse. General letters in the New Testament include Romans, Ephesians, the Pastorals, 1–2 Peter, James, and Jude. There are no general homilies in the New Testament, and only one among the Apostolic Fathers: *2 Clement.* In the analysis of individual compositions below, we shall focus on Romans, James, and 1 Peter.

General letters (except Romans) tend to be both *late* and *pseudonymous.* The second-century church preferred to understand apostolic letters in terms of their universal applicability rather than in terms of the particular situations in which they originated. The Muratorian Canon (ca. A.D. 170) articulates this view. After observing that Paul wrote to *seven* churches (a symbol of the universal Church), the unknown author continues: "nevertheless one Church is spread throughout the entire earth." Similarly, Tertullian, arguing that Marcion's "Laodiceans" should really be called Ephesians, concludes: "But the title makes no difference, since when the apostle wrote to some he wrote to all" (*Against Marcion* 5.17.1). This tendency to understand Paul's letters in a general sense encouraged the production of pseudepigraphal letters (e.g., Ephesians, James, 1 Peter) in which past apostolic advice was understood as applicable to subsequent situations, and conditions.

One group of New Testament letters belonging to the category of general letters are the so-called Catholic letters or General epistles. These include seven compositions by authors other than Paul: James, 1 Peter, 2 Peter, 1 John, 2 John, 3 John, and Jude. The designation "catholic" (meaning "universal"), first attested in Eusebius (*Church History* 2.23.24), was used because most of them lack specific destinations. The Johannine "letters," however, do not fit the category very well. First John is a deliberative homily rather than a letter, and is directed toward the specific theological problem of the heretical beliefs of secessionist Christians. Second and Third John are circumstantial letters. The Catholic letters may have been individually attracted to an existing collection of Pauline letters, or they may have been grouped in short collections. The word count in each letter suggests that a collection of Johannine letters has been placed within an earlier collection of letters, with Hebrews introducing both collections: Hebrews (4,942 words), James

(1,735), 1 Peter (1,669), 2 Peter (1,103), 1 John (2,137), 2 John (245), 3 John (219), Jude (456).

Romans

Romans is the only letter of Paul written to a Christian community he had neither founded nor visited. In other letters the historical situation of the recipients can usually be inferred with some confidence. A central issue in the study of Romans is whether it is a circumstantial letter written in response to the actual situation of Roman Christians (i.e., deliberative in purpose), or whether Paul's theological argument simply reflects his position on important issues unconnected with the situation in Rome (i.e., epideictic in purpose). Yet analyzing Romans in terms of deliberative or epideictic categories is not very helpful. Paul's main purpose in writing Romans was to present the gospel he proclaimed (Rom. 1:15) as a means of introducing himself and his mission to the Roman Christians because he intended to pay them a visit (1:10–15; 15:22–29), and use Rome as a staging area for a mission to Spain (15:24). If Romans was intended to present the gospel to the recipients for the purpose of converting them to the Christian faith, the letter would be protreptic (i.e., symbouleutic), like the later *Epistle to Diognetus.* However, since his intention was to present his gospel so that they will know more about its character and his mode of argumentation, Romans is primarily *epideictic* in intention. Yet Romans must be understood at two levels. While Paul's presentation of his gospel in Romans 1–11 is epideictic in its present context, in the prior setting of his ministry of preaching and teaching it was *protreptic,* i.e., its primary function was to demonstrate the truth of the Christian gospel and to convince the hearers to commit themselves to it and become Christian converts. The complex theological argumentation presented in Romans 1–11 and the paraenetic section in Rom. 12:1–15:13 must have been developed by Paul during many years of preaching and teaching (even the task of composing Romans must have taken many months).

Romans is also unique in that in it Paul makes extended use of diatribe style throughout Romans 1–11. The diatribe was a classroom style featuring the Socratic method of indictment and persuasion to lead students out of ignorance and error and to the truth. The imaginary opponents, hypothetical objections, and false conclusions that permeate diatribe rhetoric do not reflect the position of specific opponents whom the teacher attacks, but rather a range of possible objections. Paul's presentation of his gospel in Romans

1-11, therefore, is not occasioned by the *specific* epistolary situation, but rather introduces his *general* theological views and teaching style. Paul presents himself as a Christian teacher and preacher, and the letter he sends is a surrogate for "preaching the gospel" (1: 11-15). The concentrated Old Testament exposition in Romans (particularly dense in Romans 9-11) underlines the didactic character of the letter. The use of the diatribe in Romans suggests that Paul is not polemicizing against, for example, Jews or Judaizers in Romans 2. Hypothetical opponents cannot be used to reconstruct the epistolary situation in Rome.

The paraenetic section of Romans (12:1-15:3) is introduced by an epistolary *parakalein* clause which functions in a transitional way: "I appeal to you therefore, brethren." Since Paul uses the term *parakalein* to address those he regards as brothers (cf. Philemon 8-10), that is the approach he uses in Romans. Some regard the exhortation in Rom. 12:1-13:14 as general (dealing with responsibilities Christians have for each other, endurance in the face of persecution, subjection to governmental authority, and love as the fulfillment of the commandments), but view the paraenesis of 14: 1-15:13 as specifically directed toward the situation in Rome (the problem of "strong" and "weak" Christians). The emphasis in Rom. 14:1-15:3, however, is not based on particular problems and polarities among Roman Christians, but is a generalized form of a problem which Paul had already treated in 1 Corinthians 8-10 (the problem of whether or not the meat of animals sacrificed to pagan idols should be eaten or not). Those who thought eating improper were the "weak," those who thought it permissible were the "strong."

In the exordium (Rom. 1:1-15), Paul inserts an expansion (vs. 2-6) into the epistolary prescript (vs. 1, 7), which describes Paul's apostolic commission to the nations and the nature of his gospel, anticipating two main concerns in the body of the letter. The exordium concludes with a thanksgiving (vs. 8-12). The exordium states the problem or subject at the beginning (he wants to visit them and strengthen them with some spiritual gift), while the peroration (14: 14-16:23) repeats it at the end. Romans 1:16-17 is the thesis or proposition of the letter: the gospel brings salvation to all who believe, the Jew first and then the Gentile. Notices of Paul's impending visit frame the letter (1:10-15; 15:22-29), and the main part can be understood as an elaborate self-introduction.

The textual history of Romans is more complicated than that of any other Pauline letter. Very early (ca. A.D. 100), Romans circulated in three different forms. The longer (and more original) recension consisted of the present sixteen chapters. Two apocopated versions were also in circulation, one with fourteen and one with fifteen chapters. The phrase "in Rome" (Rom. 1:7, 15), missing from some manuscripts, was omitted from the fourteen-chapter form of the text. All these modifications suggest an early attempt to universalize a letter that already had a general character. Romans concludes with a secondary doxology (16:25–27); Pauline doxologies are not normally at the very end, nor are they as lengthy. The doxology was added as a conclusion to the shortened text of Romans (various manuscripts place it after 16:24, after 14:23, after *both* 14:23 and 16:24, after 15:33, or omit it altogether). Though often regarded as part of an originally separate letter to Ephesus, Romans 16 probably belonged to the original, longer text of Romans.

1 Peter: A Paraenetic Encyclical

The author of 1 Peter was concerned not only with the conduct of Christians undergoing persecution (1:6; 3:13–17; 4:1–2, 12–19) but also with the attendant experience of social ostracism and alienation (1:1, 17). The extensive paraenetic sections of 1 Peter provide catalogs of recommended conduct in situations of opposition and persecution (with Christ serving as a model). The experience of alienation is met theologically by clarifying both the heavenly and eschatological inheritance of Christians. This epistolary situation was apparently shared by many Christian congregations scattered throughout western Asia Minor toward the end of the first century A.D. Consequently, 1 Peter has the character of an encyclical addressed to "the exiles of the dispersion in Pontus, Galatia, Cappadocia, Asia, and Bithynia" (all located in Asia Minor, possibly reflecting the route of the envoy carrying the letter). Encyclicals were used in Tannaitic Judaism (A.D. 70–200) for a variety of religious and administrative purposes. The designation of Christians in the "diaspora" is obviously modeled on Jewish conceptions.

The unknown author of this pseudepigraphal letter selected an *indirect* approach to meeting the situation of Anatolian Christians toward the end of the first century A.D. The attribution of this letter to the Peter of a generation earlier not only reveals a problem of authority in the Christianity of that period, it also suggests how letters really written before A.D. 70 should be understood: paradigmatically in terms of the limited types of situations that recur in Christian experience.

The Greek of 1 Peter (written between A.D. 70 and 90), along with James and Hebrews, is some of the best in the New Testament.

Many scholars have regarded the bulk of 1 Peter 1:3–4:11 as a baptismal sermon (many allusions to baptism permeate the first three chapters: 1:3, 18, 22–23; 2:2–3, 9–10, 21, 24–25; 3:21), though no baptismal liturgy is actually preserved in the letter. Allusions to baptism are used as a basis for the author's paraenetic concerns. Paraenesis therefore pervades 1 Peter 1:3–4:11 (1:13–17, 22–25; 2:1–3; 2:11–3:22), almost as much as in 4:12–5:11. To this baptismal sermon was appended a hortatory section (4:12–5:11), together with an epistolary prescript (1:1–2) and postscript (5:12–14), turning the whole into an encyclical letter.

For Further Study

On Early Christian Letters Generally: Nils A. Dahl has written the short but important article "Letter" in *Interpreter's Dictionary of the Bible*, suppl. vol. (Abingdon Press, 1976), pp. 538–541. The best discussion, really a research report, is W. G. Doty, *Letters in Primitive Christianity* (Fortress Press, 1973). A good recent discussion is J. L. White, "New Testament Epistolary Literature in the Framework of Ancient Epistolography," *ANRW* II.25.2 (1984), 1730–1756. An older detailed study focusing on Pauline letters is that of Otto Roller, *Das Formular der paulinischen Briefe: Ein Beitrag zur Lehre vom antiken Briefe* (Stuttgart: W. Kohlhammer, 1933). For a more recent overview, see John L. White, "Saint Paul and the Apostolic Letter Tradition," *CBQ* 45 (1983), 433–444.

On Epistolary Formulas: Klaus Berger, "Apostelbrief und apostolische Rede: Zum Formular frühchristlicher Briefe," *ZNW* 65 (1974), 191–207; Carl J. Bjerkelund, *Parakalo: Form, Funktion und Sinn der Parakalo-Sätze in den paulinischen Briefen* (Oslo: Universitetsforlaget, 1967); John L. White, "Introductory Formulae in the Body of the Pauline Letter," *JBL* 90 (1971), 91–97. *Subscriptions:* Gordon J. Bahr, "The Subscriptions in the Pauline Letters," *JBL* 87 (1968), 27–41. *Thanksgivings:* Peter Thomas O'Brien, *Introductory Thanksgivings in the Letters of Paul* (Leiden: E. J. Brill, 1977); Paul Schubert, *Form and Function of the Pauline Thanksgivings* (Berlin: Töpelmann, 1939).

On Constituent Literary Forms: *Autobiographical Statements:* George Lyons, *Pauline Autobiography: Toward a New Understanding* (Scholars Press, 1985). *Benedictions:* L. G. Champion, *Benedictions and Doxologies in the Epistles of Paul* (Bristol, 1934); Robert Jewett, "The Form and Function of the Homiletic Benediction," *ATR* 51 (1969), 18–34. *Confessions:* Vernon H. Neufeld, *The Earliest Christian Confessions* (Wm. B. Eerdmans Publishing Co., 1963). *Doxologies:* J. K. Elliott, "The Language and Style of the Concluding Doxology to the Epistle to the Romans," *ZNW* 72 (1981), 124–130. *Hymns:* J. H. Charlesworth, "A Prolegomenon to a New Study of the Jewish Background of the Hymns and Prayers in the New Testament," *JJS* 33 (1982), 265–285; Reinhard Deichgräber, *Gotteshymnus und Christushymnus in der frühen Christenheit* (Göttingen: Vandenhoeck & Ruprecht, 1967). **Paraenetic Forms:** David L. Balch, *Let Wives Be Submissive: The Domestic Code in 1 Peter* (Scholars Press, 1981); Abraham J. Malherbe, *Moral Exhortation, A Greco-Roman Sourcebook* (Westminster Press, 1986); N. J. McEleney, "The Vice Lists of the Pastoral Epistles," *CBQ* 36 (1974), 203–219; M. Jack Suggs, "The Christian Two Ways Tradition: Its Antiquity, Form and Function," in *Studies in New Testament and Early Christian Literature*, ed. by D. E. Aune (Leiden: E. J. Brill, 1972), pp. 60–74; David C. Verner, *The Household of God: The Social World of the Pastoral Epistles* (Scholars Press, 1983). **Topoi:** The best succinct treatment of Hellenistic *topoi* is T. Conley, "Philo's Use of *Topoi*," in David Winston and John Dillon, *Two Treatises of Philo of Alexandria* (Scholars Press, 1983), pp. 171–178. There are several discussions of *topoi* in Paul: David G. Bradley, "The *Topos* as Form in the Pauline Paraenesis," *JBL* 72 (1953), 238–246; Terrence Y. Mullins, "Topos as a New Testament Form," *JBL* 99 (1980), 541–547 (thinking to correct Bradley he defines a form that is really an enthymeme); John C. Brunt, "More on the *Topos* as a New Testament Form," *JBL* 104 (1985), 495–500 (who argues that *topos* means only "argument"). **Travel Plans:** Robert W. Funk, "The Apostolic *Parousia:* Form and Significance," in *Christian History and Interpretation: Studies Presented to John Knox*, ed. by W. R. Farmer, C. F. D. Moule, and R. R. Niebuhr (Cambridge: University Press, 1967), pp. 249–268. See also Terrence Y. Mullins, "Visit Talk in New Testament Letters," *CBQ* 35 (1973), 350–358.

On Epistolary Styles of Discourse: *Greco-Roman Rhetoric:* The books of George Kennedy are valuable: *The Art of Persuasion in Greece* (Princeton University Press, 1963), *The Art of Rhetoric in the Roman World* (Princeton University Press, 1972), and *Greek Rhetoric Under Christian Emperors* (Princeton University Press, 1983). Particularly relevant is his *New Testament Interpretation Through Rhetorical Criticism* (University of North Carolina Press, 1984). See also W. Wuellner, "Greek Rhetoric and Pauline Argumentation," *Early Christian Literature and the Classical Intellectual Tradition*, ed. by W. R. Schoedel and R. L. Wilken (Paris: Editions Beauchesne, 1979), pp. 177–188. *Diatribe:* Previously the standard discussion was Rudolf Bultmann, *Der Stil der paulinische Predigt und die kynisch-stoische Diatribe* (Göttingen: Vandenhoeck & Ruprecht, 1910). The most important treatment is now that of Stanley K. Stowers, *The Diatribe and Paul's Letter to the Romans* (Scholars Press, 1981); see also his article, "Paul's Dialogue with a Fellow Jew in Romans 3:1–9," *CBQ* 46 (1984), 707–722. *Sermons or Homilies:* Joseph Heinemann, "Preaching: In the Talmudic Period," *Encyclopedia Judaica*, XIII, cols. 994–998; idem, "The Proem in the Aggadic Midrashim—A Form-Critical Study," *Scripta Hierosolymitana* 22 (1971), 100–122; Folker Siegert, *Drei hellenistisch-jüdische Predigten* (Tübingen: J. C. B. Mohr [Paul Siebeck], 1980); Hartwig Thyen, *Der Stil der jüdisch-hellenistischen Homilie* (Göttingen: Vandenhoeck & Ruprecht, 1955).

Letter Collections: *Paul:* C. P. Anderson, "The Epistle to the Hebrews and the Pauline Letter Collection," *HTR* 59 (1966), 429–438; J. Finegan, "The Original Form of the Pauline Collection," *HTR* 49 (1956), 85–104; H. Y. Gamble, "The Redaction of the Pauline Letters and the Formation of the Pauline Corpus," *JBL* 94 (1975), 403–418; E. J. Goodspeed, *Introduction to the New Testament* (University of Chicago Press, 1937), pp. 210–239; C. L. Mitton, *The Formation of the Pauline Corpus* (London: Epworth Press, 1955); L. Mowry, "The Early Circulation of Paul's Letters," *JBL* 63 (1944), 73–86.

On Paul: One of the most useful tools for studying the forms, themes, and structures of the Pauline letters is *Pauline Parallels,* by Fred O. Francis and J. Paul Sampley, 2nd ed. (Fortress Press, 1984). An excellent treatment of Paul is J. Christiaan Beker, *Paul the Apostle: The Triumph of God in Life and Thought* (Fortress Press, 1980). See also Ronald F. Hock, *The Social Context of Paul's Ministry: Tentmaking and Apostleship* (Fortress Press, 1980); E. A. Judge, "St. Paul and Classical Society," *Jahrbuch für Antike und Christentum* 15 (1972), 19–36; and Wayne A. Meeks, *The First Urban Christians: The Social World of the Apostle Paul* (Yale University Press, 1983).

On Select New Testament Letters and Homilies: *Romans:* Harry Gamble, Jr., *The Textual History of the Letter to the Romans* (Wm. B. Eerdmans Publishing Co., 1977); Robert Jewett, "Romans as an Ambassadorial Letter," *Interpretation* 36 (1982), 5–20; R. J. Karris, "Rom 14:1–15:13 and the Occasion of Romans," *CBQ* 25 (1973), 155–178; W. Wuellner, "Paul's Rhetoric of Argumentation in Romans: An Alternative to the Donfried-Karris Debate Over Romans," *CBQ* 38 (1976), 330–351. *1–2 Corinthians:* Hans Dieter Betz, *Second Corinthians 8 and 9: A Commentary on Two Administrative Letters of the Apostle Paul* (Fortress Press, 1985), contains an excellent bibliography and history of research. See also Rudolf Bultmann, *The Second Letter to the Corinthians,* tr. by R. Harrisville (Augsburg Publishing House, 1985); Hans Conzelmann, *1 Corinthians: A Commentary on the First Epistle to the Corinthians* (Fortress Press, 1975); Robert M. Grant, "Hellenistic Elements in 1 Corinthians," in *Early Christian Origins: Studies in Honor of Harold R. Willoughby,* ed. by A. P. Wikgren (Quadrangle Books, 1961), pp. 60–66; and Robert Jewett, "The Redaction of 1 Corinthians and the Trajectory of the Pauline School," *JAAR* 46 (1978), 398–444. *Galatians:* Hans Dieter Betz, *Galatians: A Commentary on Paul's Letter to the Churches in Galatia* (Fortress Press, 1979); idem, "The Literary Composition and Function of Paul's Letter to the Galatians," *NTS* 21 (1974–75), 353–379. *Philippians:* David E. Garland, "The Composition and Unity of Philippians: Some Neglected Literary Factors," *NovT* 27 (1985), 141–173 (extensive up-to-date bibliography on the subject); Gerald F. Hawthorne, *Philippians,* Word Biblical Commentary, vol. 43 (Word Books, 1983). *1–2 Thessalonians:* H. Boers, "The Form-Critical Study of Paul's Letters: 1 Thessalonians as a Case Study," *NTS* 22 (1976), 140–158; Helmut Koester, "I Thessalonians—Experiment in Christian Writing," *Continuity and Discontinuity in Church His-*

tory: Essays Presented to George Huntston Williams, ed. by F. F. Church and T. George (Leiden: E. J. Brill, 1979), pp. 33–44; A. J. Malherbe, "Exhortation in First Thessalonians," *NovT* 25 (1983), 238–256; idem " 'Gentle as a Nurse': The Cynic Background to 1 Thess. 2," *NovT* 12 (1970), 203–213; B. A. Pearson, "1 Thessalonians 2:13–16: A Deutero-Pauline Interpolation," *HTR* 64 (1971), 79–94. *Philemon:* F. F. Church, "Rhetorical Structure and Design in Paul's Letter to Philemon," *HTR* 71 (1978), 17–33; Norman R. Petersen, *Rediscovering Paul: Philemon and the Sociology of Paul's Narrative World* (Fortress Press, 1985); John L. White, "The Structural Analysis of Philemon: A Point of Departure in the Formal Analysis of the Pauline Letter," in *Society of Biblical Literature: 1971 Seminar Papers* (Scholars Press, 1971), I, 1–47. *Hebrews:* Two excellent commentaries: James Moffatt, *A Critical and Exegetical Commentary on the Epistle to the Hebrews* (Edinburgh: T. & T. Clark, 1924), and Herbert Braun, *An die Hebräer* (Tübingen: J. C. B. Mohr [Paul Siebeck], 1984). An important recent study is Graham Hughes, *Hebrews and Hermeneutics: The Epistle to the Hebrews as a New Testament Example of Biblical Interpretation* (Cambridge: University Press, 1979). The important earlier study of Ernst Käsemann (1957) is now available in English: *The Wandering People of God: An Investigation of the Letter to the Hebrews,* tr. by R. A. Harrisville and I. L. Sandberg (Augsburg Publishing House, 1984). *1 Peter:* F. W. Beare, *The First Epistle of Peter* (Oxford: Basil Blackwell, 1970); J. H. Elliott, *A Home for the Homeless: A Sociological Exegesis of 1 Peter, Its Situation and Strategy* (Fortress Press, 1981).

The Letters of Ignatius: The best recent commentary with a large bibliography is William R. Schoedel, *Ignatius of Antioch: A Commentary on the Letters of Ignatius of Antioch* (Fortress Press, 1985). Old but indispensable: J. B. Lightfoot, *The Apostolic Fathers: Clement, Ignatius, and Polycarp,* 2 parts in 5 vols. (Baker Book House, 1981; repr. of 1889–90 ed.). See also Hermann J. Sieben, "Die Ignatianen als Briefe: Einige formkritische Bemerkungen," *VC* 32 (1978), 1–18.

7

The Apocalypse of John
and Ancient Revelatory Literature

The Apocalypse (or Revelation) of John belongs to a type of ancient revelatory literature called "apocalypse." The word "apocalypse" itself is a transliteration of the Greek noun *apokalypsis* (the Latin term *revelatio* is a synonym) meaning "uncovering." By the first century B.C. it denoted "revealing (of secrets)," or "(divine) revelation." The first occurrence of the term in apocalyptic literature is in Rev. 1:1–2 (written ca. A.D. 95), a sentence intended to function as a title:

> The revelation of Jesus Christ, which God gave to him, to show to his servants what must soon take place; and he made it known by sending his angel to his servant John, who bore witness to the word of God and to the testimony of Jesus Christ, even to all that he saw.

When the Apocalypse was copied on papyrus rolls, early in its textual history, a simplified form of this initial sentence, "Apocalypse of John" (using the shortest possible title and the author's name in the genitive, following ancient conventions), was used as a title, or subscription at the *end*. When the Apocalypse was copied in page form, the title was moved to the *beginning*. Because the Apocalypse was called the "Apocalypse of John" (Muratorian Canon 71), or just the "Apocalypse" (Irenaeus 5.30.3; Tertullian, *Against Marcion* 4. 5.2), during the second century, the term *apokalypsis* was used of similar types of Christian texts (*Hermas*, Vision 5, title). While an apocalypse is a first-person vision report of a transcendent reality, ancients used the term more broadly (e.g., among the Coptic-Gnostic apocalypses, the *First Apocalypse of James* is a revelatory dialogue, and the *Second Apocalypse of James* is a revelatory discourse). *Apokalypsis* in Rev. 1:1 refers to a revelatory experience not a literary work (cf. Paul's use of an identical phrase in Gal. 1:12). The author described his work as a "prophecy" (Rev. 1:3) or a "prophetic book" (22:7, 10, 18–19). Ancient texts now called "apocalypses" that predate the Apocalypse of John neither contain the term much less use it of a particular literary genre. Only the later Jewish apocalypses such as *2 Baruch* and *3 Baruch* use *apokalypsis* as a literary designation in their titles. The fifth century A.D. Cologne Mani Codex refers to the works of Adam, Sethel, Enosh, Shem, and Enoch as apocalypses.

What Is Apocalypticism?

"Apocalypticism," a term introduced by German scholars early in the nineteenth century, is used of the types of eschatological belief systems reflected in apocalypses, with the biblical apocalypses of Daniel and Revelation as primary models. The subject becomes clearer if apocalypticism is divided into four related aspects: (1) "apocalyptic eschatology," a *system of religious beliefs;* (2) "apocalypticism" and "millennialism," *forms of collective behavior* based on those beliefs; (3) "apocalypse," a *type of literature* giving written expression to those beliefs; and (4) "apocalyptic imagery," the *language and conceptions* of apocalyptic eschatology found in bits and pieces in a variety of ancient literary settings.

Apocalyptic Eschatology

As a system of belief, apocalyptic eschatology centers on a cosmic drama based on a pessimistic eschatological dualism. The present evil world order (controlled by the human collaborators of an evil supernatural being and his allies) will shortly be terminated by divine intervention and replaced with a new and perfect order. The people of God, an oppressed minority during the present age, fervently expect either an imminent visitation of God or the appearance of his specially chosen agent or messiah. The change in eras will occur violently through a final series of battles between the forces of light and darkness. The outcome is never in question since the latter are destined for defeat and destruction. The new age will be preceded by a time of suffering followed by the judgment and punishment of the wicked and the resurrection and reward of the righteous. "Eschatology," a term meaning "an account of the last things," is apocalyptic eschatology without the pessimistic dualism and expected crisis.

The scenario just described, with many variations, owes much to the kingship ideologies of ancient Near Eastern enthronement rituals. In Assyria, Egypt, Israel, and Persia, the coronation of a new monarch was mythically understood as a symbol of cosmic renewal based on the divine triumph over chaos and the creation of a new order of peace and prosperity. Apocalyptic eschatology, the ideology of resistance and protest, was a response to the overthrow and suppression of a divinely ordained native kingship by a foreign dynasty, often accompanied by forced changes in native customs and laws, social degradation, and economic exploitation. Rather than focusing on the cosmic significance of a change in rulers or the advent of a new dynasty in the present, apocalyptic eschatology fantasized about the restoration of order by projecting a supernatural deliverance into the future.

Apocalypticism and Millennialism

As a system of beliefs, apocalyptic eschatology cannot be separated from the spectrum of religiously motivated collective behaviors of which it is the ideological expression. Since "collective behavior" covers anything from fads to organized social movements, the term "apocalypticism" may be used to represent more elementary forms of collective behavior and "millennialism" the more complex. Apocalypticism is a supernaturalist collective response to the shared experience of "relative deprivation," i.e., group perceptions of discrepancy between legitimate expectation and reality and the resultant feeling of alienation, brought on by foreign domination, suppression of native kingship, and economic exploitation. Communication and interaction of various types are essential to collective behavior, and the writing of apocalypses is one mode of communication in which the inchoate beliefs of the group find articulation and direction. Other types of "communication" can include gestures, rumors, rioting, graffiti, speeches, circulation of tracts, and acts of terrorism. It has been plausibly argued that Daniel 7–12 is an apocalyptic manifesto connected with the Maccabean rebellion (ca. 165 B.C.). The social settings of other Jewish apocalypses are much more speculative. It is likely that resistance literature in the form of apocalypses was a means of expression wholly separated from millennial movements themselves, i.e., a learned and scribal phenomenon which nevertheless gave both expression and shape to popular religious sentiment.

"Millennialism," a term describing a complex form of collective behavior widely used in cross-cultural studies of religious movements inspired by the vision of a utopian society, owes its currency to the Apocalypse of John. Revelation 20:4–6 speaks of the messianic kingdom of Christ during the 1,000–year interval between the

Second Coming and the Final Judgment. The term "millennium," literally meaning "(period of) 1,000 years," connotes the era of perfection and bliss expected by certain types of religious movements. Millennial movements (alternately designated nativistic, revitalistic, and cargo movements) have been intensively studied in recent years by social scientists. These movements are animated by the fantasy of a salvation to be imminently realized by group members on a totally transformed earth and accomplished by supernatural means.

British sociologist Bryan Wilson has synthesized numerous studies of religious movements of protest. Focusing on social movements stimulated by supernaturalist reactions to social change, he has proposed an ideal typology of seven types based on how these movements respond to the world: (1) the "conversionist" response (people must be transformed), (2) the "revolutionist" response (the world must be transformed), (3) the "introversionist" response (the world must be abandoned), (4) the "manipulationist" response (perceptions must be transformed), (5) the "thaumaturgical" response (specific ills can be relieved miraculously), (6) the "reformist" response (the world rust be amended), and (7) the "utopian" response (the world must be reconstructed). Some of these movements tend to crystallize around a charismatic leader to provide a certain amount of organizational stability.

Millennial movements were not uncommon in Judaism during the Hellenistic and Roman periods. Several revolutionary movements that appeared from the Roman conquest of Palestine (63 B.C.) to the first Jewish revolt (A.D. 66–74) are described by Josephus. The Jewish revolt against Rome in A.D. 66 was shortly followed by the crystallization of the Zealot revolutionary party (ca. A.D. 67–68). The Qumran community, a separatist Essene sect, was an introversionist movement, while John the Baptist's movement had a conversionist emphasis. The Jesus movement blended conversionist and thaumaturgical emphases, both calling people to repentance and miraculously curing their ailments.

Apocalypses

Jewish apocalypses flourished in the late Second Temple period, 200 B.C. to A.D. 100. Daniel 7–12, long regarded as the oldest Jewish apocalypse (ca. 165 B.C.), may be antedated by the oldest sections of the composite apocalypse *1 Enoch*, the *Book of the Watchers* (1–36), and the *Book of Heavenly Luminaries* (72–82), both third century B.C. Many more apocalypses were written during the generation following the destruction of Jerusalem by the Romans in A.D. 70 (e.g., *2 Enoch, 2 Baruch,* and *4 Ezra*). Some later Jewish texts, lacking political concern and emphasizing cosmological speculation, reflect the transformation of apocalyptic into Merkabah (Chariot) mysticism. They include *Hekalot Rabbati, Merkaba Rabba,* and *3 Enoch* (third century A.D. and later). Of the three earliest Christian apocalypses, the Apocalypse of John (ca. A.D. 95) follows many conventions of Jewish apocalypses, and the *Shepherd of Hermas* (composed in stages from ca. A.D. 90 to 150) blends Jewish and Hellenistic revelatory traditions. The *Apocalypse of Peter* (ca. A.D. 135) closely follows Hellenistic conventions. Compositions similar to Jewish apocalypses were produced in Persia and Egypt. In Egypt, eschatological resistance literature written during the Hellenistic and Roman periods includes the *Demotic Chronicle,* the *Lamb of Bokkhoris* (both third to second century B.C.), and the *Oracle of the Potter* (ca. 130 B.C.). Early evidence for apocalyptic eschatology in Persia (i.e., pre-Sassanian, before A.D. 221) is found in the *Oracle of Hystaspes* (ca. first century B.C.) and Plutarch, *On Isis and Osiris* 369F–370C (died ca. A.D. 120). While apocalyptic eschatology permeates Iranian religious literature, no *independent* apocalypses are found in Iranian tradition, though they occur as parts of larger compositions.

The many distinctive literary features of apocalypses are sometimes listed in serial form under the dubious assumption that such lists adequately describe the genre. Major traits of apocalypses typically listed include pseudepigraphy (using the name of a famous person as a pen name), historical reviews presented as predictions (often involving the periodization of history), reports of visions or dreams, the use of bizarre imagery, the presence of a supernatural revealer to explain the meaning of visions (particularly important when visions are seen on earth and contain more symbolism), emphasis on the revelation of cosmic mysteries including special knowledge about the end of the world, and guided tours of superterrestrial and/or subterrestrial regions.

The apocalyptic genre should rather be described in terms of a paradigm of the interrelated features of form, content, and function. In *form* an apocalypse is a first-person prose recital of revelatory visions or dreams, framed by a description of the circumstances of the revelatory experience, and structured to emphasize the central revelatory message. The *content* of apocalypses involves, in the broadest terms, the communication of a transcendent, often eschatological, perspective on human experience. Apocalypses exhibit a threefold *function:* (1) to legitimate the message (and/or the messenger) through an appeal to transcendent authorization, and

(2) to create a literary surrogate of revelatory experience for hearers or readers, (3) so that the recipients of the message will be motivated to modify their views and behaviors to conform to transcendent perspectives. The density of this definition requires a more extensive explanation below in our analysis of the Apocalypse of John.

Apocalyptic Imagery

Even though apocalyptic eschatology is the idiom of both millennialism and apocalypses, it is not limited to those contexts. Various themes and motifs, either individually or in clusters, appear in a variety of literary settings that should not on that account be regarded as apocalypses or reflections of millennial movements. For example, notions such as the visitation of God, the Kingdom of God, the resurrection of the dead, the tribulation, and similar apocalyptic conceptions can appear in various texts either singly or in clusters. Does their presence suggest the presence of apocalyptic eschatology or can these individual conceptions simply be formally repeated even though they have lost their vitality? Apocalyptic language and motifs, for example, occur frequently in the teachings of Jesus and the letters of Paul, but scholars have sometimes denied that one or both are apocalyptists. This suggests a problem of definition that the limited nature of the surviving texts prevents us from solving.

Types of Ancient Revelatory Literature

All cultures of the ancient Mediterranean world and the Near East had a revelatory worldview. It was assumed that communication between the human and divine worlds was necessary for achieving and maintaining social and individual welfare. This need for special knowledge, unavailable through conventional channels, lies behind the widespread phenomenon of divination, the interpretation of *symbolic* messages from the gods. Oracular or prophetic divination, messages from the gods in *human language*, became the basis for many types of revelatory literature. "Oracle" is a term derived from the Latin *oraculum*, used both for a divine pronouncement about the unknown or the future and for the place where such pronouncements were given. The terms "prophecy" and "prophet" are derived from a family of Greek words used to translate the Hebrew root *nb'* ("prophet," "to prophesy"). Both Judaism and Christianity usually avoided using *mantis*, the pagan Greek term for prophet.

The term "oracle" has come down to us through Greek and Latin literature and is often associated with inspired responses to inquiries. The words "prophecy" and "prophet," on the other hand, have been transmitted through Judeo-Christian tradition and are often connected with unsolicited inspired speech. Actually, *both* refer to the same cross-cultural phenomenon though reflecting different cultural idioms. Modern anthropological studies of third-world cultures use the terms interchangeably.

Israelite-Jewish Revelatory Literature

In ancient Israel and Canaan, prophecy was an oral phenomenon until the eighth century, when the great classical prophets arose beginning with Amos and Hosea in Israel, and Micah and Isaiah in Judah. These prophets were not usually writers, but had followers who wrote down individual sayings and speeches that were later organized into larger compositions that in turn became the basis for the formation of Old Testament prophetic books (Isa. 8:1; 30:8; Jer. 30:2; Ezek. 43:11). One of the original reasons for recording prophetic oracles was to authenticate the words of the prophets in anticipation of their fulfillment (Isa. 8:16–22; 29:11–12; 30:8–14; Hab. 2:2–3; Jer. 30:2–3). Another reason was to provide a substitute for the prophet's presence (cf. Jeremiah's three prophetic letters, Jer. 29:1–23, 26–28, 31–33). Prophecy functioned in several ways in ancient Israel, for there were court prophets (salaried by the king), temple prophets (salaried by temple authorities), and freelance prophets who were independent of both court and temple. The heyday of the free prophets extended from the eighth to the sixth centuries B.C., when Israel was profoundly affected by her expansionist neighbors, Assyria, Babylonia, and Persia. Free prophecy was partly a conservative protest movement attempting to revitalize ancient theocratic ideals thought endangered by a compromising monarchy seeking entangling foreign alliances in the interest of national security. Thus the free prophets whose oracles are preserved in the Old Testament constituted a powerful political and social force in Israel with no real analogue in Greek or Roman history.

By the second century B.C. the prophetic writings received the kind of sacrosanct status accorded the Pentateuch earlier. It was at this point that Jewish apocalyptic works (portions of *1 Enoch* and Daniel 7–12) began to be written. The prophetic section of the Jewish scriptures was not revered out of antiquarian curiosity, but because the ambiguity associated with prophecy made these books a continuing source of revelation (cf. the use of Jeremiah in Dan. 9:2 and the eschatological reinterpretation of Habakkuk in the Qumran *Commentary on Habakkuk* [4QpHab]). Philo of Alexandria, author of extensive biblical commentaries, thought of the Pentateuch as a collection of oracles. The Jewish scriptures thus served as a paradigm for written revelation in a way unique in the ancient world.

The relationship between prophecy and apocalyptic in Judaism continues to be debated. Some emphasize the alien character of apocalyptic and propose foreign (usually Iranian) influence, while others view apocalyptic as an inner-Israelite phenomenon that developed either out of mantic wisdom (as distinguished from proverbial wisdom) or out of prophecy itself. *Mantic wisdom* included skill in dream interpretation attributed to sages like Joseph and Daniel in the Old Testament, while *proverbial wisdom* is exemplified by the aphorisms of conventional wisdom found in the books of Proverbs and Sirach. The strong Jewish presence in the eastern Diaspora (Babylonia) for more than a millennium, beginning with the early sixth century B.C., served as a conduit for Mesopotamian traditions in Palestinian Judaism. It is now widely recognized that prophecy did not cease with the last of the Israelite prophets (Haggai, Zechariah, and Malachi), but simply took different forms appropriate to changed social and political circumstances. Apocalyptic writers often claimed inspiration, either explicitly or implicitly (*1 Enoch* 91.1; 93.1; *2 Enoch* 22.4–13; *4 Ezra* 14; *2 Baruch* 6.3; 10.1–3), but this should not always be understood as a challenge to the status of the "canonical" scriptures.

Revelatory literature in early Judaism is largely limited to genres closely associated with apocalyptic eschatology: (1) apocalypses, the central feature of which is the dream or vision report (as separate units or framed by host genres such as the testament), (2) revelatory discourses, (3) revelatory dialogues, and (4) revelatory revisions of Scripture.

A *testament*, a speech of a dying patriarch modeled after Joseph's deathbed speech (Gen. 49), can stand alone or be incorporated into other genres (cf. the testament of Abraham in *Jubilees* 20–22). Testaments consist of three basic elements: (1) a biography of the patriarch, (2) exhortation to his descendants, and (3) a deathbed forecast of the future. This is obviously related to the threefold structure of legends, visions, and admonitions, characteristic of many apocalypses (e.g., *2 Enoch* and *2 Baruch;* Daniel lacks admonitions; Revelation lacks legends), and reveals a basic compatibility between the testament and the apocalypse. Testaments with pronounced apocalyptic segments include the *Testaments of the Twelve Patriarchs,* the

Testament of Abraham, and the *Testament of Moses*. The *Testament of Levi* contains the following constituent elements: (1) a narrative of an otherworldly vision (chs. 2–5), (2) a narrative of a this-worldly vision (ch. 8), (3) a section of admonitions (chs. 10–13), (4) a prophecy of the future (chs. 14–18), all framed and punctuated by biographical legends (chs. 1, 6–7, 9, 19).

A *revelatory discourse* is a "prophetic" speech that may contain a historical review presented as a prediction of future events and/or an eschatological description of the events immediately preceding and following the end of the age. It is not an apocalypse because it is not presented as a dream or vision report. Revelatory discourses are usually part of the testament form found in all of the *Testaments of the Twelve Patriarchs* (cf. *Test. Simeon* 5.4–6; *Test. Levi* 14–18; *Test. Judah* 22–25; *Test. Issachar* 6; *Test. Zebulon* 9), and in *Test. Moses* 2–10; *Test. Adam* 3.1–12; *Test. Sol.* 15.8–12, though not in the Testaments of Abraham, Isaac, Jacob, and Job. They can also be included in revelatory revisions of Scripture (cf. *Jubilees* 23). In the New Testament, the Olivet Discourse found in Mark 13 and parallels has this form.

A *revelatory dialogue* is a conversation between a human recipient of revelatory and a supernatural revealer, not necessarily to express a variety of opinions, but to use the human recipient as a foil for the presentation of the revelatory message. Dialogues are appropriate in the context of visionary guided tours of heaven or hell (cf. *1 Enoch* 21–36; *Apocalypse of Abraham* 12–14), or symbolic visions (Dan. 7: 15–28; 8:15–27). The substantial use of dialogue in *4 Ezra* and *2 Baruch* between the seer and an angel of God, in which real problems are raised by the seers in a discussion concerning theodicy, does not appear to be a straight-line development from early Jewish revelatory dialogues but shows Greco-Roman influence.

Revelatory revisions of Scripture are a creative way of dealing with the normative status of the Torah and the Prophets, which left only limited ways of justifying dissident practices: *eisegesis* (manipulating the meaning of the text to reflect the opinion of the interpreter), *modification* (attempting to change the sacred writings, either by additions or deletions or by composing documents that might supplement the collection) or actual *revision* (rewriting the offensive portions so they will reflect "correct" opinion). *Eisegesis* is, of course, the least radical approach, particularly in the absence of historical-critical methods, and is reflected in the biblical commentaries of the Qumran Essenes, the Mishnah of rabbinic Judaism, and the early Christian interpretation of the Old Testament in the New. *Modification* is more radical, and is evident in changes introduced into the Samaritan Pentateuch, the Greek additions to Daniel and Esther, and perhaps the composition of some apocalypses. *Revision* is the most radical solution of all, since it involves replacing an earlier revelatory writing with an updated version; an example is the rewriting of Genesis 1 through Exodus 12 by the author of *Jubilees* under the guise of a secret revelation.

Greco-Roman Revelatory Literature

The revelatory literature of the Hellenistic and Roman periods is largely based on *oracles.* The Romans, heirs of the elaborate Etruscan science of divination, made little use of oracles, while the Greeks placed a high value on them, though they also used many other forms of divination. Oracles could be assembled in collections (analogous with the early stages in the formation of Old Testament prophetic books) and expanded into oracular discourses or oracular dialogues. These four literary types presuppose the phenomenon of possession trance, i.e., possession by a supernatural being enabling the medium to speak on behalf of the god. A fifth literary form, the vision report (the central feature of Jewish and Christian apocalypses), is based on the phenomenon of *vision trance,* i.e., visions, hallucinations, or out-of-body adventures.

Greek oracles were usually short (two to four lines) and were pronouncements, in verse or prose expressed in the first person, of the inspiring deity (usually Apollo) in response to inquiries made at oracle shrines by individuals or representatives of states. When some Greeks had problems digging a canal, they sent messengers to Delphi to ask Apollo the reason. He reportedly replied in verse (Herodotus 1.174):

> The isthmus neither fence with towers nor dig through,
> for Zeus would have made it an island, had he so desired.

This oracle is in the form of an *enthymeme,* a statement accompanied by a supportive reason. Most oracles dealt with matters of ritual, as does this prose oracle quoted by the Athenian orator Demosthenes (*Oration* 21.53):

> The prophet of Zeus in Dodona commands: To Dionysus pay public sacrifices and mix a bowl of wine and set up dances; to Apollo the Averter sacrifice an ox and wear garlands, both free men and slaves, and observe one day of rest; to Zeus, the giver of wealth, a white bull.

Often the inquirer would receive a written copy of the oral response. If the inquirer were an emissary of a city-state, the responses might be deposited in state archives. The staff at oracles sometimes deposited oracular responses in temple archives. Particularly important oracles might be engraved on stone for all to see, and many of these have survived, though none from Delphi, the most important of the ancient oracle sanctuaries of Apollo. Most of the preserved oracles were placed in literary settings as oracle stories, a form favored by Herodotus. The ambiguity of oracles provided a market for professional oracle interpreters *(exēgētai)*, who operated in the vicinity of oracle sanctuaries.

Many *oracle collections* existed in the ancient world, but only some of the *Sibylline Oracles* have survived. Since the ambiguous meaning of oracles meant that their fulfillment was uncertain, oracles were collected by itinerant *chrēsmologoi* ("oracle expounders") who provided readings and interpretations. The collections, which circulated under the pseudonyms of Orpheus, Musaeus, and the various Sibyls and Bakides, were not collections of responses but rather unsolicited oracles believed uttered by a Sibyl or a Bakis (generic names for legendary itinerant prophetic types, the former always female, the latter always male) and could be quite lengthy. In form many sections of the *Sibylline Oracles* are really revelatory discourses. The Romans kept an official collection of Sibylline oracles for consultation in times of national emergency. The legendary character of the various Sibyls (more than forty were distinguished by the end of antiquity) means oracles attributed to them were really pseudonymous literary products.

The *oracular dialogue* has a complicated literary pedigree as one of the many types of the dialogue that developed in Greco-Roman culture. The philosophical dialogues of Plato and Aristotle became literary models throughout the rest of antiquity. They were emulated in Rome during the first century B.C., later by Plutarch and Lucian. Many dialogues are essays cast into an artificial dialogical form. As an independent literary form, dialogues are usually placed in a conventional setting (e.g., temple dialogues occur in or near a sanctuary, symposia are dinner dialogues, and peripatetic dialogues place conversation in the framework of a stroll). One special form of dialogue is the *erōtapokrisis* ("question-and-answer"), a didactic form modeled on teacher-pupil conversation. This type of dialogue omitted any setting and was adapted as a literary vehicle for revelatory teaching from a supernatural being in a catechetical style (e.g., many Hermetic tractates and the three Coptic-Gnostic dialogues *Hypostasis of the Archons, Thomas the Contender,* and *Dialogue of the Savior*). Rather than developing directly from conventional dialogues, or *erōtapokriseis*, oracular dialogues derived from the simple oracular question-and-answer scheme. Oracle questions often had two parts, e.g.: Shall I or shall I not do such-and-such? and, To which god or goddess shall I sacrifice to ensure success? (Thucydides 1.134.4; Xenophon, *Ways and Means* 6.2–3; *Anabasis* 3.1.5–7; Dionysius, *Roman Antiquities* 1.23.4). Lucian has preserved an oracular dialogue between a wealthy Roman and the oracular deity Asklepios-Glykon (*Alexander* 43). Many of the revelatory spells in the magical papyri provide instructions on conducting question-and-answer dialogues with supernatural revealers. A literary adaptation of the oracular dialogue is found in the sixth book of Vergil's *Aeneid,* in which the hero Aeneas receives a guided tour of Hades by the Sibyl and his deceased father Anchises, and asks about some of the sights. Vergil used as a model *Odyssey* 11, where Odysseus, without a guide, holds conversations with a succession of ghosts in Hades. Though the dialogue form is not really present in the Apocalypse of John, it is found in highly developed form in the *Shepherd of Hermas.*

The *oracular discourse* was another way of expanding conventional oracular responses. The oracular discourse could easily be changed into an oracular dialogue, the history of some Coptic-Gnostic dialogues. Fictional prophetic speeches occur in Greek literature, like the doom oracle of Theoclymenus (*Odyssey* 20.351–357), and the underworld speeches predicting the future adventures of various epic heroes (e.g., *Odyssey* 11.90–137; Vergil, *Aeneid* 6.756–859). Book 3 of the *Sibylline Oracles* (mid-second century B.C.) contains several oracular discourses (97–161; 162–195; 196–294; 350–380; 381–387; 388–400; 401–488; 545–656; 657–808). There tend to be two types of oracular discourses, those which predict judgment, frequently connected with a historical review presented as a forecast (e.g., *Sib. Or.* 3.97–161, 401–488), and those which exhibit a two-part schema, the prediction of tribulation followed by deliverance (e.g., *Sib. Or.* 3.350–380; 545–656; the Potter's Oracle).

Reports of dreams or visions are common in Greco-Roman literature, and exhibit striking similarities to those of ancient Near Eastern cultures. Revelatory experiences can take place in an earthly setting (as in most dreams) or could involve ascent (to heaven) or descent (to the underworld). Further, they tend to be narrated in indirect discourse and inserted in a variety of host genres, such as history, biography, novels, and letters (e.g., Dionysius, *Roman Antiquities* 1.57.3–4; Plutarch, *Lucullus* 12.1–2; *Eumenes* 6.4–7; Philostratus, *Life of Apollonius* 4.34). One kind of literary form that has many points of similarity to Jewish and Christian apocalypses is the narrative of an ascent or descent to the supernatural world (described by Greeks with characteristic latitude as a *mythos,* "story"). These accounts are all fictional pseudonymous narratives either reported in the first person or secondarily related by a supposedly reliable informant. Examples are Plato's Myth of Er (*Republic* 10.13–16), the Dream of Scipio (Cicero, *Republic* 6.9–26), the visions of Timarchus (Plutarch, *On the Genius of Socrates* 21–22), Thespesius (Plutarch, *On the Delays of Divine Justice* 22–31), and Menippus (Lucian, *Icaromenippus*). Most of these apocalypses consist of journeys in which the postmortem rewards of the righteous and/or punishments of the wicked are seen and reported for the purpose of instilling a fear productive of correct behavior when these experiences are narrated (Diodorus 1.2.2). They are not connected with collective behavior based on the experience of relative deprivation, unlike many Jewish apocalypses. Further, they are always constituent elements of larger literary forms, unlike their Jewish and Christian analogues (though the Dream of Scipio was preserved separately because of the commentary on it by Macrobius).

Early Christian Apocalypticism

John the Baptist and Jesus

Early Christianity began as a Jewish millennial movement that survived the death of its leader, Jesus of Nazareth. If the movement begun by John the Baptist was a conversionist movement (change the world by changing people), that of Jesus—his successor—combined conversionism with thaumaturgy (change world conditions by miracles). These movements, of course, were just two of many possible responses to experiences of alienation and deprivation. The Qumran community were introversionists (they abandoned the world) while the Zealots were revolutionists (they tried to change the world). Apocalyptic eschatology provided an ideological basis for these movements as well as more elementary forms of apocalypticism found in first-century Palestine. Jews outside these circles were considered enemies as much as the Romans. Like John, Jesus was an apocalyptist who proclaimed the imminent arrival of the Kingdom of God, implying that the acceptance of his credibility as proclaimer was critically important. With the exception of the lengthy revelatory discourse in Mark 13 and parallels (see below), predictions of Jesus that have a claim to historicity include (1) announcements of the imminent arrival of the Kingdom of God (Mark 1:15; Matt. 10:7–8; Mark 13:30); (2) predictions of the destruction of Jerusalem and the Temple (Mark 13:2; 14:58; Luke 13:34–35; Matt. 23:37–39; Luke 19:41–44; 23:28–31); (3) predictions of the coming Son of Man (Matt. 10:32–33 and par.; Luke 12:8–9; Mark 8:38 and pars.). These all center on an imminent divine visitation bringing both judgment and salvation, the central feature of apocalyptic eschatology. The message of Jesus is epitomized by the two-part structure of many of his sayings, the first part referring to the present decision of man, and the second to the future response of God (Matt. 23:11–12; Mark 8:35; Matt. 5:7; 18:3). These sayings are appropriate in a conversionist movement since human transformation is regarded as a necessary prelude for the transformation of the world.

Earliest Christianity

The apocalyptic ideology of the movements of John the Baptist and Jesus of Nazareth was the framework within which the earliest Palestinian Christians understood the mission and message of Jesus and their own position in the world which would imminently end. The so-called "Q-Community," which apparently flourished ca. A.D. 30–60 in Palestine, compiled the sayings source Q, which has a strong apocalyptic orientation. Of the six sayings about the future coming of the Son of Man, five emphasize the theme of judgment (Luke 11:30=Matt. 12:40; Luke 12:40=Matt. 24:44; Luke 17:24=Matt. 24:27; Luke 17:26=Matt. 24:37–39; Luke 17:28=Matt. 24:37–39), while one has both salvation and judgment (Luke 12:8–9=Matt. 10:32–33). Many judgment sayings are also found (cf. Luke 10:12=Matt. 10:15; Luke 10:14–15=Matt. 11:22–23; Luke 13:35=Matt. 23:38–39). Since these sayings are all presented as sayings of Jesus it is not possible to distinguish clearly between original words of Jesus and creations or embellishments by the early community.

The eschatological discourse of Jesus in Mark 13 is the most extensive apocalyptic discourse in the Gospels (a shorter one occurs in Luke 17:20–37, based on Q). Both Matthew (24:1–37) and Luke (21:5–36) extensively reworked Mark 13:1–37. In Mark 13, paraenesis is mixed with prediction. The largest part of the discourse describes the woes preceding the end (vs. 5–25). The end itself is introduced by the Son of Man, who comes with clouds and gathers the elect (vs. 25–27). The discourse concludes with a long section emphasizing the need for watchfulness (vs. 28–37). Another early (ca. A.D. 100) eschatological discourse is found in *Didache* 16. It begins with an exhortation to watchfulness (vs. 1–2), followed by a description of endtime sufferings (vs. 3–5), followed by the appearance of three signs: the first in heaven, the second the sound of the trumpet, and the third the resurrection of the dead (vs. 6–7). Finally the Lord comes on the clouds (v. 8). Even though this discourse appears to be a pastiche of elements from Mark 13 and parallels, its basic structure is independent. As in the Apocalypse of John, the evils of the last days receive great attention.

The Apocalypse of John

The traditional date of the Apocalypse, ca. A.D. 95, toward the end of the reign of Domitian (Irenaeus, *Against Heresies* 5.30.3), still appears probable. Though all Jewish and most Greco-Roman apocalypses are pseudonymous, the author's claim to be "John" rings true (1:1, 4, 9; 22:8). Since his work is a real apocalypse, pseudonymity is not an invariable feature of the genre. Though tradition identifies this John (often called the Elder) with John the Apostle, it is unlikely stylistically that the same person wrote both the Gospel and the Apocalypse. Though this John is otherwise unknown, the fact that he was a voluntary or involuntary exile on the island of Patmos (1:9) suggests an upper-class status (otherwise the penalty might have been death). John does not call himself a prophet (he comes close in 22:9), but he does designate his book a "prophecy" (1:3; 22:7, 10, 18, 19). He seems to be a member of a prophetic circle (22:9 compared with 22:16) and may have traveled a defined circuit, since he was intimately acquainted with the situations of the seven Christian communities he addresses.

The Form of the Apocalypse

Structurally the Apocalypse is an extended vision report (1:9 to 22:9), framed by an epistolary prescript (1:4–8) and postscript (22:10–21), and conventionally introduced by a title (1:1–2, linked to a blessing on reader and hearers in v. 3). In the main portion of the work the author utilizes a variety of segmenting composition techniques characteristic of episodic structures.

The title in 1:1–2, prefacing the epistolary prescript, suggests the secondary significance of the letter framework. The Apocalypse does not exhibit an epistolary structure, with the exception of the framing text units in 1:4–8 and 22:10–21. In this respect the Apocalypse is unique: *no other apocalypse is framed by epistolary conventions*, for the pseudonymity of other apocalypses would necessitate a fictional receiver as well as sender. Prophetic letters are found in the ancient Near East (e.g., the Mari letters), and in connection with the Israelite figures Jeremiah and Baruch (Jer. 29:1–23; *2 Baruch* 77.17–19;

Paraleipomena of Jeremiah 6.18–25; 7.24–34). The prescript itself is quite unusual. Though containing the conventional references to sender, addressee(s), and greetings, a doxology is added (elsewhere only in Gal. 1:5), ending with the customary "amen" (cf. Phil. 4:20; Rom. 11:36; 1 Tim. 1:17). The prescript concludes with the insertion of two prophetic oracles (1:7–8). Their unconventional use at this point abruptly presents the hearers with the two focal concerns of the author: the juridical function of the imminent Parousia (v. 7) and the divine authority of this prophetic book (v. 8): " 'I am the Alpha and the Omega,' says the Lord God, who is and who was and who is to come, the Almighty" (God himself speaks only here and in 21:5–8). There are no epistolary parallels to this complex prescript, though judgment theophanies can introduce prophetic and apocalyptic texts (cf. Micah 1:2–4 and *1 Enoch* 1:3–9).

The end of the Apocalypse (22:10–21) can be construed as an epistolary postscript, a role usually limited to v. 21. The postscripts of ancient Greek letters often summarized the body, which is how 22:10–21 functions. The publication instructions in v. 10 ("Do not seal up this prophetic book") have a counterpart at the conclusion of Daniel (12:10), just as the numerous parallels to the "integrity formula" in vs. 18–19 are usually placed at the beginning or end of compositions (cf. the conditional curses in Gal. 1:8–9). Mention of the Parousia and an "I am the Alpha and Omega" formulation occur in vs. 12–13, as in Rev. 1:7–8, and the destinies of the righteous (inclusion) and the wicked (exclusion) are touched on in vs. 14–15 reiterating the words of God in 21:6b–8. The authorization of the message (I Jesus have sent my angel to the churches with this message, v. 16, reiterating Rev. 1:1) moves into an invitation to "come" (v. 17).

The Apocalypse of John is more structurally complex than any other Jewish or Christian apocalypse, and has yet to be satisfactorily analyzed. Like other apocalypses, it is constructed of a sequence of episodes marked by various literary markers such as the repetition of formulaic phrases ("I saw," "I heard," etc.), and by such literary devices as ring composition, intercalations (though never interrupting narrative sequence), the technique of interlocking (the use of transitional texts that conclude one section and introduce another), and various structuring techniques (the use of septets and digressions). Revelation 1:19 is often taken as reflecting the basic structure of the Apocalypse: "Now write what you see, what is and what is to take place hereafter," with "what is" representing Rev. 2–3 and "what is to take place hereafter" referring to Rev. 4:1–22:9. This is acceptable, but not very illuminating.

Revelation 1:9–3:22 constitutes a prophetic call narrative placed in an initial position, just as the inaugural visions of Old Testament prophets were placed before collections of their oracles (Ezek. 1: 1–3:11; Isa. 40:1–11; Jer. 1:4–10). Perhaps an even closer parallel is the divine commissions to write, frequently narrated at the beginning of Greco-Roman compositions (Pausanias 1.21.2; Aelius Aristides, *Oration* 48.2; Callimachus, *Causes* 1.1.21–24). Like many ancient call visions, this one consists of a description of circumstances (1:9–10), the vision proper (1:11–20), including a commission to write (1:11, 19), and a reaction (1:17). The inaugural vision continues through the end of chapter 3, with reiterated commands to write prefacing each of the proclamations to the seven churches.

From 4:1 to 22:9 the setting shifts from earth to heaven (though the perspective oscillates between heaven and earth). The author emphasizes four series of seven: the seven proclamations (2:1–3: 22); the scroll with seven seals (4:1–8:1); the seven trumpets (8: 2–9:21; 11:15–18), and the seven bowls (15:1–16:21). Revelation 10:1–11:14 is *intercalated* into the trumpet sequence. The vision concludes with 17:1–22:9, which is composed of the Babylon vision (17:1–19:10) and the New Jerusalem vision (21:9–22:9), with the Parousia and Judgment vision (19:11–21:8) as an intercalation, and thereby emphasized. The Babylon vision and the New Jerusalem vision begin and end with so many similarities that the main vision must extend to 22:9. Within this scheme Rev. 11:18–14:20 contains three digressions (using mythological material appropriate for digressions, cf. Plutarch, *Moralia* 855D; Quintilian 4.3.12), focusing on the past, present, and future: (1) past: the vision of the woman and her child (11:19–12:6, 13–17), with an intercalated description of a heavenly war (12:7–12); (2) present: visions of the beasts from the sea and the earth and the demands they make on humankind (Rev. 13); and (3) future: Revelation 14 contains a miscellany of heavenly scenes and proclamations.

Among the many constituent literary forms of the Apocalypse are the seven "letters" of Rev. 2–3. They are not really letters but prophetic proclamations patterned after ancient royal and imperial *edicts*. Like each of the seven proclamations, edicts begin with the name and title(s) of the king or emperor followed by a verb of declaration (Latin *dicit*, Greek *legei:* "says" or "declares") followed by the remainder of the edict addressing the recipients in the second-person plural. Even the stereotyped "I know" phrase found in each of the seven proclamations has a close parallel to an edict of Claudius (Josephus, *Ant.* 19.280–284):

Tiberius Claudius Caesar Augustus Germanicus, of tribunician power, speaks [*legei*]: "Since I have known [*epignous*] from the beginning that the Jews in Alexandria called 'Alexandrians' were joint-colonizers with the Alexandrians . . ."

The sixteen hymns or hymnlike compositions of the Apocalypse are another important constituent form (4:8c, 11; 5:9b–10, 12b, 13b; 7:10b, 12; 11:15b, 17–18; 12:10b–12; 15:3b–4; 16:5b–7b; 19:1b–2, 3, 5b, 6b–9). Some of the units can better be described as doxologies or acclamations (5:13; 7:10, 12; 19:1). Several units are combined to form antiphonal structures, constituting eight hymnic interludes (4:8–11; 5:9–14; 7:9–12; 11:15–19; 12:10b–12; 15:3b–4; 16:5–7; 19:1–4, 5–8). Though containing many traditional elements, they are not derived from early Christian liturgy but are literary creations of the author. Uniformly intoned by various figures in the heavenly throne room, the hymns function as counterparts to imperial court ceremonial (cf. Dio Cassius 59.24.5; Tacitus, *Annals* 14.15). In Pergamum, the location of one of the seven churches, a permanent thirty-six-member imperial cult choir was established to hymn the divine Augustus. The hymns of the Apocalypse, like speeches in historical works, are devices to advance the "plot." In Jewish apocalypses angelic hymns of praise to God are occasionally mentioned (*2 Enoch* 18:8–9; 19:3; 42:4; *Apocalypse of Zephaniah*, frag. A; *3 Enoch* 24–40; *Apocalypse of Abraham* 18.3), but with the exception of the Sanctus, rarely quoted (*3 Enoch* 20.2; 39.2; cf. *Apocalypse of Abraham* 17:6–21).

The author also inserts a number of prophetic oracles, a fact that not only lends credence to his prophetic self-conception but also suggests a close relationship between prophecy and the apocalyptic genre in early Christianity. Sixteen of these oracles are paired, with the second part functioning to amplify the first (1:7–8; 13:9; 14:13; 16:15; 19:9; 21:5–8; 22:12–15; 22:18–20). There are several paraenetic salvation-judgment oracles (chs. 2–3; 13:9–10; 22:18–20), three announcements of salvation (14:13; 19:9; 22:7), and one announcement of judgment (18:21–24). A very particular type is the eschatological theophany oracle in 16:15; 21:3–4; 21:6–8; and 22: 12–15. Scattered throughout the Apocalypse are seven beatitudes (1:1; 14:3; 16:15; 19:9; 20:6; 22:7, 14).

The Content of the Apocalypse

The content or message of the Apocalypse is inseparable from its eschatological perspective. Unlike many Jewish apocalypses, it

avoids cosmological speculation for an exclusive focus on eschatology. The author writes during the interim between the death
and resurrection of Jesus and the imminent Parousia. What is his
message? It is expressed in succinct form in the speech of God in
Rev. 21:6–8:

> And he said to me, "It is done! I am the Alpha and the Omega, the
> beginning and the end. To the thirsty I will give water without price
> from the fountain of the water of life. He who conquers shall have this
> heritage, and I will be his God and he shall be my son. But as for the
> cowardly, the faithless, the polluted, as for murderers, fornicators,
> sorcerers, idolaters, and all liars, their lot shall be in the lake that burns
> with fire and brimstone, which is the second death.

For John there are two categories of people, the righteous and the
wicked (22:11), and the latter predominate. Christians are in a life-
and-death spiritual struggle (12:17) in which some will "conquer"
and others will fail. Conquest is really a martial metaphor, perhaps
used in response to "victory," an important motif in Roman imperial propaganda. Christians must "conquer" (seven times in chs.
2–3; 12:11; 15:2; 21:7), just as the Lamb both has conquered (5:5)
and will conquer (17:14). Jesus paradoxically conquered through
death (1:18; 2:8; 5:6, 9, 12), and followers of the Lamb must do the
same (2:10, 13; 6:9–11; 7:14; 14:13; 20:4), and extravagant salvific
promises are made to them (2:7, 11, 17, 26–28; 3:5, 12, 21). When
used of Christians, the verb "to conquer" is always intransitive, for
it is a passive experience expressed by synonyms like "endurance"
(2:2–3, 19; 13:10; 14:12) and "keeping" ("what is written in this
prophetic book," 1:3; 22:7, 9; "my works," 2:10; "my word," 3:8;
"the commandments of God," 12:17; 14:12, etc.). Those who do
not conquer are fallen Christians (cowardly, faithless, polluted) and
nonbelievers (murderers, fornicators, sorcerers, idolaters, liars), according to the vice lists (9:20–21; 21:8, 17; 22:15), who will eventually experience the second death (2:11; 20:6; 21:4, 8).

Most items on the vice lists fit the stereotypical behavior that Jews
attributed to pagans, indicating that John operates with a "we"/
"they" dichotomy which excludes many Jews (2:9; 3:9). The author,
speaking only through various supernatural revealers, expresses
strong approval and disapproval of various behaviors, though rarely
are ethics directly enjoined. The behavior required is largely framed
in *negative* terms: *not* eating idol meat (2:14, 20); *not* worshiping the
beast or receiving his mark (13:15–17; 14:9–10; 19:20); *not* being
defiled by women (14:4). All of this suggests that the basic issue is
one of irreconcilable cultural conflict. Christians, who are heirs of

many Jewish cultural and religious traditions, are seen in conflict
with the dominant Greco-Roman culture in western Asia Minor.
John finds very few totally enthusiastic Christian allies, for (judging
by Rev. 2–3) there are several Christian orientations. "Jezebel" and
the Nicolaitans represent a liberal tendency, embracing cultural
accommodation, that is strongly represented in Pergamum and
Thyatira, though markedly unsuccessful in Ephesus. Most Christians espouse a centrist position and are judged by John's Jesus as
persons who have departed from works done at first (2:5), or whose
works are imperfect (3:2), or who are lukewarm (3:15f.). They also
tolerate liberal elements: "Jezebel" and the Nicolaitans (2:14f., 20).
John himself represents the apocalyptic tradition of nonconformity
and opposition to the insidious influence of the dominant alien
culture. He has allies in Ephesus, Smyrna, and Philadelphia; some
adherents in Thyatira (2:24f.), but few in Pergamum, Sardis, and
Laodicea. John is supported, the revelatory visions of the Apocalypse disclose, by God himself.

The Function of the Apocalypse

The function of apocalypses is usually understood in terms of
social setting, a subject about which little is known. The Apocalypse,
for example, is often thought to have arisen in response to a Domi-
tianic persecution, but this proposal lacks historical substantiation.
Yet crises are a matter of perspective, and it is still probable that
John wrote to console and encourage Christians in a situation he
perceived as critical.

Apocalypses, like other works, have explicit and implicit *literary*
functions, which have the advantage of being found in the text itself.
Two functions are relatively explicit. First, the use of the apocalyptic
genre *legitimates* or *authorizes* the message (1:1–2; 19:9; 21:5; 22:6,
16). Second, the eschatological emphasis on the imminent return of
Jesus provides a *sanction* for the necessity of an immediate response
to the message (1:7; 16:15; 22:7, 12, 20). John emphasizes these
functions by explicitly framing the Apocalypse with both emphases
(1:7–8; 22:12–13). A third important function is implicit in the literary structure of the Apocalypse. Paradoxically, supernatural revelations are thought to conceal that which they reveal, a perspective
reflected in the widespread belief in oracular ambiguity. Revelatory
literature, including apocalypses, is potentially the means for further revelations. In the case of the Apocalypse this is facilitated in
two ways. First, the work is constructed like a maze concealing the
central revelatory message (expressed in most complete form in

Rev. 21:6–8). Second, explanations of the visions are few and far between (1:20; 7:13–17; 17:6b–18); the hearers must use their imaginations to understand them. These two factors together legitimate the Apocalypse, for the hearers can experience for themselves the revelatory experience narrated by John.

Christian Apocalypses in Transition

After the Apocalypse of John, Christians continued to write apocalypses and the genre evolved considerably. Since Christianity had no native kingship traditions or myths of cosmic renewal of its own upon which to draw, it used those of Judaism. John's utilization of archaic mythic images, following Jewish apocalyptic tradition, was based on the assumption that Christians constituted a new people of God, the successor to Judaism. The increasing separation of Christianity from Judaism meant that apocalyptic eschatology, the idiom of nations deprived of a divinely ordained king, became less meaningful and functional. Individual eschatology (the fate of individuals in the afterlife) became increasingly important as the increasingly popular visions and tours of hell suggest (e.g., the Apocalypses of Peter and Paul).

The Shepherd of Hermas

The *Shepherd of Hermas* is a composite work that developed in stages from ca. A.D. 90 to 150, in or near Rome. It consists of three sections of five Visions, twelve Mandates, and ten Parables. Visions 1–4, which make up the oldest segment, were written in expectation of an imminent persecution. The revealer is an old woman modeled on the Sibyl (Vis. 2.4.1). Vision 5 to Parable 8 constitute a later unit introduced by Vision 5. Parables 9 and 10, which conclude the work, were added last of all. The supernatural revealer is now the Shepherd, whence the title.

Hermas reflects a blend of Jewish and Hellenistic traditions. The central theme of the work is the possibility of a second (and final) repentance. Traditionally repentance was regarded as a once-for-all act connected with baptism (Mand. 4.3.1), but to Hermas was revealed the possibility of a second repentance (Vis. 2.2.4–5; Mand. 4.4.4). The Shepherd represents the victimized poor (the "pious poor" of Jewish tradition have an analogue in the innocent poor, over against the unjust rich, stock figures of Greco-Roman declamations); he condemns those who are wealthy, involved in business, and socially ambitious and calls for a new and final repentance involving the rejection of "double-mindedness."

Is the *Shepherd of Hermas* an apocalypse? Although some label it a "pseudoapocalypse" because it lacks eschatological themes typical of many Jewish apocalypses, it fits the definition of the apocalyptic genre defined above. Like the Apocalypse of John, it is not pseudonymous and was written to be read before congregations (Vis. 2.4.3; 1.3.3–4; cf. Rev. 1:3; 22:18), unlike its Jewish analogues but like its Greco-Roman counterparts. Composed in an episodic style typical of apocalyptic literature, *Hermas* contains two apocalypses, Visions 1–4 and Vision 5 to Parable 10. Visions 1–4 begin with a novelistic introduction (1.1.1–2), followed by reports of four earthly visions, each with several elements: (1) rapture by a spirit to the place of revelation; (2) preparation for revelation (prayer, fasting); (3) the vision itself, consisting of a dialogue between the revealer and Hermas. The stupidity of Hermas' questions is emphasized in the dialogues. The message of this apocalypse is summarized in a statement by God himself in Vision 2.2.5–7, announcing a final opportunity for repentance to those who have denied him in the past. The function of the work is to provide supernatural legitimation for the revelatory message, which is sanctioned by the imminent persecution.

The second apocalypse (Vis. 5 to Par. 10) begins with an extensive vision in which the Shepherd appears to Hermas and commands him to write the Mandates and Parables that follow (Vis. 5 to Par. 1.11). As in the Apocalypse, the revealer introduces himself with an "I am" predication and concludes the inaugural interview with a conditional blessing and curse on those who hear the commands. The Mandates are largely paraenetic. Mandates 1–2, 9 are in the form of revelatory discourses by the Shepherd, while the rest are revelatory dialogues. The Parables contain six visions (2–4, 5, 6, 7–8, 9, 10) in which the Shepherd suddenly appears to Hermas and through dialogue explains the allegorical significance of various natural phenomena (an elm and a vine, Par. 2; leafless trees, Par. 3) or a story (the parable of the vineyard, Par. 5.2–7).

Like the Apocalypse of John, *Hermas* contains a variety of constituent literary forms. Several types of prophetic oracles, identifiable on form-critical grounds, have been embedded in Hermas. This provides further evidence for the connection between prophecy and the apocalyptic genre in early Christianity. Four salvation-judgment oracles are found in the Visions (2.2.6–8; 2.3.4; 3.8.11–9.10; 4. 2.5–6), each with conditional threats and promises, and all using the coming persecution as a sanction. Two oracles of assurance are preserved in the Mandates (12.4.5–7; 12.6.1–3), while six paraenetic salvation-judgment oracles are evident in the Parables (6.1.4; 9. 23.5; 9.24.4; 9.28.5–8; 9.31.3–32.5; 9.33.1). Parables (or allegories) were used in Jewish apocalypses (*1 Enoch, 4 Ezra, 2 Baruch*) and also play a significant role in *Hermas.* The term occurs more than thirty times. They both reveal and conceal divine truth (Mand. 10.1.3–6; cf. Mark 4:11–12).

Hermas has also been used as a quarry for examples of the Jewish-Christian homily. Some of the prophetic oracles described above have been designated homilies, since they are formulated as addresses in the second-person plural. Among the shorter forms, four beatitudes occur (Vis. 2.2.7b; 2.3.3; Par. 2.10; 9.29.3b; cf. 5.3.9; 9.30.3), and a woe oracle in Vision 4.2.6, and several catalogs of vices (Mand. 5.2.4; 6.2.4–5; 8.3, 5; 12.2.1) and virtues (Mand. 5.2.3; 6.2.3; 8.10).

The Apocalypse of Peter

The *Apocalypse of Peter,* composed ca. A.D. 135, is one of the first *pseudonymous* Christian "apocalypses." Written originally in Greek, it survives only in an Ethiopic translation and some less reliable Greek fragments. The revelation is set on the Mount of Olives, with the disciples asking about the Parousia and the end of the world (1). Peter asks the meaning of the parable of the fig tree, and receives a tortured allegorical explanation (2). Jesus' right hand contains an image of the future fate of both sinners and righteous (3), and in response to Peter's question, he describes the future judgment (4–5) and Parousia (6). He then describes the eternal tortures that sinners will experience, with the punishments often fitting the crime (7–12). The righteous will receive their reward in Acherusia or the Elysian Fields (13–14). The work ends with the disciples accompanying Jesus to a holy mountain where they receive a vision of Moses and Elijah (15–17).

This "apocalypse" is not an apocalypse at all, but a revelatory discourse of Jesus regarding the future with only two brief questions by Peter (2, 3) at the beginning of the discourse, and three in the closing scene (16). The setting of the discourse is modeled after the Olivet Discourse at the beginning (Mark 13 and pars.), and the Transfiguration account at the end (Mark 9 and pars.). It is not a *guided tour* of hell, for no guide and no trip is involved. Martha Himmelfarb has shown that the frequent use of demonstrative explanations ("this is/these are"; the language of tour guides) is a style characteristic of some Jewish "tour" apocalypses but absent from Greco-Roman analogues (there are exceptions, however; cf. Vergil, *Aeneid* 6; Cebes, *Tabula*, passim). The focus on the sins and punishments of the wicked reflects an amalgam of Jewish, Christian, and particularly Greco-Roman underworld mythology. Like the Greco-Roman descriptions of the underworld (Diodorus 1.2.2), this apocalyptic discourse functions to instill a fear that will provoke approved behavior in the readers.

Gnostic Apocalypses

Even though Gnosticism emphasized realized eschatology, the notion of a future (though not imminent) consummation was retained. A two-part schema, envisioning tribulation followed by the complete destruction of the world and the reintegration of the divine world, occasionally occurs (*On the Origin of the World* 125. 32–127.17; *Paraphrase of Shem* 43.28–45.31). In conformity with Gnostic presuppositions, the total destruction of the physical world is emphasized, and no new creation is envisaged. This ideology cannot appropriately be labeled apocalyptic eschatology.

The Coptic-Gnostic apocalypses, part of the find at Nag Hammadi in Egypt in 1946, exhibit great variety. Some documents are entitled apocalypses and conform to the genre (*Apocalypse of Peter; Apocalypse of Adam; Apocalypse of Paul*), while others have the label but are not really apocalypses (*First Apocalypse of James; Second Apocalypse of James*). Two documents are not labeled apocalypses, but exhibit the appropriate generic characteristics (*Concept of Our Great Power; Paraphrase of Shem*). Further, there are apocalypses not identified as such (*On the Origin of the World* 125.32–127.17; *Asclepius* 70.3–74.17) which are parts of larger compositions.

For Further Study

General: The best recent introduction to Jewish and Christian apocalyptic, with an excellent bibliography, is Christopher Rowland, *The Open Heaven: A Study of Apocalyptic in Judaism and Early Christianity* (Crossroad Publishing Co., 1982). A popular survey is available in D. S. Russell, *Apocalyptic Ancient and Modern* (Fortress Press, 1978). The current state of research on apocalypticism is reflected in David Hellholm, ed., *Apocalypticism in the Mediterranean World and the Near East* (Tübingen: J. C. B. Mohr [Paul Siebeck], 1983), with thirty-four essays by prominent scholars. Another important collection of essays is Jan Lambrecht, ed., *L'Apocalypse johannique* et l'apocalyptique dans le Nouveau Testament (Gembloux: Duculot, 1979). Still useful is D. S. Russell, The Method and Message of Jewish Apocalyptic, Old Testament Library (Westminster Press, 1964). The older work by Paul Volz, Die Eschatologie der jüdischen Gemeinde im neutestamentlichen Zeitalter (Tübingen: J. C. B. Mohr, 1934) is still the classic discussion of Jewish eschatology. The best introduction to the problem of genre is John J. Collins, ed., Apocalypse: The Morphology of a Genre, Semeia 14 (1979), with articles identifying and analyzing Jewish, Christian, Greco-Roman, and Persian apocalypses.

On Apocalypticism and Millennialism: The most comprehensive discussion of millennialism is Bryan R. Wilson, Magic and the Millennium: A Sociological Study of Religious Movements of Protest Among Tribal and Third-World Peoples (Harper & Row, 1973). Also valuable is Sylvia Thrupp, ed., Millennial Dreams in Action: Studies in Revolutionary Religious Movements (Schocken Books, 1970). Egyptian, Persian, and Jewish apocalypses are put in historical context by Samuel K. Eddy, The King Is Dead: Studies in Near Eastern Resistance to Hellenism 334–31 B.C. (University of Nebraska Press, 1961). Martin Hengel does the same for Judaism in Judaism and Hellenism, tr. by John Bowden, 2 vols. (Fortress Press, 1974).

On Jewish Apocalypses: The texts of Jewish apocalypses in annotated English translations with competent introductions are available in James H. Charlesworth, ed., The Old Testament Pseudepigrapha, vol. 1: Apocalyptic Literature and Testaments (Doubleday & Co., 1983). An excellent discussion of Jewish apocalyptic is John J. Collins, The Apocalyptic Imagination: An Introduction to the Jewish Matrix of Christianity (Crossroad Publishing Co., 1984). Also useful is Michael Stone, Scriptures, Sects and Visions: A Profile of Judaism from Ezra to the Jewish Revolts (Fortress Press, 1980). For a discussion of the Hekalot literature and the movement from apocalyptic to merkabah mysticism, see Ithamar Gruenwald, Apocalyptic and Merkavah Mysticism (Leiden: E. J. Brill, 1980).

On Other Near Eastern Apocalypses: C. C. McCown's older article "The Hebrew and Egyptian Apocalyptical Literature," HTR 18 (1925), 357–411, has been superseded by the careful discussion of Jan Bergman, "Introductory Remarks on Apocalypticism in Egypt," in AMW, pp. 51–60.

On Ancient Revelatory Literature: Comprehensive discussion of Greco-Roman, Israelite-Jewish, and early Christian material with an extensive bibliography is found in D. E. Aune, Prophecy in Early Christianity and the Ancient Mediterranean World (Wm. B. Eerdmans Publishing Co., 1983). For a comprehensive discussion of the testament genre with its constituent future forecasts, see Eckhard von Nordheim, Die Lehre der Alten: I. Das Testament als Literaturgattung im Judentum der hellenistisch-römischen Zeit (Leiden: E. J. Brill, 1980). Pheme Perkins, The Gnostic Dialogue: The Early Church and the Crisis of Gnosticism (Paulist Press, 1980), has a competent introductory discussion of types of dialogue. John J. Collins, The Sibylline Oracles of Egyp-

tian Judaism (Scholars Press, 1972), is basic. For translation of texts dealing with revelatory magic, see Hans Dieter Betz, ed., *The Greek Magical Papyri in Translation* (University of Chicago Press, 1986). The most adequate discussion of Delphic oracles is Joseph Fontenrose, *The Delphic Oracle: Its Responses and Operations* (University of California Press, 1978). For a Greek edition with French translation and commentary on the Chaldean oracles, see Edouard des Places, *Oracles Chaldaïques* (Paris: Belles Lettres, 1971). On the Greco-Roman vision form see John S. Hanson, "Dreams and Visions in the Graeco-Roman World and Early Christianity," *ANRW* II.23.2, 1395–1427.

On Early Christian Apocalypticism: Christopher Rowland, *The Open Heaven: A Study of Apocalyptic in Judaism and Early Christianity* (Crossroad Publishing Co., 1982), is the most thorough recent discussion of early Christian apocalypticism. For a popular treatment, see Paul S. Minear, *New Testament Apocalyptic* (Abingdon Press, 1981). J. Christiaan Beker, *Paul's Apocalyptic Gospel* (Fortress Press, 1982), is also useful. Elisabeth Schüssler Fiorenza touches an important question in "The Phenomenon of Early Christian Apocalyptic," in *AMW*, pp. 295–316. Lars Hartman, *Prophecy Interpreted: The Formation of Some Jewish Apocalyptic Texts and of the Eschatological Discourse, Mark 13 Par.* (Lund: Gleerup, 1966), analyzes sequences of motifs in Jewish apocalypses and select New Testament texts. Several important articles are found in Adela Yarbro Collins, ed., *Early Christian Apocalypticism: Genre and Socail Setting, Semeia* 36 (1986).

On the Apocalypse of John: For competent discussions of the date, authorship, and social setting of the Apocalypse, see Adela Yarbro Collins, *Crisis and Catharsis: The Power of the Apocalypse* (Westminster Press, 1984). The problem of genre is discussed by David Hellholm, "The Problem of Apocalyptic Genre and the Apocalypse of John," in *Society of Biblical Literature: 1982 Seminar Papers*, ed. by Kent H. Richards (Scholars Press, 1982), pp. 157–198. On structure, see the first chapter of Adela Y. Collins, *The Combat Myth in the Book of Revelation* (Scholars Press, 1976), and Elisabeth Schüssler Fiorenza, "The Composition and Structure of the Book of Revelation," *CBQ* 39 (1977), 344–366, in conjunction with Charles H. Giblin, "Structure and Thematic Correlations in the Theology of Revelation 16–22," *Biblica* 55 (1974), 487–504.

On Later Christian Apocalypses: Non-Gnostic texts in translation with detailed introductions are available in Edgar Hennecke, *New Testament Apocrypha*, ed. by Wilhelm Schneemelcher, tr. by R. McL. Wilson et al., vol. 2 (Westminster Press, 1966). Translations of the Coptic-Gnostic apocalypses are available in James M. Robinson, ed., *The Nag Hammadi Library in English* (Harper & Row, 1977). Important studies on the Shepherd of Hermas include David Hellholm, *Das Visionenbuch des Hermas als Apokalypse*, vol. 1 (Lund: Gleerup, 1980), on structure and genre, and Carolyn Osiek, *Rich and Poor in the Shepherd of Hermas: An Exegetical-Social Investigation*, ed. by Bruce Vawter, *CBQ* Monographs, 15 (Catholic Biblical Association of America,

1983), on recent research and an analysis of the book's message. On the *Apocalypse of Peter*, see Martha Himmelfarb, *Tours of Hell: An Apocalyptic Form in Jewish and Christian Literature* (University of Pennsylvania Press, 1983), who links it with sixteen later Christian and Jewish "tour" apocalypses. On Gnostic apocalypses, see Martin Krause, "Die literarischen Gattungen der Apokalypsen von Nag Hammadi," in *AMW*, pp. 621–637, and George MacRae, "Apocalyptic Eschatology in Gnosticism," in *AMW*, pp. 317–325. An important work on Gnosticism generally is Kurt Rudolf, *Gnosis*, tr. by R. McL. Wilson (Harper & Row, 1983).

Index
of Selected Subjects

Index
of Selected Biblical Passages